SUPPING
with THE
DEVILS

HUGO
YOUNG

SUPPING
with THE
DEVILS

Political Writing
from Thatcher to Blair

ATLANTIC BOOKS
LONDON

First published in 2003 by Atlantic Books, on behalf of
Guardian Newspapers Ltd.
Atlantic Books is an imprint of Grove Atlantic Ltd.

All these pieces originally appeared in the *Guardian*, except for

'Moral? Poof!', pp. 3–10, *Not the Guardian*; 'Margaret Thatcher's execution',
pp. 11–18, *Not the Guardian*; 'Maggie and me', pp. 19–21, *Memories of Maggie* by
Iain Dale; 'John Major's life and coming death', pp. 22–44, *The New Yorker*; '
The undeniable French connection', pp. 91–9, *London Review of Books*; 'Heading for
estrangement', pp. 126–9, Guardian Unlimited; 'It's just not cricket', pp. 153–64,
Observer Sport Monthly; and 'Muffled by the Woolsack', pp. 195–8, *Not the Guardian*.

2 4 6 8 10 9 7 5 3 1

A CIP catalogue record for this book is available
from the British Library

ISBN 1 84354 116 5

Typeset by FiSH Books, London
Printed in Great Britain by CPD, Ebbw Vale, Wales

Design by Philip Lewis

Grove Atlantic Ltd
Ormond House
26–27 Boswell Street
London WC1N 3JZ

CONTENTS

INTRODUCTION

WHEN I FIRST READ NEWSPAPERS, there were no political columnists. A man called William Connor sounded off in the *Daily Mirror* with flamboyant verve, more style than substance, about everything under the sun. But he needed to disguise himself behind the name Cassandra to acquire the authority which a named mortal apparently wasn't allowed. And he wasn't political, as such. The violent prejudices of John Gordon seasoned the *Sunday Express*. But the political commentator as we know him or her, privileged as to space, freedom and regular byline, did not exist. I don't think the *Manchester Guardian* or *The Times* retained anyone resembling a columnist. For one thing, *The Times* was then written entirely without bylines, except for weekly ruminations on the books page by one Oliver Edwards, which turned out to be the pseudonym of the editor, William Haley, reporting, bizarrely, on his daily study of recondite works of Victorian literature. The *Guardian* vested all celebrity in its reporters Alistair Cooke, Victor Zorza, Harry Boardman and many others whose distinguishing feature was the brilliance with which they broke the rule of the icon of the Manchester tradition, C. P. Scott. His most famous journalistic utterance was something about comment being free and facts being sacred. Nowhere was this austere sentiment ignored to greater effect than in the pages of the paper he had owned for fifty years.

During my time as a newspaper writer, the absence of columnists has been comprehensively made good – or possibly the reverse. Not long ago, running into an acquaintance who worked for the government, I found him in a state of disbelief. He had been asked, on behalf of Prime Minister Blair's office, to compile a list of all national newspaper columnists to whom Downing Street might want to get a political message across. His survey wasn't yet complete, but so far he had counted no fewer than 221 of them. That figure included Sunday as well as daily papers, and the definition of the political was probably generous, encompassing women's pages and sports pages and arts pages as well as people like me who spend most of their space mainlining on public affairs. But the transition from zero to 221-plus registers a change in the priorities of journalism for which there is only one good thing to be said. At least, with so many, we cancel each other out.

When political columns began, which was just about when I first got a job on Fleet Street, each paper tended to have one columnist, who thus acquired an oracular authority no journalist deserves. In our case, at the *Sunday Times*, it was William Rees-Mogg, who, week after week, was the only named political voice. He seemed to be stupendously important. His demand in 1964, for example, that Sir Alec Douglas-Home should quit the leadership of the Conservative Party, was met with instant obedience. Home was positively sheepish in his subservience to the prophetic word. He openly admitted that this single piece by Rees-Mogg had pushed him over the edge. Today that could not happen. There are no oracles, only a cacophony of rival voices. But I can't think of many other virtues in a state of affairs that has so reordered the space and, often, the prestige afforded to columnists on the one hand and reporters on the other. Reporting is the bedrock of journalism, while columns seem more like the shifting sands of tide and fashion: undisciplined, unreliable and possibly, in the basic scheme of things, unnecessary.

This mordant thought presses deeper when a publisher urges one to put together between hard covers a collection of writings from the work of a couple of decades. Much of the point of columns, indeed of all exercises in daily journalism, is their transience. Most of a columnist's output is written for the morning after, not the years beyond. This transience is a mighty privilege at the time, and I enjoy every column day that comes round, as it does in my case twice a week. For me, the performance of trying to make sense of what's happening is a kind of drug. But is the stuff worth preserving for longer? Probably, I think, only as a form of reporting in itself. Less as a series of discrete argumentative pieces written at the time, than as a kind of chronicle or tableau of a period and some of the issues that concerned it. That, at any rate, is how I now justify what follows.

Going through the miles of words from which this collection is drawn forces me to clarify something else that's more open to debate. There are two questions that have knocked around my head ever since I began writing a political column, first in the *Sunday Times* and now in the *Guardian*. I'm not sure I've ever got them completely sorted. There's no clear-cut answer to either. But it seems important for a columnist to work out what he's doing on both counts. For whom, in the end, is he writing? And, trickier still, on whom is he depending?

William Rees-Mogg was the first columnist I knew, and years ago I asked him the first question. Did he have anyone in mind as the core audience for his Augustan Sunday sermons? He replied immediately and with memorable precision: an overworked doctor in Leamington Spa. A good answer, I thought, though not one universally agreed. When Peter Jay was an economics columnist on *The Times*, he favoured erudition no matter how few people could take it in. He once replied to a baffled reader who complained that he didn't understand what Jay was talking about, by saying that the piece in question was only meant to be read by three people, distributed between the Treasury and the Bank of England. That could be an important audience. The abstrusest economic issue is sometimes worth putting into journalism. And Jay went on to become the most lucid explicator of economics who has ever appeared on BBC television. But for a newspaper columnist it somehow doesn't seem enough to write only for a stratospheric élite.

My own attitude is more vulgar. I assume an audience of the maximum number of *Guardian* readers interested in public affairs, and see the job, above everything else, as explanation rather than persuasion. The columnist should try for scoops of fact, but may more readily discover scoops of interpretation. That's what I mean about the primacy of reporting. I sometimes take a strong line about a controversial subject. The reporting comes through a distinctive prism. But I think what I'm mostly doing, more often and more usefully than sounding off, is to convey some more or less important truths about present moods and future probabilities as seen by the actors in the political game. For the most part I've been less interested in influencing events and the ministers who make them, than in enlightening readers who may want to understand what is going on. I don't see myself as a player, more as a watcher, a finder-out, a discloser, an alerter, a reporter.

On the other hand, a columnist can't pretend that's the whole story. Some of the pieces preserved here are different. Sometimes the job is plainly to put some weight behind a struggle where there's a possibility of influencing events. For me, that has usually been on bits of legislation to do with civil liberties, where small clauses can have big results. Occasionally, I think I've helped push the boulder back up the hill, shaming legislators into moving in directions the government did not want. So, even if one doesn't write for the political class, one can't avoid being read by them, or sometimes profiting from their mesmerized belief that newspapers have great influence. They know the *Sun* reaches more voters than the *Guardian*, but a Labour government especially worries about what the *Guardian* says because a lot of Labour movers and voters read the *Guardian* and we therefore become part of a virtuous circle that sometimes carries our words spiralling upwards to the seat of power. I think this rests largely on an illusion. Very seldom do ministers need to pay attention to what any columnist writes. But I'm happy to bask in the milieu that just occasionally says otherwise.

It seems important, however, for journalists to know their limits. In the end we are not players, and shouldn't ever aspire to be. We're not responsible for action. We criticize decisions but never make them, which is fair enough: the critic has his role in a democratic society. But we don't have to compromise to get results. We seldom work or live anywhere near the street, as most MPs have to do once a week when they meet their constituents. Equally, we're not negotiating with the IRA, or privy to the secret threats from world terrorism, or having to make the best of life alongside George W. Bush.

That's why it's best that the columnist stays faithful to his first audience, rather than write to an agenda that only three people can understand or determine. We shouldn't be writing primarily for the actors or the experts. In the United States, where columnists are far more important than they are here, writing for a scattered audience that thirsts for an Olympian authority they can believe in, the columnist is more often a player. President Lyndon Johnson actually went to Walter Lippmann's house one evening in 1964 to ask him what to do about the Vietnam War. Lippmann had a long record, beginning at the Versailles Treaty in 1919, straddling the worlds of politics and journalism as if there wasn't much difference between them. He was a figure of huge authority, especially in foreign policy, who was allowed by politicians, and allowed himself, to be an intimate part of their world even while churning out his columns. Other American journalists go into government and back again, apparently undamaged. Others again become the slaves of this or that President, party and personal allegiance voiced shamelessly through their writing. In their world, there's no such thing as detachment. That tradition isn't wholly absent from Britain either. Some of the biggest names in journalism saw it as their duty in the 1980s to become editorial auxiliaries to Mrs Thatcher's onslaught on the shape of the British state. They wrote for and on behalf of the reigning political class, half in and only half out of the game. But I can't think of a single one whose reputation as a journalist was improved by the experience.

This begins to merge with the second question, and it may already be plain how I'm going to answer it. What is the right relationship between political columnists and the politicians about whom they write and on whom, to some extent, they depend? Having fixed on our audience, what about our source material? The audience is entitled to expect us to be insiders, to know what's going on. But I think they need also to rely on us being outsiders, ultimately.

If we purport to be telling it like it is, we can't avoid talking to politicians. We need to have relations with them. They own the truths we like to think we're reporting. What they say they think is news even if they don't really think it. The line they're spinning is at least half the story, and the columnist, sometimes unlike the front-page reporter, has the advantage of being able to expose the spin and deride it. But he obviously has to talk around, to be able to do that. He must sup with the devil constantly. Besides, finding out is not a pain. Many ministers and officials I've known have been excellent company: serious, gossipy, instructive, and knowing a lot more than I do about subjects I care about. I've had hundreds of such conversations in my life as a columnist, most of which I've had the time to note legibly and file away (will memoirs one day beckon?). One needs to keep in as 'insiderish' contact as possible with all politicians and officials in the relevant fields of interest. The columnist owes it to readers to know as much as he can conceivably find out. Though writing, I contend, as an outsider, he must discover as an insider.

But, for me, there's a limit to the intimacy. It's the only way I feel comfortable. I can think of no more than three politicians I've regarded as friends. Friends, in this business, are poison to the work. That's a social tic I can't shake off. For example, I've had few politicians in my house, for the possibly ignoble reason that I'd find it hard to be honestly disagreeable about them in print after that.

Such fastidiousness is not an advantage for a columnist. It cuts off some of the inside dope. But I think it keeps the water purer. It goes along with another piece of 'outsiderdom' — again a personal taste — which is a lifelong inability to form any party political allegiance. I don't claim social and political detachment as a universal virtue. I just can't get away from it. Some might call it cowardice, or a cop-out, perhaps even self-deception. Shouldn't columnists be arguing and reporting from a systematic declared position, which comes close to aligning them with a party? All I can say is that my own constitution is different. In recent years, more political journalists than ever have been happy to associate themselves with a political party or political causes, in and out of print. Some of them seem willing to climb on interest-group, and even party, platforms at the sniff of a television camera. I'm pretty startled by that. I think there should be more austerity — except that abstinence from active politics strikes me not as self-sacrifice but simple professional-ism. Isn't journalism enough? So it's as the outsider that this columnist writes, paying whatever price that might entail by way of contact, engagement and the agreeable illusion of being a player in the great game of government.

That's the mentality out of which these pieces come. Some are columns written for the morning after, which still seem to me to have life. The passing of Margaret Thatcher and the entry of Tony Blair produced longer efforts, written under the same conditions, which means they're pretty rough but perhaps evoke the moments. To cover the triumvirate of prime ministers I've had most contact with, I've included a *New Yorker* profile of John Major, written just before he was destroyed. From the whole period, though, I've cut out all day-to-day pieces that recorded the ceaseless ups and downs. They truly were written for the day, or possibly week, and have no further interest.

Apart from pure politics, my strongest interests turn out to have been pretty steady. There are pieces here about the style and method of politics, as much as the content. There is quite a lot about the law and judges, an abiding fascination ever since I found I was the only journalist on the *Sunday Times* with a law degree. Home Office issues – immigration, freedom of information, abuse of police power – are a category that puts all governments under the jaundiced eye of a liberal (that much of an allegiance I obviously own up to) journalist. This may sound like a pretty conventional attitude for any newspaperman. If the separation of journalism from politics doesn't mean journalists constantly challenging the extension of arbitrary authority, what's the point of not being a politician? All the same, I sometimes feel the press's attention to the evolving details of this everlasting problem, visible under every government but especially in the years bracketed by Thatcher and Blair, has been shallow and episodic.

The thread running through the collection extends such themes. It concerns, one way or another, the nature of the British state. Much of that, of course, emerges in the power struggles of high politics that are the raw material of the political columnist's life. The operation of the state is always our big subject. But other facets, both of power and state, have been a regular preoccupation of mine. One is the triangle formed between Church, state and liberty. The role of churchmen both English and Roman keeps coming back. I've also been interested, for example, in how little, or how much, politicians have intervened to shape British cultural life, broadly defined, whether by putting up the abomination called the Dome, or trying to end hunting, or demolishing the occasional inconvenient work of art like Rachel Whiteread's *House*. Ireland, on the other hand, which cut deep into the Thatcher–Major–Blair years, is an aspect of state power that always eluded my sympathetic understanding. I reckon it's the subject I've written worst about. So I have left it out.

Britishness in all its manifestations, though, has become a major problem for modern politicians, and it reaches deep into what used to be called foreign affairs. Over the years covered by these pieces, perhaps the most striking development – the biggest category shift – has been the liquidation of that term as a meaningful point of distinction. British politics are now inseparable from the globalized world in which they have to operate. It has to be understood that most foreign affairs have become domestic, which makes it more natural and necessary for a columnist to keep plunging into them.

So I've written increasingly about America, often in the context of war though with occasional irresistible sideshows such as the un-British sport of baseball. I supported two wars, in the Gulf and the Balkans, while being an early dissenter on Iraq. But here especially, perhaps, the duty of elucidation falls more heavily on the columnist than simple side-taking, and I hope the complexities, and my sense of agonized indecision, show through the prose. Permeating each of these conflicts has been, for the British, another problem about the nature of the state: how much (as in the Gulf) or how little (as in Bosnia) does Britain continue to be enmeshed with Washington's interpretation of our supposedly concordant national interests? I think this question, once regarded as settled, is likely to become the greatest that faces Britain in the first decade of the twenty-first century. It means that a British newspaper columnist finds himself writing about the likes of Bill Clinton or George W. Bush quite naturally, as if they were our domestic politicians.

Which is more than can be said, yet, of any Continental European leader. But the European Union, of course, is the place where, most of all, the distinction between foreign and domestic is blurred to the point of invisibility. The Eurosceptic press continues to deny that, valiantly treating Europe as a foreign country. But it is fighting against the ineluctable facts. And here I have to concede that there's been a breach in my detachment. Europe turns out to be the one great question that draws me towards a systematic and committed allegiance. Only in mid-career, to my shame, did I begin to understand that, for Britain, Europe is the issue overshadowing all others. I seldom wrote about it at all, until I was working on a biography of Margaret Thatcher and was forced to understand, through the contradictory virulence she brought to this defining issue of her premiership, how vitally it infused the workings of the British state and the evolution of the British political class. So I've become a supporter of integration, perhaps sometimes to the impatience of *Guardian* readers to whom the only excuse I can offer is that by now, after the heady 1970s and the combative 1980s, pro-Europeanism has returned, alas, to being an unfashionable position.

This is not as copiously represented here as it might be. Count yourselves lucky. Enough is enough. Refer to future columns, the way they were always meant to appear.

Hugo Young
Hampstead, February 2003

ANCIEN RÉGIME

Moral? Poof!

MARGARET THATCHER, it turns out, is not entirely without first-hand experience of South Africa. She went there once, as Secretary of State for Education and Science, to open an observatory. She does not make too much of this distant episode, but it has left a vivid impression and remains in the present tense. Could she say, I asked her yesterday, after she had sent Sir Geoffrey Howe, the Foreign Secretary, on his way, that she had seen apartheid in operation?

'You have to be very careful saying that just because you've been to a country you've seen it,' she replied. 'But I've seen the operation of apartheid in a number of respects. The first thing you see when you get off at Johannesburg airport is that you go into a hotel which is totally non-colour-conscious. You go into a dining room and there's all colours and backgrounds. So your first impression of South Africa is rather different from what you've been led to believe.'

Soon, however, you came across other things, which were different from Britain. Mrs Thatcher had not been to Soweto or any other township. But she had seen both sides of South Africa, including the part where apartheid apparently did not exist. 'I've seen it on occasions where there's no apartheid, and I've seen it when there is apartheid. And I don't like apartheid. It's wrong.

'Let me make that clear, apartheid is wrong. It has to go, and it is going.'

The question is how to speed its departure. Despite the events of recent weeks and months, the Prime Minister is an unswerving believer in the virtues of contact, dialogue, persuasion. She had made a start, she reminded me, when she had received President Botha at Chequers last year and told him that forced removals of black communities were 'totally and utterly and particularly repugnant to us'.

Their meeting and subsequent correspondence had been fruitful. 'Those have been stopped now. Things are coming in the right direction. Naturally one wishes them to come faster.'

I suggested that this process might now have come to a halt. 'What leverage do we have through mere persuasion, particularly when the main characters in the drama won't even see our Foreign Secretary?'

Mrs Thatcher deployed the quiet voice of incredulous affront. 'I'm sorry, that's absolute nonsense. President Botha's seeing the Foreign Secretary. He was alway going to see the Foreign Secretary.'

'But Sir Geoffrey had wanted to see him this week.'

'You have to try and arrange a date. I run eight, nine, sometimes twelve engagements a day. I can't just fit people in. Let's look on the positive side, and not try to make every single difficulty in this country, difficulties which don't exist. Mr Botha will see Sir Geoffrey Howe. 'Course he will. The question is arranging a date which is mutually convenient.'

'But wasn't it a bit humiliating that the trip was set up so publicly and then Botha said he wouldn't be available?'

Mrs Thatcher said it might have been better if they could have arranged the whole thing more quietly. But there would certainly be a meeting, and we should meanwhile look on the positive side, which consisted of fulfilling the terms of the last EEC communiqué outlining the need to get negotiations started between the South African government and black political leaders. Negotiation, not sanctions – the Rhodesian way.

'But Rhodesia survived sanctions only because it had South African support. Surely there is no South Africa to support South Africa?'

'South Africa has colossal internal resources. A colossal coastline. And whatever sanctions were put on, materials would get in and get out. There's no way you can blockade the whole South African coastline. No way.'

So, I asked, was there no economic pressure which, in the Prime Minister's view, would have any effect?

The banks, she thought, who had pressed for repayment of the South African debt last year, had had some effect. But the main influence came from people inside South Africa who were fighting against apartheid. And who were these? Above all, industry, 'and

4

some of the political parties'.

'But the question is whether governments, your government, can and should add to that pressure?'

'You're talking about economic pressure,' said Mrs Thatcher. 'I'm talking about how to bring about negotiations.' And here she launched into an attack on past policies. South Africa should never have been isolated by the world. 'I think we should have had more contact. We would have influenced her more. She would have been able to see that multiracial societies do work in other countries. They do, of course, have certain problems in Kenya and Uganda. But South Africa would have been much more influenced to come our way.'

As it was, even the moderates, black and white, would respond badly if they saw the West just hitting out at their country.

'So are you saying there is no form of hostile pressure which is appropriate?'

'Let me say what I'm saying,' she responded, in a voice which had now long assumed the deliberate and emphatic timbre familiar at Prime Minister's Questions. 'There is no case in history that I know of where punitive, general economic sanctions have been effective to bring about internal change.

'That is what I believe. That is what the Labour Party in power believed. That is what most of Europe believes. That is what most Western industrialized countries believe. If that is what they believe, there is no point in trying to follow that route.'

So sanctions, first of all, would not achieve the desired effect. But that was only the beginning of the case against them.

We now approached the central thrust of the prime ministerial argument, that part of it which elicited her most withering scorn. But there was a moment of calm before the storm, even a brief, flickering line of self-doubt, concerning a point over which 'people, if I might say so, seem to be confused – although they might make the same allegations about myself'.

The matter in question was the *moral* case for sanctions. 'I must tell you I find nothing *moral* about people who come to me, worried about unemployment in this country, or about people who come to us to say we must do more to help Africa – particularly black Africans.

'I find nothing *moral* about them, sitting in comfortable circumstances, with good salaries, inflation-proof pensions, good jobs, saying that we, as a matter of *morality*, will put x hundred thousand black people out of work, knowing that this could lead to starvation, poverty and unemployment, and even greater violence.'

I tried to intervene. 'So the black leaders who ...'

But Mrs Thatcher was thumping the table. 'That to me is *immoral.* I find it repugnant. We had it at the Community meeting. Nice conference centre. Nice hotels. Good jobs. And you really tell me you'll move people around as if they're pawns on a checkerboard, and say that's moral. To me it's *immoral.*'

'So how do you read the motives of the black leaders in South Africa, Bishop Tutu and many others, who are actually in favour of economic sanctions?'

'I don't have to read them. I can tell you there are many, many people in South Africa, black South Africans, who hope to goodness that economic sanctions will not be put on.'

'How do you know that?'

'Huh. You've heard Chief Buthelezi say that. He said it in this room.'

'That's one.'

'But seven million Zulus. He said it on the doorstep of Downing Street. I've heard it, too, from some of my ... from some other people, here in this room. Here in this room.'

'All right. But Tutu, Mandela, the ANC, the UDF, also represent a large segment of opinion – which you reject.'

'I totally reject it. Because I find it very difficult to know how they can turn round and say "Put our people into acute difficulty. They've got good jobs. They're looking after their children. But pursue a policy which can lead to children being hungry." I find it very difficult indeed.'

So sanctions, far from being moral, were positively immoral; and, as we have already seen, they would be ineffective. A third objection could also be made, and here one suddenly became aware of scores, nay hundreds, of unseen visitors who have passed through Mrs Thatcher's drawing room and had some of the elementary facts of life explained to them, particularly the dire occasions for retaliatory action which are afforded by the geography of southern Africa.

'I sometimes get the map out and say, look at it. Have you looked at how goods are going to get in and out of Zambia and Zimbabwe. Close Beit Bridge and how are you going to do it? That's the maize route. When there was a drought, that's the route through which maize went to keep people alive.

'I ask them, have you looked at it? Have you looked at the poverty and hunger and starvation – just when we're after all trying to give things *to* Africa, to see she doesn't suffer in this way?'

The voice was shaking now, at this spectacle of a continent which displayed such inexplicable moral inconsistencies. 'I find it astonishing, utterly astonishing, that on the one hand we're doing everything to help Ethiopia, everything to relieve poverty and starvation, everything to get the right seeds, the right husbandry. And at the same time we're suggesting that you turn people who are in work, out of work. And add to the problems you've already got. When people call that moral, I just *gasp*.'

Nor would the retaliation stop with the impoverishment of black Africa. There was also the West's strategic interest in certain raw materials – and here too the moral issue kept breaking through.

'Platinum comes in quantity from only two places, South Africa and the Soviet Union. Are people who say there's a moral question suggesting that the world supply of platinum should be put in charge of the Soviet Union? And there are other things. Your chemical chrome, your vanadium, and of course gold and diamonds. They would have a fantastic effect on the economy of the Soviet Union.

'To me it is absolutely absurd that people should be prepared to put increasing power into the hands of the Soviet Union on the grounds that they disapprove of apartheid in South Africa.'

These lectures have evidently borne fruit. 'I go through these things with some people, and they say: No one told us, no one explained this to us.'

The rest of the world, however, would seem to be looking for deeper and different explanations. Particularly the Commonwealth. There was, as the Prime Minister had early in our conversation conceded, a desire at least for some mark of disapproval of apartheid to be made. 'Signs and gestures,' she called them.

This was why Britain had agreed to the EEC package last year. But this hadn't been enough. 'The Commonwealth wanted more. So we did krugerrands. And we put the extra gold coins in. And we've done no promotion of tourism. And various other things. But I don't know anyone in power in the Western world who is suggesting punitive sanctions.'

'But they are suggesting bigger gestures, aren't they?'

Indeed they were, she said. But I had lit the blue touchpaper again. 'All right. Supposing you start with fruit and vegetables. That would be 95,000 people, blacks and their families, out of work. *Moral?* Poof! *Moral?* No social security. *Moral?*

'Up would go the prices here. Some of it would be sold out of the coastline, through third countries, re-marked, and perhaps come in at a higher price. And the retaliation we could have to things we export to South Africa! What is *moral* about that?'

This raised a question even about the gestures we had already taken part in. Insofar as they were designed, in a minor way, to inconvenience South Africa, they were surely open to objection from the Thatcherite point of view.

'We've gone along with the gestures and signals,' she said, 'because I recognize that people want to do something more than words.'

'But you don't really believe in them?'

'I don't believe that punitive economic sanctions will bring about internal change.'

'But even the gestures you're not keen on?'

(Pause.) 'I don't think the gestures are very effective. We withdrew our military attaché from South Africa. That means we don't get as much information as we should otherwise. Often you argue against the big things, the really damaging things that would cause unemployment. So you accept much smaller things, as we did.'

A few weeks ago, in the early stages of the sanctions crisis, the Prime Minister had formulated what struck me as a classic Thatcherite utterance, when she said: 'If I were the odd one out and I were right, it wouldn't matter, would it?' I now reminded her of this, and asked whether she was really so indifferent to the opinions of allies, Commonwealth colleagues, and so forth.

She said this had all been a familiar experience for her. There were many times when she had been the one to put arguments that no one else actually liked to put. She won some, she lost some, but the times she lost it was, it seemed, invariably because her antagonists were moved more by emotion than by reason. 'If you're alone, you only operate really by persuading. Your only way of persuading is by argument.'

So was she now winning the argument, from this lonely eminence? Apparently she had more allies than we could know about.

'Look, in the world in which I live, sometimes you make the argument and sometimes people do not express their own views, knowing you will express yours. And they hope to goodness that you'll win your argument. Many people.

'In the world where I live, sometimes there's a public view and a private view.' This wasn't, of course, her own problem. 'So often, my own converge,' she chortled, with legitimate pride. But she understood other people's difficulties and took comfort from their tacit backing.

Standing on her own high ground of unshakeable consistency, Mrs Thatcher is especially contemptuous of her political opponents – 'people who took the same view as we do when they were in power, and voted in the United Nations the same way we did.'

I suggested, in Labour's defence, that the internal situation had drastically changed since Denis Healey was in power and Dick Crossman was composing his diaries. Political upheaval had hugely escalated, and the government was weaker.

'And apartheid has been reduced,' Mrs Thatcher snapped back. 'There's practically no apartheid left in sport.'

'Due to a boycott,' I replied.

'Well.' Short pause. 'Due to a boycott. Due partly to a boycott. Not economic sanctions. A political thing.'

The prohibition against mixed marriages had also gone. 'As a matter of fact, I think it's the thing that signals the end of apartheid.' The pass laws were also going. And enforced removals. And job reservation. Even the Group Areas Act, Mrs Thatcher claimed, was 'starting to go'.

There were now 'many black people with professional qualifications and of considerable substance'. Their only problem was that they couldn't live where they wanted, and couldn't take a proper part in government. 'Those are the things to which you've got to address your minds and your action. I think we've done quite well by persuasion, particularly in the last eighteen months. But by *non-economic* ways. And we should go on that way.'

The next test is the mini-Commonwealth conference in early August. By then Sir Geoffrey will have made his rendezvous with Botha, and Mrs Thatcher hopes that Bishop Tutu will follow. After all, she had opened the door to the bishop in London. 'He asked to see me. Of course I saw him. I don't just refuse to see people. I very much enjoyed talking to him.'

Even though she didn't agree with him? 'We got just a little bit more understanding between us, and if we went on talking I think we would again.'

She gave me a foretaste of how her emollient self would greet the Commonwealth. 'Emotions will be running high,' she predicted. 'And when that happens, you just have to let them run high and keep very calm yourself. Because it doesn't help if you let your own emotions run high, even though they feel as though they're running high.'

Her job would be steadfastly to remind her seething interlocutors of some of the facts. 'How many of you have states of emergency? How long have you had them? How many of you detain people without trial? How many have had censorship? How many of you have excluded people on racial grounds?'

I wondered whether they might not get irritated if she started talking to them like that. Wouldn't it be a little patronizing?

'It's not patronizing. That's just putting the facts to them. Patronizing? What's patronizing about putting the facts? The Commonwealth's been strong enough to survive all those things. It's not for me to be patronizing. I try not to be. Not for us to be patronizing to South Africa either. We don't live there.'

So the Commonwealth is duly warned. There was an impassioned calmness about Mrs Thatcher yesterday. She appears to be ready, as ever, to attack.

'We can still get through, if we will', she said at the end. 'We can still help to get negotiations started.' But to this end she did not sound like a politician preparing to agree to a single thing that much of the world expects of her.

Margaret Thatcher's execution

SHE DIED AS SHE HAD LIVED, in battle. It was a quite extraordinary end, but it was in keeping with everything important that had gone before. There was a continuity, not only in the texture of these events but in the circumstances of her long life and swift demise. Just as her triumphs were often rooted in her zest for combat, her refusal to listen to advice and her unwillingness to admit that she could be wrong, so were these the sources of her last predicament. Until yesterday, when all three habits were finally broken.

It is a shocking way to go. Having lost no vote either in the Commons or in the country, she was yet disposed of by the unaccountable will of fewer than four hundred politicians. There has been nothing like it in the democratic era: no verdict apparently so perverse and unprovoked delivered by a governing party against a leader upon whom it had fawned and under whom it had grown fat for so many years. Many Conservatives will be thunderstruck by what they accomplished yesterday; some, even among those who did the deed, will be ashamed. For the first time in her prime ministership she provoked, while not requesting it, the human sympathy reserved for a helpless creature at bay.

The symmetry between the life and death was none the less compelling. She was a leader of lurid style and risky habits, especially in the field of personal relations. Aggressive to a fault, she spent years scorning not only consensual policies but the consensual demeanour. With nerveless indifference, she was prepared to see the larger portion of her friends as well as enemies in high places depart the scene as a direct result of her behaviour. A kind of rough justice therefore now prevails, its chemistry precipitated by the most enduring victim of these gross habits, Geoffrey Howe. She who lived by fire and insult cannot wholly complain when the ultimate insult repays her.

These have, however, been years that will not be forgotten. The Callaghan era might never have happened, for all that history makes of it. This is less true of the periods to which Harold Wilson and Ted Heath attach their names, but what lingers from them is notoriety more than fame. The Thatcher era will be different, and nowhere more so than in the evidence it offers that personality can be the single most potent contributor to the pattern of events. For better or for worse, this will truly and for ever be called the Thatcher era. She was a creature of her times. Although as a minister under Heath, she showed an opportunist's capacity to find different times congenial enough, from the mid-seventies she rode the tide of liberal economics and anti-state politics with missionary aplomb. All reformers need circumstance to coincide with destiny. But character matters more. There were things that happened which would, I think, have happened quite differently without her.

The first was the Falklands War. It was a prime example of ignorance lending pellucid clarity to her judgement. Surrounded by ministers who knew what war was and dithered at its prospect, she understood what the soldiers wanted and shirked neither the military consequences nor the huge political risk. This quality of leadership was justly rewarded. She was, in fact, especially decisive in war. But for her it is also certain that American bombers would not have been allowed to bomb Libya from British bases in April 1986.

Second, the conduct of economic policy in the early eighties owed almost everything to her moral fibre. It may have been a failed policy, but it was hers. She was committed to an economic theory and committed against caring about unemployment. When Lord Hailsham told her, in July 1981, that she would destroy the Conservative Party as surely as Herbert Hoover led the Republicans to oblivion in 1932, she spat in his eye. Blood on the streets did not alarm her, any more than the self-starvation of Irish republicans. She worried not about the jobless masses but the looted shopkeepers: a priority which, nine years later, no longer seems odd.

Third, and for similar reasons, the dethroning of trade-union power would have taken a different course without her. She acted out with utmost seriousness the anti-union prejudice which most other Tories shared but which many of them had not dared to deploy. Public sector strife, culminating with the 1984 coal strike, was permitted to drag out as ministers watched with almost sadistic fascination. But without the gimlet eye of their leader upon them, their record suggests that they would have lost their nerve well before the desired 'demonstration effect', which always mattered more than the money, was achieved.

With Mrs Thatcher's fourth irreplaceable mark, we reach more contentious territory: the region, in fact, where hubris and nemesis met, to ultimately catastrophic effect. Few qualified observers doubt that her stand against the European Community achieved a British advantage in the early days, which was unavailable by other means. By asking reasonable questions in a wholly unreasonable manner, she secured more of 'our money' from Brussels. A decade's combative diplomacy made for a quite different British presence. Arguably, we counted for more in Europe, in a constructive as well as a critical role, in 1985 than in 1975.

But here came the first source of her trouble. The mark in Brussels became a kind of curse at home. Her elemental convictions about nationhood and sovereignty were not the feelings of significant colleagues. The issue became an emblem of the style as well as the content at the heart of her difficulties. It showed the falsity of this distinction. With this leader the style *was* the woman.

In modified form, this was also a key to her fifth uniquely personal policy, the poll tax. It is the only tax in the Western world to have grown more out of character than reason. Reason, as expressed by Nigel Lawson and the Treasury, said that it would be unjust, unworkable and insupportably expensive. Character, sticking blindly with a Thatcher commitment dating from 1974, insisted that it must go forward and enlisted – another consistent trait of these years – the incautious support of enough meekly compliant ministers for the blame to spread.

Policies alone, however, do not define the place she will take in the annals. The intangibles are perhaps more important and may ensure her name a longer life. Thatcherism embodies a style and a set of values that will take a long time to disappear from British politics. At the least, they may be the model of what to avoid: a memory studiously honoured in the breach. More likely, they will endure as an example others cannot neglect.

As a leader, she developed abrasiveness into an art form. She despised, above all, consensus: the goal of most other leaders but not her. She inveighed against it with as much vigour in November 1990 as she did before she became Prime Minister. As a leader, also, she needed to know everything and often seemed to do so. There never has been a leader better briefed, with readier riposte, more scornfully employed against her ignorant enemies. This most formidable capacity was some kind of answer to those who charged her, accurately, with an insatiable desire to interfere in every minister's business. Hardly anything moved in Whitehall without her approval; but for hardly anything that happened did she fail to have a detailed justification.

As well as this ambiguous virtue, however, she had a plainer one. She did not want to be liked. The least likeable of all leaders, according to consistent opinion poll findings, she none the less won three general elections. In this she was wholly admirable. She did not pander to the people. They often remarked on how much they hated her, even as they admitted to a grudging respect. This quality, often described as a flaw, did much for the moral calibre of our politics. No other leader in our time, I guess, will be so easily willing to resist the desire to please.

She used this harshness to establish a more prominent British presence in the world. Of all the people bewildered by what has happened, none flounder in deeper astonishment than foreigners from all over. For most of them, Margaret Thatcher has given a passable imitation of the Britannia whom, during the Falklands crisis, she shamelessly sought to personify. Before her, a series of faceless men, usually in grey suits, trod the global stage pretending to an influence that depended on past glories some of them could almost remember. They rarely said or did anything worthy of report on an inside page of the *New York Times*.

In the Thatcher era, the image has been different. During the Reagan years, moreover, image proclaimed more than mere appearance. Through their shared ideology, they formed a society for the mutual support of leaders determined to abolish the post-war consensus. Mrs Thatcher visited Washington often, was invariably fêted and, if an election year loomed, nationally drafted for the presidency. She had a very special relationship with Mr Reagan and, as the interlocutor with Mr Gorbachev, a special role in the dialogues that led to the ending of the Cold War. When that ice age broke up, moreover, it was to the Thatcher model that many of the newly free countries consciously turned for guidance on the modalities of the free market. All this was due to her personal charisma. Evangelism and showmanship captured the East, beginning in the Soviet Union shortly before the 1987 election. Some might say that the influence thereby attained was a little illusory. How could a weak country like Britain aspire to change the world, especially when Germany was becoming so manifestly the dominant power in Europe? But that only serves to reinforce the Thatcherite point: without her peculiar quality of conviction, proclaimed by her flamboyant personality, Britain would have continued to take its proper place as an increasingly obscure island off the shore of north-west Europe. It is a destination her successor will have the greatest difficulty in avoiding.

So this defiance of historic inevitability may not last long. There were signs of it waning well before she fell. Developments in both East and West were beginning to relegate Britain back into the second division. What the lady spoke for at home, on the other hand, could expect a longer shelf-life. It was here that her legacy had the best chance of surviving, if only because some of it has been seized by her opponents.

She spoke, as no one else did, for business Britain. Not just for big business but, rather more, for small. Detached from her party, she could easily have been a latter-day Poujadist, expressing the economic but also the social philosophy of little-England shop-keeping, the world from which she sprang. In entrepreneurship, in profit-making, in market-place success she saw the unalterable foundations of a successful society. She never deviated from this philosophy, and never tired of reiterating its principles as a guide to human conduct. Doubted and even despised during the seventies, these at last became conventional wisdom in the eighties.

Nowhere was this more apparent than in the Labour Party. Arguably, the new model Labour Party was one of her most important creations. She often vowed not to leave politics until socialism had been scorched off the face of Britain. One more term, she thought, would finally disabuse the country as well as Labour that the politics of the Left had any future. A pseudo-socialist

Labour Party has outlived her, which she will deeply regret. But the pseudery is significant. In Labour rhetoric, the virtues of private property and market economics have replaced ancient promises to dismantle the integument of the capitalist system. By departing, Mrs Thatcher may have removed Mr Kinnock's favoured electoral target: but she leaves an Opposition more anxious to retain than remove a fair amount of what she has done.

She also leaves an economy which, for all their railing, is stronger than it was. Maybe the most history will be able to say is that the Thatcher years decelerated British decline. Certainly the wondrous miracle, which many of her former colleagues were pointing to in their obituary tributes yesterday, takes its reality only from an assumption about where we might have been without the medicine she administered in the early eighties. Even so, if we grant that all political careers can be said to end in failure, with their grand promises never fully achieved, this career can be deemed less of a failure than many.

There were failures, however. And of many candidates for consideration, two strike me as reaching close to the heart of the Thatcher experience. Just as there were the positive events unattainable without her, so were there the negative: specific and peculiar to her person.

The first concerned her attitude to government itself, and in particular the role of the state. She came into power determined to reduce it. Most Tory leaders have said as much, but she was the first who announced a conscious mission to abandon paternalist aspirations and get government, even benign government, off the people's backs.

This was conspicuously accomplished in only one department, that of state ownership. The privatizing of productive business will never be reversed, and even the utilities are likely, under Labour, to remain outside the public sector. Selling council houses and cheap shares in gas switched a few million people from being clients of Labour, as the party of public ownership, to being clients of the capitalist party.

But elsewhere, Mrs Thatcher's relations with the state ended in confusion, futility and contradiction. One of her famous axioms was that no such thing as society existed: which postulated a dismantling of the collective institutions that propped society up. This did not happen. Her sentiment was widely regarded with ridicule and incomprehension, even among her own supporters. Society at large showed no inclination to assume its disintegrating role. Quite the opposite. Every test of public opinion showed that in her didactic task, of persuading people that the state could not be benign, she failed.

But her actions also countermanded her ambition. In the Thatcher years, there were many ways in which the central state grew more – not less – powerful. In finance, in education, in health services, the edicts of the centre overrode those of the locality, as local government was substantially undermined. She was aware of this paradox. In schools and hospitals, a species of market choice was supposed to stand substitute for local democracy. But in the end the gentlemen, and un-gentlewoman, in Whitehall knew best. We were told that this would be temporary. But a government of different temper will find a lot of new instruments in place, the tools of Mrs Thatcher's rage for action, conveniently ready for use.

Add to this the curtailments of civil liberties, notably concerning free expression, and the Thatcher era will go down as one in which state power increased. All Tory leaders have been vigilant in defence of the state's policing power. But a special edge was given this trait by this Prime Minister. Her own experience with terrorism, always an underrated aspect of her psyche, made her an unyielding proponent of media curbs which touched upon it. She was in favour of freedom as long as it could be paid for: a less reliable defender of the intangible liberties of man.

The second failure concerned, in the end, her view of what political leaders were meant to be and do. She had the vices of her virtues. This was what finally engulfed her.

She was strong, but put excessive weight on strength. She accumulated more personal power than any peacetime Prime Minister in history; and in that guise will interest the constitutional historian for many years. But she saw too little value in the art of compromise. Leadership, for her, was equated too often with the satisfaction of her will. How often, when challenged with being over-mighty, did she deride the notion of a leader who gave precedence to other virtues than strength. She was a conviction politician, but too often scorned the reasoned statement of different convictions, sometimes by her closest colleagues. Argument she relished, as long as she won, but persuasion she neglected. Give-and-take and the other techniques of sweet reason were alien to her nature. This made for abrasive and often decisive government, but it was fatally disabling for any kind of collective leadership. For surprisingly many years, it wrought no lasting damage.

The collective was willing to put up with its uncomradely supremo because, essentially, it was persuaded that she was going in the right direction: and in any case she kept on winning elections.

But at the end, over Europe, the one issue on which the Conservative Party was prepared to concede that it was most seriously divided, the obedience of the collective – beginning with Nigel Lawson and ending with Geoffrey Howe, and not forgetting the destruction wrought by Nicholas Ridley in between – collapsed.

Behind Mrs Thatcher's political method lay a vision of Britain, but perhaps more importantly, also a vision of herself. Although insecurity was never entirely missing from her makeup, it coexisted with even less confidence in the ability of anyone else to do what she was doing.

For many years she thought she was irreplaceable, a judgement which grew not out of simple vanity so much as an assessment of Britain's plight and what she could contribute to it. When the tumbrels began to roll two weeks ago, she still could not credit that this verdict was being revised. Nor could many other people. Some still cannot. Having broken the rules and beaten the system often in the past, she seemed capable of doing it again. It was almost an offence against nature to suppose that she could not.

But finally the system, which says that this is Cabinet and not prime-ministerial government, reacted. There was a point beyond which it declined to be flouted. This point was identified by an age-old reflex: the perception that an election was about to be lost and power surrendered to the other side. No fear exceeds that of politicians faced with the loss of office, not even fear of the avenging virago across the table. So in the end, in a drama whose outlandishness aptly reflected the years before, she went.

Maggie and me

MARGARET THATCHER, seventy-five this week, knew from the start that I wasn't likely to be 'one of us'. I worked for the *Sunday Times*, then an independent and liberal paper. I had all the wrong instincts, being neither a Conservative nor someone who believed political journalists should have other than sceptical connections with politicians. About the only thing we had in common was a birthday. Despite all this, we got on quite well, more to her credit than to mine.

It was partly, no doubt, a matter of prudence. The *Sunday Times* was a very big paper with a lot of politically uncommitted readers. I did several interviews with her when she was Prime Minister. The first was preceded by her personal search for Nescafé. If that happened at Number 10 today, you could be sure there had been a meeting of spin doctors beforehand, to assess precisely what impression should be made. But the early Thatcher was a cosmetic artefact only when she appeared on television. Her personal coffee-making wasn't, I thought, done for effect. Like her obsession with turning off the Downing Street lights, it was the extension of Grantham housekeeping into the prime-ministerial world.

There were two reasons, I think, why I survived for ten years as an acceptable interviewer and occasional off-the-record conversa-tionalist. First, Thatcher always liked an argument. It was a mode of discourse she found irresistible. The very fact that I was so plainly not in her camp became a virtue. I was bestowed with 'convictions', and even principles. Once allotted this label, I never seemed to lose it.

One of the things Mrs Thatcher said, intimidatingly, to an early civil servant was that she usually made up her mind about a man in ten seconds – 'and I rarely change it'. So, perhaps, it was with me. Her encompassing of me within her invincible power of persuasion was due, however, to the second feature of our relationship. I'm sure she never read a word I wrote. I retained my place in the tent of the acceptable because she never knew what I really thought, since she was a stranger to my columns. These became, as the years went by, critical to the point of savagery. I questioned her honesty as much as her wisdom. I impugned her motives, ridiculed her judgement and even cast doubt on her sanity. I remained, unread, within the pale.

One thing Thatcher certainly did not read was my biography of her, *One of Us*. And after all, why should she? Who would want to read what purported to be a detailed account of her life and thought, when knowing that every nuance, however honestly chronicled, was bound to be not quite how it really was?

The last time I met her was in what could, none the less, be called a biographical context. The occasion was the annual Christmas party given by the American Ambassador. A long queue was lining up to shake his hand, and suddenly my wife and I found that Lady Thatcher and her husband had materialized beside us. This wasn't long after she had ceased to be Prime Minister, and she could still not quite credit that she had to queue at all. A frisson of doubt on her face plainly revealed an inner impulse to march up to the front and be greeted without delay. But Denis decided against such a display of amnesia as to who they now were, and the two of them therefore faced ten minutes imprisoned in our company.

The talk, led by her, immediately turned to writing. This was a subject which used to attract little but her scorn. She once asked me in very public company when I was going to get down to some proper work – building wealth, creating jobs, etc – instead of wasting my time with journalism. It was one of the regrets of my life that I had lacked the presence of mind to say: 'After you, Prime Minister'.

But now, she told me, she had just completed the first volume of her memoirs. She was now a writer. The book had been a great labour, she said. But I wouldn't know anything about that, would I? Because I was a professional journalist. I was incredibly lucky, she added with patent reproach. A note of envy was even detectable. It was all so easy for me.

She, on the other hand, had had to labour at getting it all down. She had written every line of the first draft herself, she said, although that nice John O'Sullivan had helped her rearrange some of the words into a better order. But it was essentially all her own work. In recent years, she has taken up her life as a politician, albeit surrounded by a court rather than colleagues, and certainly not by journalists invited to give her an argument. Long ago, I resumed my original distance, and she, in more exaggerated form than ever before, the delusions of unchallengeable, world-correcting rightness. But I bask in the moment when, with ego pumping in a new direction, she was briefly 'one of us', absolving us writers, just for a year or two, from being 'one of them'.

John Major's life and coming death

IN POLITICS, one rule has the force of history behind it: if at the time of an election most people feel richer than they felt at the last one, they will vote for the person they believe to have been responsible for their prosperity. This rule, which imposed itself so emphatically in the United States last November, is taken to have universal application. For a decade, mounting middle-class affluence kept a Conservative, Margaret Thatcher, in power in Britain as surely as it did a Socialist, the late François Mitterrand, in France.

Across the whole of Europe, Britain now stands out as the financial leader. Among the Continent's major economies, Britain's is the fastest-growing, having outpaced France's and Germany's for four years, and it is also the most attractive to investors. Personal disposable income has continued to rise and, after years of fearful caution, consumer confidence has begun to follow it. Unemployment in Britain continues to fall, even as it climbs in Germany, and the Organization for Economic Co-operation and Development, the most authoritative monitoring body for the developed world, predicted in December that Britain's financial eminence would continue through 1998.

For Prime Minister John Major, the presiding genius of economic recovery, this prediction comes at the perfect time: on 1 May, if not before, there will be a general election. His party, the Conservative Party, has been in power for nearly eighteen years; he has led it for more than six; and there is enough evidence of prosperity to suggest that the historic axiom should still hold. Major invokes it every day, reminding the country, with only modest hyperbole, that it now has a better prospect of inflation-free, export-led growth than it has had at any time since the First World War.

Something, however, has gone wrong. The country appears not

to be listening. While reeling off the rosy economic statistics, the Prime Minister has yet to find a way of dealing with a more dismal figure – the finding of innumerable opinion polls that he's trailing the Labour Party by almost twenty points. The polls have been like that, or worse, for three years. Somehow, the old determinism is being thwarted. Instead of another laboratory test proving the ascendancy of the wallet over everything, a different experiment is being conducted – one in which the nation looks deeper into both itself and its leader, and finds problems that he and his party seem incapable of resolving. In particular, a Great Question presents itself: Where does Britain belong? In Europe? Out of Europe? In mid-Atlantic? On its own?

This historic choice is on the verge of defeating a man whose most reassuring credential when he succeeded Margaret Thatcher, in 1990, was that he had no historic vision of the kind with which she had alarmed the nation and impressed the world. He was uncannily prefigured by the character whom Joseph Heller described in *Catch-22*, the infamous Major Major: 'Even among men lacking all distinction he inevitably stood out as a man lacking more distinction than all the rest, and people who met him were always impressed by how unimpressive he was.' That it should fall to this man both to put the Tory Party in its soundest economic position for decades and to render it, on the larger question, unelectable is a bizarre apotheosis. But then bizarrerie has long attended him.

He was born in Worcester Park, a forgettable patch of suburbia on the southern edge of London, in 1943. His childhood is a morass of rememberings and forgettings. He doesn't like to talk about it, perhaps because it was so odd. 'Every time I've done so,' he told me recently, 'it has been distorted. Not necessarily by the person to whom I was talking and who wrote about it, but by the secondary comment that latches upon what was said when I had been talking to someone: "There he is again, talking about his background and trying to make political capital out of it." It's a crude point. And that's happened repeatedly. My background is unusual, and I concede that. It is unusual even if I wasn't a Tory. I am happy to concede that. But we have rich and diverse backgrounds in the United Kingdom. Why should that be strange?'

Major's father was sixty-three when he was born, and was

something of an exotic. In his early life, he had been a clown and a conjurer, a revue artist who took his touring company around the country: a small-business man, therefore, as well as a much travelled raconteur. He was born Tom Ball. That Britain later elected a Prime Minister called Major, bringing Heller's creation improbably to life, is owed to the fact that Tom Ball and his partner needed a stage name. She called herself Kitty Drum. Kitty Drum became his wife, and Drum and Major trod the boards as a double-act from the early 1900s until Kitty died, in 1928, felled backstage by a piece of scenery. Although Tom remarried – and left the theatre – his fourth child was named John Major. He was registered for school as John Major-Ball, a double-barrelled surname on which the boy insisted until he was a teenager. The hyphen betokens a certain class distinction, and Major has said that he didn't like it. Not long ago, however, one of his old teachers, Derek Esterson, gave television viewers a different story. 'If you didn't use the hyphenated form, he objected very strongly,' Esterson said. 'It was more or less a standing joke with the class. I would call the register, and if I didn't always use the hyphenated form he would jump up and shout "Major-Ball, sir".'

The childhood wasn't easy. By the 1940s, Tom Major-Ball was a more orthodox businessman, but not a very successful one, having turned to making garden ornaments while raising a family with his second wife. The austerities of the war and the period after it were not good for the market in garden gnomes: they were, after all, a discretionary purchase, and people stopped buying them. Business fluctuated to such disastrous effect that Tom had to sell his house and move his wife and children from the sedate gentility of Worcester Park to a two-room flat on the border between Brixton and Camberwell – inner and more squalid suburbs – where the kitchen was on the landing, the bathroom was two floors down, and West Indian immigrants were filling up the neighbourhood.

During the impressionable years between twelve and fifteen, Jack Major-Ball, as he was known, lived a straitened existence in a rough part of the inner city. His father, older than many boys' grand-fathers, was going blind, and, though he continued to turn out the garden gnomes, he was ashamed of the penury into which his family had sunk. He was also heavily in debt. This he attributed partly to inflation, which had a devastating effect on small-business people like him, and partly to petty bureaucrats in the Town Hall, who kept getting in the way of enterprise. The household, evidently, was not immune to political lectures of a Conservative persuasion, along with fecund storytelling by an old showman from another age.

If Major had been an American politician, it is likely that such a background would have been exploited, the familiar tale of struggle that finally ends in triumph. In fact, he has hesitated to make much of it, and instead has shown many signs of wanting to forget it. If Major had been an American, he would also probably have had a decent education. But he had a problem with school. He discharged himself at the age of sixteen, over feeble objections from his parents, and in adult life he has continued to complain unsentimentally about his school experiences. 'Anyone who thinks school days are the happiest days of your life should have their bumps felt,' he told an early biographer, Penny Junor. 'In my experience, school had to be endured before life could be enjoyed.' To Anthony Seldon, who has begun work on another biography, he is still making the point: 'I didn't like the shepherding together of lesser beings who were being told that they had to be subservient and to respect greater beings who happened to be schoolmasters.'

The language of the unreconstructed truant contrasts, however, with a certain embarrassment about the results. When prominence first exposed Major to routine media inspections of his past, his school records turned out to be closed; the local authorities had sealed off the archive. There was difficulty in establishing whether he could even remember which O-levels – the first-stage tests then universal in British schools – he had taken. The answer proved to be three while he was at school, followed by three a little later – a miserable performance.

For the 1992 election, his first as Party Leader, Major was persuaded to make a campaign film that took him back to his roots, the pollsters and spin doctors having told him that there were votes in it. He put the filming off half a dozen times. When the limousine finally trundled down Coldharbour Lane, Brixton, Major's reaction seemed perfectly rehearsed. 'It's still there,' he gasped. 'It's still there.' But this wasn't rehearsed. The surprise was genuine. He hadn't been back for decades. Life had carried him, mercifully, into another world.

It had done so, moreover, without stopping at the most familiar platform of all – a university. Modern Britain has had many upwardly mobile leaders: Margaret Thatcher's father was a corner grocer, and her predecessor, Edward Heath, was raised by a small-time builder. But Heath and Thatcher followed the familiar path from a state grammar school to Oxford University, the great dissolver of underprivilege for all who are bright enough to seize their opportunity. By the time Margaret Thatcher left Oxford, she had met half of Winston Churchill's Cabinet on their trips to address meetings of young Tories.

By leaving school at sixteen, Major cut out all chance of university. 'Would I change what I did? No,' he said when I asked him. 'Would I have liked to have been at university with the opportunity of reading the books that people say I haven't read, but in fact I have, and all sorts of other things? Yes, of course I would have liked that. Who wouldn't like the opportunity for a lot of reflection and educational thought?' This void makes him conspicuous among world leaders. Bill Clinton attended Georgetown, Oxford and Yale Law School; Helmut Kohl, the German Chancellor, probably Major's most important interlocutor, holds a doctorate from Heidelberg; François Mitterrand was a law graduate of the faculty of political science at the Sorbonne; Boris Yeltsin got a degree in civil engineering after five years at a technical college in the Urals; and even Saddam Hussein apparently studied law. John Major went nowhere at first, except into a series of dead-end jobs of the kind awaiting any school dropout. He worked as a clerk for the London Electricity Board, helped out with the gnomes, was unemployed for many months, was turned down when he applied to be a bus conductor.

Late last year, the annual Lord Mayor's Banquet was once again held in the ancient Guildhall in the City of London, the financial centre. This is put on every year to honour the Prime Minister of the day. The current Lord Mayor is a hard-nosed City accountant, but on this night he was in his role as high-establishment figure, costumed in a robe, silver buckled shoes, and a tricorn hat, greeting guests after they were floridly announced and then made to walk a gauntlet of fifty paces. Ambassadors, jurists, and military top brass all sported an array of regalia, and for the grandest of them a personal chorus of trumpets issued from somewhere in the rafters. The Lord Chief Justice was in his full-bottomed wig, and the Archbishop of Canterbury wore a ceremonial skirt that matched his purple breeches. Last in line was the Prime Minister.

At her zenith, Margaret Thatcher attended the banquet wearing a high Tudor ruff and collar that shamelessly recalled a celebrated portrait of Queen Elizabeth I. Her successor, who appeared in plain white tie and tails, is not so obviously cut out for grandeur. He merited a double fusillade of trumpets, but the applause dribbled out dutifully as he and his wife, Norma, walked up the aisle. Norma, a once-timid housewife who has blossomed as a biographer and small-scale historian, looked apologetic. As it happened, I was watching these proceedings from the gallery above, standing behind a camera. As the mayoral group swivelled to look up for a photograph, I found myself looking directly into Major's face. He was calm, unblinking, easy-smiling behind large spectacles, acquiescent in the preposterous theatricals laid on for his greater glorification. This was politics, British politics. When, at the end of a long evening, he finally prepared to speak, I saw him glancing at the clock: the Lord Mayor's introductory rotundities had gone on too long, and the Prime Minister's own soundbites would be too late to be the top story on the television news. The speech, when it came, was all about the British economic miracle. Major's vowels have never entirely shed the nasal whine typical of south London. Neither cadence nor climax graced this oratory, and the statistics were hard going at that hour of the night. But he appended allusions to British Nobel Prize winners, Oscars, Broadway triumphs of English shows, and *Newsweek*'s recent, and entirely arbitrary, designation of London as the coolest city on the planet, all of it evidence, he lumpenly concluded, that 'Britain is back in business – and it's back to stay.'

Brixton is only two miles away from the Guildhall. Not long after the banquet, I tried to find out how Major had felt about the piquancy of the shift. His reply was typical of a man who has raised ordinariness into his own bathetic art form: 'I have never felt overwhelmed by coming here from Brixton, ever, and everyone's background leaves its own imprint and I dare say mine has as well. But I don't see any reason why someone from the back streets of

Brixton hasn't as much right to be in Downing Street as someone who went to Eton, Oxford, the Guards, and the Inns of Court.'

For John Major, the turning point towards high politics was supplied, with raw directness, by politics itself. After he left school, he joined the Young Conservatives. There he immediately found himself at home. The brooding youth discovered a community he could relate to. Lonely and largely friendless – he was the youngest in the family by eleven years – he began to enjoy a social life. Having been previously confined to the charmless square mile of suburban London, he now travelled to alluring seaside resorts where British parties held their annual conferences. He became, almost at first contact, a politics junkie.

Somewhere along the line, Jack Major-Ball disappeared into the troubling past, and John Major emerged as a young man whom local politicians could rely on to work the streets and harry the enemy in a largely working-class part of London that the Labour Party had run since the beginning of time. The activity brought him, quite suddenly, to life. It was the start of an apprenticeship: though he would take up a low-level career in banking, he was, for the next twenty years, preparing for his entry into the holy of holies, Parliament itself.

From the Brixton streets, he graduated to unglamorous work in local politics, eventually helping to manage the public housing in the borough. He wasn't a man of ideas. Political management was his forte, and a kind of gawky, unfailing politeness was his readiest tool for securing results. He came without baggage. When, in 1976, the Party nominated him as its candidate for Huntingdonshire, a 'safe' Conservative district near Cambridge, he worked it as if he were likely to lose it, visiting every one of its seventy-seven villages and courting an electorate that, though apparently rural, was actually rather like him: the sparsely populated countryside had been steadily occupied by thousands of Londoners spilling out of the capital in the expansive sixties in search of a better life. In 1979, a general election was called – Thatcher's first, heralding a new ideological age. But for the neat, colourless young man for whom politics was the most serious thing he'd ever been paid to do, ideology was never on his agenda.

Once he was in Parliament, modesty was his style. Liked by most people, he was noticed by few, cultivated by none. It was more than three years before he got his first real job, as a junior whip, and almost another three years before he was promoted to a significant policy position, in charge of the smaller outposts of the nation's social-security system. Several contemporaries were promoted much faster and much higher. In the typical curriculum vitae of a British politician, Major's social-security job might have been expected to lead, with great good fortune and after a tortuous and lengthy climb, to a Cabinet position. Instead, in just little more than five years, he found himself Prime Minister.

It turned out that he *had* been personally noticed, by Mrs Thatcher. She was ever on the lookout for likely young men – seldom young women – who seemed plausible supporters of her hard right-wing approach to economic and social questions, and she had selected him for a social-security job similar to the one in which she herself had started ministerial life a quarter-century earlier. Perhaps it was an auspice. He had qualified, in her famous phrase, as One of Us, which was to say that he could safely be admitted to her camp of true Conservatives who were certain to be loyal to the leader against the attacks of softer, wetter, Tories. There had been many favourites who came and went. By the mid-eighties, when Thatcher was at the height of her pomp, the Tory abattoir was lined with the corpses of men – Cecil Parkinson, Leon Brittan, and John Moore, to name but three – whom she had identified as destined to sit one day alongside her, perhaps with a claim on the succession. Major was different.

He survived, however, in ironic circumstances. Although he was instinctively loyal, he was never one of Thatcher's dogmatic disciples. It was enough for her, apparently, that he had no compelling ideas one way or the other. He did agree with her doctrine of monetarism: that the supply of money was the prime cause of inflation, that full employment should be abandoned as a political objective, and that the early-twentieth-century economist John Maynard Keynes was a fossil whose teachings had no place in modern policy. He offered no argument against the painful rigours that Thatcher had inflicted on British society. While other Tories sometimes rebelled, Major went along with the anti-trade-union, market-dominated, welfare-curbing priorities of his patron, never uttering a squeak of protest as she capped the spending of local councils, and destroyed their power, which was essential to the increase of her own. Above all, Major was conveniently competent. Whatever job he had, he didn't drop the ball. He therefore got a big one unnaturally soon: in 1987, he was suddenly raised into the Cabinet, as Chief Secretary to the Treasury, with the task of policing all government expenditures.

Thatcher, by then, had grown ever more imperious, her rages finally provoking a series of equally furious responses among her most senior colleagues. Major entered a Cabinet in which turbulence was seething all around him, and he, with his timely aptitude of character, was its beneficiary. The Foreign Secretary, Geoffrey Howe, grappled with the Iron Virago once too often, and was pitched out of his job, as was the Chancellor of the Exchequer, Nigel Lawson – both men great beasts in the political forest. On each occasion, the same amenable replacement was standing quietly by. To call Major a cipher would be unfairly demeaning, but he seemed to be what Thatcher now needed: a competent, deferential, unchallenging, slightly puzzled loyalist – Major, Major, Major Major.

Behind this turbulence, one question loomed: the Great Question.

The Europe of today is the work of a generation of European leaders, who in the aftermath of the Second World War wanted to ensure that there would be no more war on the most warlike continent in the history of the world. To this end, in 1958 they established an economic body, the European Economic Community, known as the Common Market, to lower the customs barriers between European countries, in hope of creating greater political cohesion and, ultimately, an economic entity that would increase Europe's power in the world market – especially in its competition with the United States. Germany and France, nations ruined by war, were behind it, along with four of their neighbouring countries – Italy, Belgium, Luxembourg and the Netherlands – and in four decades the six have vastly prospered. In 1992, the Common Market became the European Union, and it has been expanded to fifteen countries. For trading purposes it is in most ways a single unit, with its workers crossing frontiers, with its internal tariffs removed, and with its economic rules increasingly harmonized between its members. The Union's next great ambition is to replace as many as possible of its national currencies by a single central bank controlling it.

In forty years, this extraordinary project has advanced by fits and starts, but a consistent feature of it has been Britain's uneasy resistance. Britain didn't join at the beginning, tried to get in in the early sixties only to be vetoed by the French leader, Charles de Gaulle, and finally entered in 1973; ever since, it has been the reluctant member of the club. Britain is the offshore island, culturally and mentally aloof from the Continent for centuries, but it is in Britain that the arguments about what 'Europe' means for nationhood have been played out with the most divisive agony. In fact, Europe has changed Britain immensely for the better. More than half of British exports now go to the tariff-free Union, and the vast increase in travel has lowered many barricades. The culinary revolution that has given London a respectable claim to being the best place to eat in Europe is only one example of what has been gained from the Continental infection. But infection is how the process continues to be seen by members of the Conservative Party, traditionally the party of the flag. This argument has become the European version of America's own: What power should belong to the states and what to the federal government? On the threshold, probably, of a single currency, even Continental politicians are beginning to wonder just how federal European politics can expect to become.

British politics is now dominated by this question. With the passing of socialism, it has become the only one that matters. In Tory politics, the pallid Mr Major, prince of operators and scourge of ideologues, has been decisively touched by it. It was instrumental in his becoming Prime Minister, and now is working towards his demise.

Thatcher's leadership was dominated by anti-Europeanism. As Prime Minister, she inherited the connection to Europe as an axiom of British polity, but from the beginning she attacked it with an aggression that, at first, inspired her party just as much as it revolted the European 'partners'. Europe, in Thatcher's eyes, was not only federalist but socialist, and was therefore an affront to much she thought she'd done as a great, consensus-defying right-wing leader of Britain. 'We have not successfully rolled back the frontiers of the state in Britain, only to see them reimposed at a European level, with a European super-state exercising a new dominance from Brussels,' she lectured the Europeans in 1988, at the height of her power and indignation.

Europe, all the same, defeated her. It was the pretext for one of the most astonishing episodes of British or any other politics. Here was a leader who had won three elections for the Conservative Party, in 1979, 1983, and 1987. By November 1990, she had helped Ronald Reagan beat down the Soviet Empire and had won the Falklands War; she was famous around the world, and most Conservative Members of Parliament owed their jobs to her all-dominating leadership. Yet that month she was ousted by these same MPs. She was, after all, only the leader of a party, not a president – a distinction central to British politics. Like all parliamentary leaders, she was the servant of her party before she could be the leader of the nation, and in 1990 her party sacked her.

On one level, the reason was simple: the MP's thought she couldn't win them the next election. Though different members of the party were in revolt for different reasons, most shared a loathing for a style of governing that had finally become intolerable. Some were concerned by the reckless way she had reformed local property taxes, the 'poll tax' that had inflamed typical householders, including many Tories, and had provoked riots in the streets. Some thought her to be genuinely demented: two Cabinet ministers told me early in 1990 that she was 'certifiably barking' – English slang for mad. And for some, the defining moment was a summit meeting of European leaders in Rome, at the end of October 1990: in response to moves toward monetary union she had administered such unbelted savagery upon her European colleagues that it convinced many MPs that she was no longer capable of defending the national interest. Since party rules made it possible to force her to stand for re-election as its leader, she was duly made to do so and, amid scenes driven by an emotionalism that matched her own, was thrown out.

The party, looking now for a leader who was Thatcher's polar opposite in style, alighted on the inoffensive grey man from Brixton via Huntingdon, calm, collected, and classless, with opinions that, as far as they could be discerned, attracted the least hostility from the largest number of MPs in what was by then a dangerously opinionated party. In particular, he was acceptable to the right, the enraged friends of Thatcher, who were determined to prevent the succession from going to the other challengers, especially Michael Heseltine (in Tory terms a pro-European lefty) or Douglas Hurd, the Foreign Secretary. Both were more fully formed politicians than Major, readier for the purple. Both had done more jobs, been longer at the top, acquired a more formidable aura. But they did not come from the Thatcherite tradition. Major did. On this basis, he won quite easily, arriving at the top, as is sometimes the perilous charm of politics, sooner than custom dictated or anyone had expected, but the calibre of his right-wingery had never been put precisely to the test. In falling so gratefully on the man whose greatest talent, a friend once said, was to leave 'everyone confident and convinced they have John as an ally', the party didn't really know what it was getting.

He did at first what the faithful wanted. Major's strength, his managerial shrewdness, was what the situation had called for, and he immediately applied it. He lowered the temperature, liquidated the worst problems, made room for British Conservatism to rediscover its distinctive quality as the most formidable election-fighting machine in Europe. Thatcher's taxation disaster, the poll tax, was deftly abandoned, and the street riots ceased. In place of her jagged nationalistic posturing, Major made emollient promises that the country would be 'at the very heart of Europe' – an aim that would now sound unimaginably inflammatory but which the party then permitted him to declare without demur. And in April of 1992 he led it to a narrow but decisive victory, consigning the Labour Party to its fourth successive defeat.

Major now had a five-year term of his own stretching ahead. It was no longer so easy for him to shelter behind a calculated lack of political definition. On many matters, he naturally adopted essential Thatcher positions with more outspoken emphasis than he had expressed in previous jobs. On the economy, for instance, he continued to observe the Thatcher agenda. The railways – a nationalized institution – were set to share the fate of the previously privatized utilities: water, gas and electricity. Trade-union powers were curtailed yet again. Major, a creature of Thatcher's age, was a Thatcherite, if only because there was nothing else he knew how to be.

But there were soon signs that he wasn't a clone. A part of the Brixton experience that never left him was the resolute hostility it gave him to any kind of racial prejudice. He was and is a humane and decent man; 'decent' indeed is the epithet that has survived through some extravagant descents into ridicule and contempt as his political power has waned. Quite early on, he offered more explicit support for gay rights than any Prime Minister before him, by warmly receiving the actor Ian McKellen in his capacity as a leading gay activist, and endorsing his nomination for a knighthood. Certain elements of the party were not amused. One of the complaints of the anti-Europe Right, which now detests him, is that he remains too vapid in every way. A senior honcho of this school, ranting to me recently, said the trouble with Major is that he 'lacks all conviction'.

'All?' I asked.

'Oh, well, he cares about the blacks and the Third World, and safe havens for Kurds. But I don't count those.'

The Right, in short, had rather mistaken their man. With Thatcher gone, he was the one thing keeping the infidel Heseltine at bay, but the other candidate, Douglas Hurd, knew very well that Major would never recite the full rightist catechism. Hurd told me, 'When he was Chief Secretary and I was Home Secretary, we used to have lunch every three or four months. I wasn't close to him, but he talked clearly about his views and they were a long way from hers. I've never understood (a) why she thought he was a protégé, and (b) why the right wing in 1990 thought, Here's our guy. I don't think he deceived anybody. I think they both just wanted to believe in him. I thought I knew differently. I was right, in almost all respects except, perhaps, the purely fiscal area.'

A more common error was to underestimate Major's intellectual capacity, the source of much condescension, when the chattering classes cottoned on to the meagreness of his education. Somewhere along the line, Major had developed a first-class brain. There seems to be no technicality he can't master. A senior Foreign Office official, a man of top-drawer arrogance, once told me he'd never known a minister to show greater intellectual facility than Major did in coming to grips with the monstrous complexities of the so-called 'hard' ECU, the virtual currency that was once making the rounds as the solution to Europe's desire for common money. Raymond Seitz, when he was the United States Ambassador in London during the Bush administration, saw a lot of Major, and was awed by his intelligence. 'Whether it was GATT or arms control or Russia, I was always impressed,' Seitz said. 'He was always prepared. He was very alert, especially to what had just happened.'

Part of this is the result of sheer hard work. His friend Chris Patten, the Governor of Hong Kong, says that Major works harder than anyone he knows. The relentless grinder overcompensates for the training he never had. 'He has this ability to run down the adrenalin, every single speck of it, and then somehow to recharge it overnight. Many nights, I'd go home and think, He's got parliamentary questions tomorrow. He's got a statement tomorrow, yet he's in a state of total exhaustion. Nothing in the tank. But by morning he'd done that extraordinary recharging process.'

Major is very good with people who don't patronize him and, perhaps for that reason, has always had women in senior posts around him. He seems more comfortable with them: looks them straight in the eye, offers them the double-fisted handshake of a tactile man who, a glib psychiatrist might conclude, wants to be loved. But he's also a watcher. Douglas Hurd, who continued as Foreign Secretary for the first five years of Major's premiership, much admired the international negotiating panache of someone whose paucity of foreign experience was evident in his never having visited the United States until he got into the Cabinet. That narrow past, according to Hurd, has been no bar to Major's success in even the widest fields, for he simply transferred to them the lifelong talents of a Brixton survivor – a street wisdom about people.

'He is passionately interested in personalities,' Hurd said. 'He's a student, a collector of people. He studies body language more than anyone else I've known. Getting into foreign affairs was like enlarging his collection. He used to say to me, because I was often with him, "But you didn't watch what his hands were doing. You didn't see what he was doing with his hair at that point."'

When I reported this to Major, his own body visibly stiffened. Plainly, I had stumbled on the protective device of an outsider from way back. 'Yes,' he said to me, his cover blown. 'I look at the body language at least as much as I listen to the words … I have always done it. It's always been there. I have been able to do that, and have done that, as far back as I can ever remember.'

He's proud of being a man of the people. 'It's deeply ingrained in him that the person who's bringing him dinner is quite as important as the person who's bringing him advice,' Sarah Hogg says. 'He treats servants in exactly the same way as ambassadors, to the annoyance of some ambassadors.' But he feels that others' condescension is always lurking.

For instance, he still can't understand why people should imagine that because he left school early he must be an unlettered philistine. Even so, in his Downing Street flat, where our main conversation took place, there didn't seem to be all that many books. My visit was a rare one. Interviews with journalists are normally held at the twenty-six-seater table in the Cabinet Room, which he uses as his office: a daily reassurance, perhaps, that he alone commands the often cantankerous characters who meet there once a week. The flat was more intimate: our knees almost met as we sat across from each other in tightly placed chintz armchairs. The adornments there which he most cares about are cricket memorabilia, and he instructed me on them piece by piece. There were a couple of decent Impressionist paintings on the wall, of which, when I asked him, he showed no knowledge, peering at them as if for the first time. They turned out to be lent, and the lender had stipulated that they shouldn't be publicly identified. Major showed more interest in a horrifically garish portrait of Joan Sutherland, the diva whose biography his wife, Norma, has written. But the books were what was bothering him. 'I find it astonishing,' he said, 'that I read this nonsense from time to time about how I don't read books … I've been a bibliophile, reading everything I can lay my hands on, since I was about four.' Over his shoulder, as we spoke, I saw anthologies of cricket writing and an Anthony Trollope collection. He said he always read for half an hour before going to sleep. A Trollope was by his bed; he was rereading *In Pale Battalions*, by Robert Goddard, a crime writer steeped in English nostalgia; and he had *Sense and Sensibility* on the go again following the success of the film. But the real library, he said, was in his private house, near Huntingdon. He added that he had extended it at both ends, partly to accommodate his groaning shelves.

In his determination not to be underestimated, Major calls to mind a contemporary with whom he might seem to have little in common. George Bush, after all, was the American version of an aristocrat. But the Age of Major matches that of Bush. Neither man was many people's obvious choice for the top job. The mentalities of both were, at best, dilute versions of the heady stuff that had intoxicated the politics of the eighties. Each succeeded a force of nature, and lived not only in the shadow of that force but under the resentful eyes of those who had worshipped the deity who was gone. Coming in as America prepared for war in the Persian Gulf, Major, the new leader of the closest military ally, was a high risk for Bush.

'Who is this guy?' they asked in Washington.

'There was no take on him,' Raymond Seitz recalls. 'He had been Foreign Secretary for only three months, and he had no record.'

Their personal affinities, as much as anything, soon got Major and Bush together. On his first visit to Washington, Major was suitably deferential, and Bush was overjoyed not to be dealing with the woman who, once Reagan had gone, imagined herself the leader of the Free World and allowed it to be known that Bush, confronted by Saddam Hussein's invasion of Kuwait, might well lack the spine to take him on. From the moment Major went to Camp David with Bush in December 1990, and told him 'I'm with you' over the Gulf, the relationship of two quiet, modest men, who would both rather like than dislike people, became agreeably productive.

Even then, though, Major could not relinquish his social insecurity, and he never has. He is still very worried about doing the wrong thing. On being invited to Bush's Kennebunkport estate the following summer, he didn't know what clothes to bring. How many short-sleeved shirts? Would there be fishing, which he'd never done? Though unpretentious, he has his vanities. Would his arms look too white under the American sun? 'You will notice,' one of Major's friends said, 'that he never gets out of a helicopter until the blades stop. He has an obsession about his hair being in place.' The hovering critics, actual or anticipated, are ever-present in the front of his mind, on large matters as well as on trivia of dress and deportment. For a man at the top of a not insignificant country for six years, he seems to get little fun out of life. 'He doesn't allow himself many treats, never goes off to the Ritz for a good meal,' a puzzled colleague said. 'It's very curious to be Prime Minister for so long and tell everybody the whole time how much you dislike it.'

Major did not demur when I put that to him. 'If you mean I don't take the perks out, I am not interested, I am not in politics for perks,' he said. 'Politics is a damned serious business,' he added before running through his workload, which, he insists, is more massive than for anyone else in his global peer group.

I got a glimpse of his humourlessness even in Huntingdon, his home and electoral base, where I followed him around one day at the end of November. Out there, people are pleased to see him. On every fourth Friday, he spends, like any ordinary Member of Parliament, a few hours with the people who elected him, advising them on their welfare claims or their housing needs. It's an impressive habit, which most recent Prime Ministers have lost soon after getting into Downing Street. It's the kind of politics that this wholly ungrand leader is most relaxed about.

The next day he attended a breakfast for a hundred and twenty small-business men and women who paid about £25 a head for the meal, a small fraction of what it costs to breakfast with Clinton. With no other journalists present, he gave them the message about British success, stressing the steady economic path, disclaiming seductions. 'I have a particular loathing of inflation,' he said, expressing his deepest economic conviction, which began with his long-gone father and his experiences with unsold garden gnomes. 'Inflation is the worm in the apple. I would loathe a short-term boom. I want steady, sustainable growth. I would rather lose the election and be able to say to people we were trying to persuade them about what is right, and didn't manage to do so, than to win it by doing the wrong thing.'

The locals were tickled. Later in the day, Major visited a shop that sold tickets for the National Lottery. The lottery, a weekly numbers game, has been one of his government's great successes, puncturing the age-old priggishness about state-sponsored gambling: in its first two years, it raised more than £2.4 billion ($3.6 billion) for the arts, sports, and charity. This visit marked the second anniversary, and I thought its only purpose was for Major to be photographed purchasing a ticket. He entered the shop, looked around, talked to staff, but failed to buy a ticket. As he was leaving, I asked him why. 'Oh, no,' he replied knowingly. 'Can you imagine what people would say if I won?'

But the odds on winning a million are beyond invisible, I said. Anyway, you could always give it away.

He paused. 'I prefer to give my money direct to charity,' he solemnly stated – a line that precisely contradicted the very selling point that had converted gambling from an unthinkable vice into a great British life-enhancer. Making further inquiries, I discovered that he had another reason for not playing the game. Major, who carries a big mortgage, has always been worried about money. How terrible it would be, he once mused to a friend, if he won a big prize and was then compelled to spend the rest of his life regretting that he couldn't, in all decency, pocket the proceeds.

So, yes, a miserable sod. And now, having arrived in office as the man with the fewest enemies, he faces the imminent loss of it as a leader with almost no friends. The very question that put him where he is today is on the verge of destroying him.

He actually began by handling the Europe issue quite well. After Thatcher's rage, Major's mildness and punctilio were greeted with as much relief by Continental leaders as they were by George Bush. He talked their language of consensus, and knew how to negotiate. The expert in body-reading was also formidably well briefed, keeping far more details in his head than grander capos like Kohl and Mitterrand, and he was rewarded accordingly.

The test had come a few months before the election, in December 1991. In the Dutch town of Maastricht, a treaty was negotiated that significantly advanced the cause of a federal Europe, committing the Union to creating a single currency within the next decade, and making important strides towards a closer collaboration on security and foreign policy. The treaty also contemplated several ways in which members would surrender some of their independence to the Union itself, with its federalizing institutions, such as its court and its Parliament, becoming more powerful. Though the Maastricht Treaty was a significant step towards more federalism, it was one that Major could accept, because he had secured two crucial exemptions: Britain, alone, retained the right to keep its own illiberal employment laws (under which hours of work, wage levels and collective rights are less securely guaranteed than on the Continent); and Britain, along with Denmark, kept open the option of not joining the scheme of the single currency. This seemed to preserve what mattered most to the Conservative Party, and when Major returned from Maastricht, his claim that it had been a victory – 'Game, set, and match,' his spokesman imprudently rejoiced – was accepted by almost all Tories. The Continentals, equally, recognized a cunning negotiator. Ruud Lubbers, the Dutch Prime Minister at the time, told me, 'There are two models for negotiation – one rational and one emotional. Most political leaders negotiate emotionally. Margaret Thatcher. Helmut Kohl. You mustn't be intimidated when someone is shouting at you. John Major is a rational negotiator. A gentleman, rational, well-briefed, well informed.'

At Maastricht, and in its immediate aftermath, Major was in top form, seeming to keep both sides happy. A handful of his diehards objected to what the Europeans were getting up to, and criticized him for declining to use his veto to stop the treaty entirely. But, on the whole, he got away with having it both ways: remaining fully inside the Union, but on Britain's own terms.

Such comfort did not last long. On 16 September 1992, five months after the election, came a humiliation that yoked 'Europe' to Major's fate permanently. Until Black Wednesday, as the dreaded day came to be known, the value of the pound was linked to that of other European currencies through the so-called exchange rate mechanism. This was designed to be a prelude to full economic union. Central banks agreed to support each other's currencies at preset parities. The pound, however, weakened during the summer of 1992, and speculators began to bet heavily against its being supported. In the days before and after Black Wednesday, the financier George Soros reputedly made over a billion dollars for his fund by selling sterling short, and buying the stronger Deutschmark, certain that the pound would be devalued, which with the parities unsustainable, it duly was.

'Coming out of [the mechanism] was a disaster. It was a political disaster. There's no doubt about that, of course it was,' Major told me. 'It was an embarrassment for the United Kingdom.'

But it was more than that. It unleashed the rage of the anti-Europe elements in his party equally upon the European Union and upon him. Their ferocity was extraordinary. From this moment, the British dialogue about Europe descended to a new level of unreason, and the press to new depths of invention. 'CAN MAJOR TAKE THE STRAIN?' shouted a headline in *The Times*, Rupert Murdoch's up-market Europhobic organ, over a text that shamelessly speculated about 'the state of the Prime Minister's mind'. Without a shred of evidence, the paper recited the gamut of stress disorders from which he was supposed to be suffering, and several right-wing columnists declared him unfit to be a national leader. Having watched six Prime Ministers at close quarters, I can say with confidence that not one of them has been subjected to a more contumacious cacophony of bile from his so-called friends, and that Europe has been at the bottom of it. Major the tactician, forever dodging and weaving between the reality of Britain's deep links with Europe and the fantasy sustained by members of his party of breaking them, has been torn apart. Major the visionary is a creature that never did exist. It was part of his job description, when he succeeded a woman whose visions had turned to nightmares, that it shouldn't exist.

The next major conference of the European Union is in June, in Amsterdam, after the British election. The next great issue will be which countries will submerge their currencies into the euro. The British position is to wait and see, a stand that keeps the country in negotiations and appeases the few pro-Europe members who remain in Major's Cabinet. Procrastinate and survive, his familiar tactic, continues. But it's obvious that the Tory Party will not accept a single currency, at least initially, and Major came closer, in talks with me, to revealing his own scepticism than he has done before. His schizoid condition continues. On the one hand, he speaks as though economic and monetary union were virtually impossible: it would involve every member-state surrendering control of interest rates and much else to a European central bank, a prospect he finds democratically repugnant. As he said, 'I wouldn't like to be the Chancellor of the Exchequer who went to the dispatch box and said, "Well, I no longer have any control over interest rates, I am sorry they have gone up three per cent, but it's nothing to do with me, Guv."'

'But that's an argument for never going into economic and monetary union,' I replied.

'Yes,' he said, 'it is an argument for never going in, and it's one we'll have to confront at some stage.'

On the other hand, he is utterly opposed to Britain's even contemplating exit from the European Union. 'That is madness. It is nonsense, copper-plated nonsense, that we would leave the European Union and form some kind of new Atlantic alliance.' In other words, Major wholly favours the European Union but almost wholly disfavours its most definitive project. The cleavage within him is complete.

Meanwhile, more and more Tories now talk about quitting Europe entirely. The rejection of Major's line – an unprecedented, organized spurning of the leader – is part of a wider degradation that includes indiscipline, rancour and sleaze. Conservatism is now openly detested by much of Britain. The country seems to have had enough, notwithstanding the rise of its economy or the respect, tinged with pity, it feels for the weak and decent leader who is about to be engulfed.

The rules governing politicians' ethics in Britain have always been lax, but it is on Major's watch that their inadequacy has been exposed. The Major years, evolving seamlessly out of the Thatcher years, have seen Tory MPs accepting bribes for tabling questions in Parliament at the behest of business clients; the National Heritage Secretary was sacked after he was caught, among other things, sucking the toes of an 'actress'; another minister resigned when it was discovered that he had fathered an illegitimate child; another was maintained in office even after he had confessed to having had five mistresses. The moral rot of one-party government has seldom become more grimly apparent to a nation that never, in any case, produced a Conservative majority among voters (although they were obviously happy to tolerate an electoral system which has preserved one in Parliament for four elections). Major, while personally horrified by the sleaze, has always been reluctant to move decisively against it, for fear of offending his allies. As he has over the issue of Europe, he has temporized. Temporizing is always what he sees best how to do.

Approaching an election that could be called any time between now and 1 May, Major is not without a plan. The Tory political programme is now a mix of consolidation and further radicalism, with still more privatizing, perhaps of the welfare state itself, in sight. But Major's principle re-election strategy rests on deploying simple fear. 'Don't Let Labour Ruin It' is the message of speeches and advertising posters. The Conservative Party still has plenty of money behind it, with a 'fighting fund' of more than thirty million dollars. Maurice Saatchi, Thatcher's advertising man, is working hard for Major. The man himself yields no ground to the common perception that the Labour Party, under modernizing leader Tony Blair, holds few terrors. He regards Blair as a phoney capitalist, leading a party that has opportunistically changed its spots, and he can't believe the people could be so gullible as to vote for him. Saatchi's advertising thus far has featured two keynote images: a shifty Blair, menacingly masked in red devil's eyes, and a weeping family group from Middle England, who are meant to convey the coarse message that a Labour government would end in tears. Major still thinks this stuff will work, although few others in his Cabinet share his confidence. He said, 'We are now on the verge, after seventeen years, of a degree potentially of stability that we haven't had for a very long time, and at that stage up pops fashionable opinion and says, "Well, they have got everything right now, so it is safe to turn to the people who oppose them in everything they have done."' In the cause of dispelling this fashionable fallacy, Major is trying to summon up a slightly new persona – that of a man who, against all odds, has achieved great things.

For the first time, he has begun to make something of that extraordinary past, apparently seeing it as a way of outfacing his challenger; Blair had a very full education, starting at Fettes College, a private school, and passing on to Oxford, which Major still pretends he never missed. The man of toil, not to mention experience, emerges from the Right to smack down the presumptions of the toff from the Left. Behind him are his real achievements. For better or worse, his government has continued to privatize public businesses and force competition on to public services. He has spent more time on Northern Ireland than all his predecessors in the seventy-six years since Irish Partition, and has done so for no better reason than that he felt it was his duty to try to produce a peace. There were certainly no easy votes in it. And then there is the economy, which he has brought to the unfamiliar pinnacle, and which, in times past, would have guaranteed election victory.

Early in his time, this cautious fellow, who seldom enters the foothills of oratory and fine phrase-making, hit upon a defining sentiment to which he was prepared to put his name. On being asked to describe his political purpose as Prime Minister, he replied that he desired to foster 'a nation at ease with itself'. It was a modest ambition, in keeping with the aura of self-effacing benignity he likes to cultivate. Perhaps it was a personal signal, too. Here, after all, is a man in search of ease with himself, trying to make sense of past and present. His picture of where he might find it reaches back to another England, where, in words he once spoke but surely didn't write himself, are found the 'long shadows on county grounds, warm beer, invincible green suburbs, dog lovers and' – paraphrasing George Orwell, a man hitherto never pilfered for Tory propaganda – 'old maids bicycling to Holy Communion through the morning mist'. The problem, however, is not the ease but the nation. That problem Major has not solved. Does Britain belong in Europe? Six years of Major have produced the answer for which he deserves to be forgotten: Maybe.

The people's triumph

SOME ELECTIONS SWEEP aside every refinement of interpretation. That is what the British, the stolid, conservative, middle-minded, middle-class British, did yesterday. Voting for the centre, they delivered a result of withering extremism. Bringing in the centre-Left, they despatched the Right into outer darkness with a conclusiveness that has never been done to it in times of prosperity and peace. Their mood may not have seemed exultant, but their decision was staggeringly emphatic. They set at nought every threat, every fear, every trumped-up charge, every scream of warning, every promise of doom the Tories could invent, and quietly did what every opinion poll said they would do: tell John Major and his shabby, busted government to get stuffed.

It was predicted, and we could not believe it. Nobody believed it: Labour, Tory, Liberal Democrat, editor, pundit. The people were often said to be mysteriously missing from the election the professionals were conducting. They were said not to know, not to have decided, not to be engaged. But the people seem to have known what they were doing all along, and were preparing long ago to do what none of the professionals could believe. The people are sovereign. Never can I recall my sense of that ancient democratic truth being so emphatically, incontestably made flesh.

This wasn't just a shift of power, a swing of the pendulum conducted by a country concerned about fair dealing in the two-party system. It wasn't merely honouring the mantra about time for a change. It was an expulsion. It said to the Tories: Get thee hence, and do not return until you have more to tell us than the insulting message that nobody else is capable of governing.

It wasn't a vote for an entirely different principle of ruling, but that isn't a reason to diminish it by one iota. Within the limits afforded by an anti-ideological age, it said that one party was wholly fit and the other wholly unfit to govern.

We had talked about a more modest Labour victory, of course: by two or three score seats perhaps. Even the victory itself, never mind its scale, could not be wholly anticipated. However obvious we felt it to be, we couldn't believe it until it happened. Only at the moment of it happening does catharsis occur. Only now, with the seats coming in and the figures finally out of reach of speculative doubt, is the new age that people have thought about for many months and years finally ushered in.

It is a victory, first of all and beyond dilution, for Tony Blair. Blair's vision may have seemed easily uttered, and it was often doubted. Many people thought it wasn't really a vision at all. Many Tories seriously convinced themselves that he was nothing but an opportunist who would do anything to win. It is true that he wanted, above all, to win. But he did so with the most personal vision, pursued with the most single-minded courage, that any modern leader has shown.

It is a personal victory, for example, far more plainly than Mrs Thatcher's in 1979. Mrs Thatcher, at that stage, had done almost nothing to reform her party or change its attitudes. She was, in 1979, the prophet of a pretty rooted Conservative status quo. The transformation of the Labour Party, by contrast, is Blair's personal work. When he determined to move far beyond what Neil Kinnock had done, virtually nobody else believed it was possible. When he decided to rewrite Clause Four, which was the key political risk he took, Peter Mandelson, his infamous alleged Machiavelli, wasn't privy to the decision. It was essentially Blair's alone.

He could do this because, at bottom, he made his own terms as political leader. If he hadn't got his way, he could have walked away from politics, as he made clear, privately at least. Far from being a careerist, he decided, probably before he became leader, that politics was only a tolerable or worthwhile activity if it could be conducted in the real world, according to the rules that connected with people's real lives. That has been a guiding star from the moment he became leader. This result could not have happened if he had ever abandoned its steady signals.

The way it was achieved, and the scale of its outcome, however, are much more than the fulfilment of an election strategy. They put the leader in an unexampled position of power to influence life and politics for the better, to place his own mark upon them. There have been other leaders of whom, if such a statement were ever made about them, it would have been right to be deeply apprehensive. Of Blair, it is not, I think, necessary. One must never forget what power can do for bad.

But Blair has principles and objectives, a mix of hard-headed idealism, that deserve the trust the country has so massively placed in him. After years in which the concept of political leadership was first defiled by manic arrogance, and then by posturing timidity, Britain has now given itself the chance to experience something quite different from either model.

But the victory is also for a party. The Blair reforms to the Labour Party have been accompanied by a change in political culture, which now admits discipline as an indispensable element. Numerous have been the times when it could have exhibited its old ways, chafing at the leader, destroying shadow ministers who sent their children to the wrong schools, passing resolutions that were a gift to nobody except Labour's opponents.

Although Labour's sheer professionalism has attracted plenty of comment, from other professionals who judge it to be several light-years ahead of anything the Tories can do, to me it is the party's political hardness that is more responsible for the opening of this new era. There are those who doubt whether it will survive. That's another thing the blind old Tories were obsessed by. One of their senior honchos sent me a note, as the election was beginning, which seriously implied that Ken Livingstone was merely awaiting the Blair victory before pouncing on the levers of power, aided and abetted by an irresistible cohort of secret socialists.

The contrast between the parties, in this respect, could not be greater. The Tories have become a rabble, and even when their rabbledom is caused in significant part by an issue on which their rebels are thought to speak for the people, this turns out to be another great Tory misjudgement.

If ever there was a party that was, in the exact sense of the word, unfit to form a government – incapable of putting together the construct that goes by that name – the Major Tories were that party, and will remain so, under whatever successor, for a good many years to come.

But most of all, this is a victory for the people. It is their wisdom that has brought it, their priorities that it will serve. One should not forget what these priorities were and are: middle-of-the-road economic management, no higher taxation, better-run public services, a limited, pragmatic agenda – but also, it would seem, massive support for the policies that were distinctive between the parties, and on which the Tories made enormous efforts to scare people witless.

The most conspicuous of these is constitutional reform. It looks as though the new Opposition won't begin to have the numbers to try and stop this. But just as important as the arithmetic is the raw political reality. Against such a massive statement from the voters, what price the House of Lords, roaring from the backwoods, citing some higher duty to obstruct their own reform, or other aspects of the irreversible changes in Scotland and Wales that, if mandates mean anything, the electorate has now endorsed?

What price, equally, the continuation of a phobic posture towards the European Union? Although Tony Blair has been careful to speak sceptically about extravagant integrationist moves, and will face a press that pays no heed to the message of a democratic majority, Labour has left itself much more room for manoeuvre than Mr Major. Major made this his single, most blood-curdling issue, imploring people to reject the party that was, as he made quite clear, dangerously 'European'. The people have given him his answer in several millions.

A very big majority, for any government, presents its own problems. Labour government itself is hard enough to imagine, after all these years. These new men and women are plunged into all the problems of governing, in none of which have they any experience, and that will doubtless bring its portion of errors and calamities in due course. Labour government on the back of a three-figure majority, crushing the Tories out of sight and confident of a five-year term, peopled by many unknown politicians, is a complete historic novelty. But it is the right event for our time. It shows that our country and its politics have a capacity for outrage, and reserves of bold vitality, that nobody could credit.

CONDITIONS OF POLITICS

The Tory war on political independence

THE HONESTY OF MINISTERS is important, and the careers of dishonest ones can be destroyed. But dishonesty, I think, is not systemic. Most British ministers are honest to a fault, at least about their personal affairs, and most MPs truthfully declare their private interests. The defaulters are random cases, too glibly deemed explicable by the decline of the times. This misrepresents what Thatcherism did. With its endorsement of buccaneering individualism at any cost, it certainly changed the climate. But that wasn't its most potent contribution. Something more pervasive than Conservative sleaze has polluted the system, and that is the Conservative war on political independence.

Ministers come and go, but quangos are for ever. They are the outposts of the Tory state, a massive growth of the Thatcher and Major years, already controlling 20 per cent of public spending, in Wales and Scotland vastly more. By 1996, their number is predicted to rise to 7,700. When the Nolan Committee turns to them, it will find itself examining not just a massive Tory bias in the way 40,000 quango appointees are selected but something more elusive and inadequately remarked: the destruction of a key pillar of British governance.

The other day, almost drowned by the Neil Hamilton tributary in the Mississippi of sleaze, the Labour Party charged that sixty-six NHS Trusts are chaired by Tories or by people connected with firms that have given money to the Tory Party, and 85 per cent of Trust members come from the predominantly Tory worlds of business, accountancy and 'political consultancy'. This is only the most recent in a series of analyses that have become a sub-industry of the academic world. As interesting as the enumeration of Tory loading was the fact that Mrs Bottomley did not deny it. Nor, these days, do other ministers. I've discussed it with several, and they don't find it remarkable. Conservative domination of unelected power has simply become accepted as a necessary auxiliary to elected Conservative government. Having given quangos so much control, why on earth, ministers ask, should they risk these appointees acting in ways they do not like?

This is a serious piece of vandalism on the body politic, for which one person is abundantly responsible. We begin to understand more clearly that Margaret Thatcher's most insidious legacy to government was the premise on which she always acted: that there is no such condition as political neutrality. Is he one of us? The question echoed not just round the Cabinet and the party but, with ever more grating resonance, throughout the public service. Upon the right answer depended preferment in the Civil Service, and in a vast range of public jobs touching institutions as far apart as the High Court bench and the Tate Gallery. In all of these Prime Minister Thatcher took an unprecedented interest, imposing a doctrine which steadily extinguished the old belief in a public service that was apolitical.

Over fifteen years, in other words, allegiance has grown into the decisive test of eligibility. Whatever justification this once had was long ago dissolved by the corruption it has produced, not of people but of a system. In the early days Whitehall had to be weaned rather abruptly away from its Keynesian, social democratic traditions, and mandarins who declined to accept this political direction legitimately suffered for it. But in pushing this therapy far beyond its limits, Thatcherites created a Civil Service that has exchanged independence for fealty, and scepticism for submission. One victim of this is the head of the Civil Service who, we currently witness, no longer enjoys his age-old credibility as an independent figure above politics. A larger victim is the taxpaying public, no longer able to trust public servants. Largest of all is public service itself, which people of substance, now required to answer to a party allegiance, no longer want to perform.

Over fifteen years, this has been an impressive degradation. One effect is to neutralize the standard Tory answer to the charge of quango-packing, which is to say that Labour governments did the same. They did not. True, there wasn't a committee in sight during the sixties and seventies that didn't have a statutory trade unionist on board. But this was the age when neutrality lived, and the Crossman/Castle/Benn diaries chronicle with irritation a Civil Service that still saw its job as being to ask a lot of awkward questions before obeying orders. Tory scions – Cockfield at the Price Commission, Lane at the Commission for Racial Equality, Elspeth Howe at Equal Opportunities – were given charge of some of Labour's most cherished projects. Independence was respected, detachment conceded as a commodity of value. Party politics was still not held to be the only mediator of truth.

It will be a pity if the Labour Party's responses to the present cycle of sleaze reflect the corrosive new orthodoxy rather than the one that prevailed when they were last in power. There's a temptation to make them do so. Mr Blair, among the reforms he demands, has been careful to ask for publication only of the party positions that quango members hold, not their political affiliations. But the danger is great, if he wins power, of a new government determined to replace the other side's political placemen and women with their own. It will take an administration of saints not to exact revenge in a quango-land that has been so mightily deformed.

This would be a grave error, the final turn-off for a cynical public. Labour should set out to restore the idea of independent public service, not consign it to the oblivion of all-party depravity. This isn't the US, where party allegiance is declared and registered. Our pattern is very different. Quite a lot of people have no allegiance, nor any organized set of positions that might add up to one. In fact, there are probably more of these than there ever were in the days when neutrality was the norm. In those days, more people did know where they stood. Now, by ironic contrast, the end of ideology and the turbulence of voting patterns speak for an electorate much less willing to be pigeon-holed.

What would restore public life more than any other change would be reinstatement of the idea of independence. The final corruption of the party mind is its blindness to any other than party truth and party advantage. The politicization of British life, a totally Marxist aspiration, was in fact achieved by Thatcherism. It's now a major cause of the Tories' problems, proof of their hubris, source of the abounding mistrust. More than erring ministers, it's what's rotten in the state.

Gluttons for inequality

IN THE GRILL ROOM at the Dorchester Hotel, London, the most expensive claret, Château Petrus, stands in the list at £960 a bottle. On Christmas Day 1994, a party of six men got through twelve bottles of the Dorchester's Chateau Petrus at a sitting. Actually, they were unable to manage the last half-bottle, which they graciously left for the wine waiter, although it was his opinion that, had they been interested in the very best rather than the most expensive claret, he could have recommended something rather cheaper, perhaps running even as little as £500 a bottle. But they did not want to stint themselves. Somebody was prepared to ante up £11,500 for the Christmas meal, and that's without the food.

Some members of the Dorchester party, according to a man who saw them, were Arabs. But this scene strikes me as a story of our own time and country as well. It is currently the most extreme display of conspicuous consumption in a short time that I have to offer: excess on a level which even lottery hysteria hasn't managed to inspire. That it could happen at all is a reminder that, when it comes to the making and spending of money, the scale of acceptable normality at the very top has edged beyond what anyone would have defended even a decade ago, at the height of Mrs Thatcher's crusade against the levellers. It is the secret British disease. We are living in new realms of financial gluttony, to which the response of public people is a doctrine of silence.

The private beneficiaries have been less quiet. That, too, is fallout from the Thatcher years. Ed Wallis, chief executive of PowerGen, says he's worth every penny, when, on top of a fourfold payrise, he is forced to account for £1.2 million he will gain from share options in a near-monopoly that was once in public hands. Colleagues in the same sector airily dismiss criticism of similar bonanzas by insisting they are *de rigueur*. Sir Iain Vallance, chairman of BT, got stroppy when his £663,000 salary was queried in the Commons, contending, with dubious relevance but memorable effect, that he worked harder than a junior doctor, whose monetary value might, in any case, be compared unfavourably with his own.

How much has this to do with government? Quite a lot. Many of the flagrant cases, most shamelessly defended by their culprit-heroes, come, like Wallis's, from the monopolistic utilities. These were handed a low share price by ministers anxious to sell them and who now enjoy, through no exceptional effort of their own, the vastly greater share prices that have made a new breed of corporate millionaires. Their bosses have grown wealthy at public expense and very little risk. They are by far the largest beneficiaries of privatization, exceeding in profit even the ex-ministers who helped put them where they are and then joined their boards.

But that is not the limit of the government's role. For these new rich are also spared, by official ordinance, embarrassment. They're the exponents of an approved philosophy, fought for by the Tories since 1979. They personify what market capitalism is about. They've done well, and why not? Their success, far from raising questions, is a kind of prize: proof that these old public businesses play big and equal in the private sector. The Prime Minister may sometimes writhe at the more grotesque implications, but he never denounces them. He deflects the problem to shareholders, unconcerned that in PowerGen the government still holds 40 per cent. He is the silent accomplice, as his predecessor was the triumphant prophet, of the age of excess.

He will pay his own price for this. The repulsive sight of these self-seeking predators, and the feeble casuistry they are sometimes obliged to venture in their own defence, is not lost on other employees in their businesses, however blithely ministers pass it by. For Labour, such episodes are a gift. Gordon Brown, the Shadow Chancellor, sometimes makes it sound as though the whole prospective budget deficit implied by his party's spending plans can be covered by an assault on windfall profits from quasi-monopolistic electricity and water businesses.

Quite rightly, he is relentless in calculating the scale of the share-option scams. He suggests, though not with much conviction, that each utility regulator should tame the option-gluttons by limiting the price increases he will countenance. Nobody doubts that Mr Brown speaks for a world which is outraged that Britain should now register more inequality of income distribution than at any time since records began last century, and a greater increase in poverty since 1979 than any other advanced country.

Yet there is something muted about Labour's response all the same. The party is cautious in the promises it makes about what it will do. It is safe to say, I guess, that not a single glass of Chateau Petrus has been drunk in the Dorchester Grill by anyone who ever voted Labour, or ever would. But the leadership still sounds more anxious to make the world safe for the Petrus-drinking classes, for fear of alienating the £10-a-bottle brigade, than standing up for an equalization that would drive an even bigger inroad than £960 a time into their taxed income.

Nobody doubts that top business executives need to be well paid. They may not deserve more than junior doctors. Some may be of less social utility than the teachers to whom Kenneth Clarke is this week applying the same brusque scorn as he did a few years ago when they learned to love him at the Department of Education. But scarcity dictates in rough-and-ready fashion the logic of most executive rewards. Risk and pressure and responsibility, and the often huge costs of making bad judgements, define the load that needs to command large financial recompense.

But that's not true of Ed Wallis's share options, and it's not the last word on the policy a party of the Left should be promoting. Among the tricks of the age of excess has been to pretend that its critics are as green-eyed as its practitioners. The politics of envy has been made to displace the politics of social justice, and Labour is still not entirely released from the consequent paralysis. The leadership issues pious hints, but will not yet promise to tax heavily incomes and options on the Vallance–Wallis scale. It lets its justified concern for the aspirational middle-class voter impede the scaling-down of plutocrats. Yet raising tax against them is not an act born of trifling envy. It would be a new statement of social norms, replacing the indecent conventions that became the texts not just of normality but virtue in the last decade. Why can't Labour make that statement, loud and proud?

Forget politics for art

BEING A POLITICAL JOURNALIST has many pleasures, but carries a serious deprivation. There are no heroes in my life and work. Politics in the modern era doesn't create the tasks that make for heroism, nor characters one would bet on showing it if called upon to do so. Looking back on 1996, I cast about for men and women to celebrate, and find none. All is cavil, compromise and feet of clay.

I have been lost in admiration a few times in 1996, but never once for a feat of politics. Yearning to indulge just occasionally in the journalism of greatness, sometimes I wish I were Michael Billington or Richard Williams.

The experiences that live with me have nothing to do with my profession. Feeling the need for something that really mattered, I never found it there. There's a whole vast interlocking industry of government and media that feeds off politics, and I am part of it, filling all these columns, servicing the rage and sometimes the vanity of other players in the game. But what, at the end of the year, is left?

The dross of argument, the sediment of Euro-rage, the multiple manipulation of truth, the impotence of power. The salient positive change of 1996, which is the solid improvement in Britain's competitive economic position, would appear to owe no more than tiller-touching to politicians, and to have made no impact on the people it should impress as the most heroic achievement of the political class. The year ends as it began: with a government the people despise, running a country whose destiny it no longer decides.

Chronicling brilliance is therefore a delight denied to people in my line of business. Mention Robin Cook and the Scott Report, and you've just about exhausted the heroic moments. The nature of the politician's trade these days is the organizing of minor triumphs and the avoiding of major calamities.

To satisfy my thirst for greatness, I look elsewhere.

Ian McKellen's Richard III will live in the memory long after the vacuous pretensions of John Redwood, scheming his way into the dustbin of history, have been exposed for what they are. It is, to me, the finest film ever made of a Shakespeare play, partly because it does not film the play but makes out of it a totally cinematic drama for modern times. Has there been a more mesmeric up-close map of conspiratorial intent than McKellen's subtly pliant visage? I doubt it.

Harrison Birtwhistle's *The Mask of Orpheus*, an extraordinary, one-off rendition, was put on at the Festival Hall in April. Here was a rebuke, among other things, to the market economics of the age: an undeviating modernist piece, a four-hour meditation on heroism and myth, for which every seat was taken. I sat just behind the composer, who was hunched next to the electronic controls that interplayed with two conductors, and felt myself to be in the presence of a creative genius, transported into other worlds.

The same thing happened with Paul Scofield, playing John Gabriel Borkman in perfect balance with Eileen Atkins and Vanessa Redgrave. This was acting in the grand manner, yet without a trace of overindulgence or other falsity.

I felt just such absorption at the first preview performance of Pinter's *Ashes to Ashes*. To be present when a great piece of poetic drama makes its opening impact on an audience, the first audience it has ever had, with the author-director visibly twitching in the circle, somehow added to the tight, minute-by-minute excitement of the work itself. Yet compared with the endless first and last nights in the political arena, which always turned out to be inconclusive, Pinter's new play was granted slight admission to the national consciousness.

To produce a level playing-field, in this contest with the barrenness of domestic political life, I have picked four British experiences. Broadening the scope, I could have added *Fargo* and *Lone Star*, two masterly American films, Cézanne at the Tate, Jasper Johns at the New York Museum of Modern Art, Haitink's *Ring*, Schiff at the Wigmore Hall. Each drove home the banality, and yet the high presumption, of the material I write about.

So did Ganguly's century at Lord's, a small Bengali batsman seeing the ball so early in his first test match that he made England's fastest bowlers look like donkey-droppers. It is, of course, asking too much that politics should produce effects analogous with these. In politics, an acknowledgement of greatness is available only yoked to allegiance. There are people who think Tony Blair is already a great man, and he has certainly done some big things to his party.

But flawless admiration comes only from the followers. A journalist could never allow himself to indulge in such a feeling for any politician. The signal instance of what happens when that professional rule is forgotten is to be found in the fate of both journalism and politics when unconditional love was poured on Margaret Thatcher. Both professions were corrupted. Just as neither a film nor a theatre critic is likely to find such simple perfection as I sometimes do in the worlds they have to follow.

All the same, this year I've envied them. In politics, it has been a year of sound and fury signifying very little. Every week we have heard an extremity of ranting and threatening, of panic followed by nullity and then more panic, of Labour's unproven promise and the government's withered strength.

Beside these mastodons, culture has continued to scale the heights, untouched by their prosings about a world they have neither time nor interest to engage with. Harrison Birtwhistle's triumph leaves Virginia Bottomley vaporizing to an empty hall. Jack Cunningham, her Shadow, had trouble recalling when he last went to the movies. They presume to change society, and in every headline and bulletin their works are forced upon us. But they don't change people. For that, you look above and beyond them, where life flourishes oblivious.

It's the *Sun* wot really runs the country!

THE DAY BEFORE the election, I interviewed Tony Blair for the *Guardian*, at what must have been the first moment when he was prepared to acknowledge to an outsider that he was going to win. He didn't know what the majority would be – around forty seemed to be his best bet – but concerning a prime contributor to this majority, whatever it turned out to be, he had no doubt. His tone was admonitory. Nobody, he vigorously insisted, should underestimate the matchless importance to his victory of the endorsement he received on the first day of the campaign from the *Sun* newspaper.

Mr Blair's gratitude to the *Sun* has been evident ever since. The messages of recognition were followed by a stream of articles ghost-written by his press secretary, Alastair Campbell, a master of this tricky craft, as well as special 'interviews' that may or may not have been delivered, like Gordon Brown's, to another branch of the Murdoch press, by fax. The hallmark of all these exercises has been their collaborative spirit. We get the sense of a Prime Minister and editor who are in this thing together, with the proprietor lurking benignly alongside – and the next election already in the sights of an unquestionably far-sighted political leader.

They were at it again this week, with Mr Campbell hacking out a column of populist reassurance, in the leader's name, on European economic and monetary union (EMU), and the *Sun* being happy to print it. The *Sun* even went as far as welcoming Mr Brown's statement of prevarication on EMU, while saying it did not agree that the abolition of the pound was constitutionally tolerable. The love-in just about continues. It will have been one of the gratifying proofs, as Downing Street surveys the scene, of the success of its chosen EMU strategy. For Downing Street seldom makes a big move without weighing carefully what the *Sun* will think.

If this attitude were based on a genuine identity of view, there might be something to be said for it. But it derives from a more ignoble emotion. It's a weakness not a strength. Calculating what the party's natural enemies, rather than its friends, might say has always been at the heart of New Labour's management style. That's what spinning is all about – except on those, more frequent, occasions when it's about rivalries between Cabinet ministers. I think it will prove to be the heel of our Achilles.

The recent history of EMU makes the point. Though the case against entry in 1999 was economic, the case against an early referendum to make it possible some time after that was political. High in the political reckoning was fear that the Murdoch press and the Rothermere press, to name but two, would not only oppose EMU but make life hell for the government up to and including the next election, withdrawing their support where they had given it, and imperilling everything Mr Blair dreams of for his second term.

Time, however, isn't going to change any of this. If the Prime Minister believes that these editors and proprietors will ever change their line on EMU, he hasn't been reading their output for the past few months and years. The case put forward by *The Times*, the *Sun* and the *Mail*, along with the *Telegraph*, has a cold religious zeal that cannot be relied on to respond to either fact or reason just because the government has decided that the balance of economic argument is now in favour of entry.

True, there are occasional signs of openness to the possibility that the economics might change. *The Times*, in its verdict on the Chancellor's statement, took care to couch its endorsement in economic terms, as if to imply that these might one day alter the case. But this was manifestly a pretence. The passion of all these papers is so extreme, their defence of national independence so adamant, that one can conceive of no conjunction of economic circumstances which might persuade them that they had been, after all, mistaken in their entire presentation of the EMU issue, and must now support it. To them it is a matter of principle, enduring, apparently, for the ages.

It follows from this that, while the *Sun* would revile the government for manoeuvring towards entry in this Parliament, it will revile it no less if it does the same in the next. Moreover, at the next election it will oppose tooth and nail the party that shows any sign of favouring what it, along with Mr Lilley, is pleased to call the destruction of the pound. It could do no other. Its entire world of Union Jacks and Queenly banknotes and red-beefed England, the stuff of its ranting for two decades, would be in danger of falling apart. These papers have such a vested interest, first, in the failure of EMU, and second, in the self-exclusion of Britain in perpetuity if EMU succeeds, that a government flirting with them risks finding its room for manoeuvre decisively foreclosed.

That's what Mr Blair is in danger of doing now. Although I think he made a bad mistake this week, I don't doubt his sincere desire to advance the integration of Europe and keep open the idea of entry into a successful euro. Unlike the *Sun*, he wants to be a good European. Unlike *The Times*, the *Mail* and the *Telegraph*, he doesn't believe that joining EMU would constitute a betrayal of the British nation. Ultimately, he cannot make common cause with them. Some time, he will have to face down the screaming and the bullying, which is the British tabloids' matchless contribution to democracy, or risk the surrender of any kind of European project. Part of the preparation of public opinion, which Mr Brown said would be integral to the five-year hiatus we have now allowed ourselves, must surely consist of doing exactly that.

In the end, it's a question of how you define leadership. Is leadership a matter of soft-soaping the editors and readers of the *Sun*? Or is the relevant constituency one whose interest is served by doing things the *Sun* does not like? This constituency could be called the nation as a whole. Its concerns are massively wider than the lowest common denominator of xenophobic prejudice to which the *Sun* consistently plays. Who, one must ask, is running this country? Who was elected by the readers of other papers? Is the European Union a threat to the sovereignty of the British government?

On present evidence, it cannot hold a candle to the *Sun*.

Safe sex and political perspective

IN THIS AGE, we gorge on intimacies. The secrets of the power élite have never been more lubriciously exposed. Whether it's Ron Davies's cruising, or Peter Mandelson's sex orientation, or Bill Clinton's private parts, we're told the lot. Taste and discretion are now unknown to the reporting of politicians. Yet we may be on the verge of discovering that this gorging, this raging torrent of supply, rests on a premise that is fundamentally false. I say this as one who believed it. I equated popular appetites with popular attitudes, and have perhaps been absolutely wrong. Wrong, though, in a large company, for whom this week ought to be a redefining moment.

Today was supposed to be the one that buried President Clinton out of sight. A month ago, after the most humiliating inquisition in the history of the presidency, he was toast. The November congressional elections would shift his condition from the perilous to the terminal, as the great American public voted more impeachers into place, sweeping away the special pleading, the sophisticated talk-outs and all the other subterfuges used by Clinton Democrats to sustain their fallen leader. Even if he survived, his presidency would cease to be. Morality aside, you just thought: what a jerk, wrecking his authority on a single easy piece, leaving the world leaderless until 2001.

But consider what has happened. The people aren't following the script. The Republicans don't look as though they will get the votes for impeachment, and might even finish up worse than they began. The scheming New York Republican boss, Al D'Amato, may be the toast. Newt Gingrich faces the looming fact, as he did soon after the apparent triumph of hard rightism in 1994, that he overreached his ambition. It seems likely that the message from the voters, after being forced to examine every aspect of Clinton's sex life including the lies he told about it, is utterly different from the analysis made by the media. This is not the first time, but the most resonant I can recall, when we've read the people wrong.

For Clinton is already showing his iron constitution. Even before today's mid-term elections, he was recovering. He went about his business, and the fever began to pass, partly because of outrage at the illicit tyrannies of Prosecutor Starr but also because sheer survival brings its own reward. The normalizing of post-Lewinsky Clinton is almost a fact of political life. He can negotiate, without any impediment, over the Middle East. He can appear in public, without being laughed at. If today the Congressional balance stays about the same, he will have gained a huge moral victory, his transgressions on the way to not mattering after all.

Why? One reason is what he stands for. Clintonism survives even the peccadilloes of its hero. That's the way it will look from Downing Street at any rate, where they're so keenly on the lookout for evidence that the durability of third-way politics transcends the worst personal setbacks. And it's true enough. Within the limits of the possible, Clinton has managed to take credit for all the gains, and blame others for most of the failures, of the past six years. The closest of his intimacies is with public opinion. He's a superlative performer in that way. But there's more to this blatant disjunction than a skilful president and Republicans bent on overkill.

People resist their reaction being taken for granted, and will vote accordingly. Added to that must be the sense that the media have simply misconceived what is going on. They've made gross assumptions about public attitudes that the people do not share. They assume that the voters want their leaders to be perfect, and that any contrary narrative they can dredge up answers a popular lust to punish all transgressors. They think their incessant revelations are doing the public's work, and sometimes God's. They're prepared to claim that their outbursts of moral indignation reflect the popular will. And so a picture builds up, whereby any disclosure is justified, and the most extreme conclusions about a politician's credibility are drawn from it.

In one way, the voters are complicit in this phoney edifice. For they do always want to read and watch the media effusions, the more intrusive the better. The public appetite for sex stories is probably insatiable. But the mistake the media make – the reason many of us seem to have got the Clinton business so badly wrong – is to assume the readers are also ferocious avenging judges, whether of Peter Mandelson, Bill Clinton, or even, close to home in Wales at least, Ron Davies.

The public, on the contrary, seem to be invariably tolerant about sex. Clinton has tested this to destruction and survived, perhaps done more than survive – and there's no reason to suppose the British public is any more bereft of perspective than the American. What afflicts both countries, if this is so, is a kind of double-take: an extravagant media judgementalism based on a claim to be able to read and represent the public mind which turns out to be thoroughly dubious. There's a serious argument to be had about whether so-and-so's personal behaviour is intrinsically rotten, disqualifying him from public work: which wasn't the case with Clinton. But the popular will, whether deployed as an alibi for moralizing or a basis for political assessment, needs to be given credit for a lot more sobriety than newspapers or television, from the highest to the lowest, usually reflect.

Stealing public funds, or profiteering from a public job, will always be another matter. Whitewater, if it added up to a row of beans, could have been tricky for the President. But on private sex, the public keeps its head. If the public man is doing a good job, who cares? The people like to know, but then don't judge. This makes politicians' paranoia about their privacy just as misplaced as media hysteria about the discoveries they make when they invade it. Behind both groups stand voters who don't seem to experience half the heat they're assumed to do, as long as the politicians are doing honest, steady, committed public work.

Wrenching the media away from sex probes may be impossible. But the Clinton story shows the high ground they claim is spurious. That's a benign and amazing outcome. Will it be heard, and listened to, and widely broadcast? Politicians don't become unpopular, or ineligible, or incredible through their private habits. Hold the front page.

Safe bets are bad politicians

THIS HAS BEEN THE YEAR of the politician as Fallen Man. Heaped upon him are expectations of virtue he can never meet, and he has betrayed them, whether with a woman in Washington or with a ministerial mortgagee in Notting Hill. It is all terribly disappointing. The defining images of 1998, if you can forget Baghdad bombings and Kosovan murders and starvation in Russia and the felling of Asian tigers and the widening degrees of social inequality to be seen in every advanced country in the world, are of vengeance wreaked on Icarus.

The gloating, naturally, has been fervid. Are not the Augean stables being scoured cleaner? Isn't the political leader being called to account for his failure as the role model, in matters moral and monetary, which he is meant to be? Maybe. By all means, let's hold these people to account. But if moral perfection is the standard, soon there will be no leaders left. The case that's forgotten in such pious lamentations is the case for the unvirtuous politician.

The politician as role model is quite a recent invention. The extension of public accountability into every cranny of his character was not an experience the predecessors of Clinton and Mandelson had to suffer. Great men had weaknesses that bear a close resemblance to modern frailties, yet still rose to the pinnacle of esteem. Was this because the weaknesses were less gross – or because they were regarded with a sense of perspective which entirely eludes the frantic scourges of the 1990s?

In 1848, the penniless Disraeli borrowed £40,000 – the equivalent today of roughly £2 million – to set himself up with a country house. Part of the money was sought from the Norwich Union, but the other two-thirds was handed out by the Conservative leader's wealthy patrons, Lord George and Lord Henry Bentinck. Nobody seems to have thought anything of the two-way indebtedness that resulted. Disraeli's biographer, Robert Blake, was unable to disentangle the exact circumstances of the loan even a hundred years later, but writes with certainty that the Bentincks 'never intended to call in the money'. This was merely the climax of a life of notorious personal fecklessness with money, which still did not bar Disraeli from serving two terms as Prime Minister, and becoming one of the most esteemed reformers in history.

In 1912, David Lloyd George agreed to buy shares in the American Marconi Co., having been put in the way of them, before they were available to the public, by the Attorney-General, whose brother happened to be a Marconi director. Lloyd George was Chancellor of the Exchequer at the time, and the British government was a coming purchaser of the wonders of Marconi wireless telegraphy. The shares rose 20 per cent the day they came on the open market. Such flagrant insider trading would now doubtless lead to exile from even the remotest purlieus of civilized life. It caused a serious crisis at the time, from which, however, Lloyd George was permitted to extricate himself by force of oratory, leading to a parliamentary vote.

Here, too, the surrounding static has a close contemporary echo. Prime Minister Asquith insisted that in the Marconi scandal only 'rules of prudence', not 'rules of obligation', had been broken. The minister had shown poor judgement but was 'absolutely unstained'. 'I acted thoughtlessly, I acted carelessly, I acted mistakenly, but I acted innocently,' pleaded Lloyd George, some decades before a politician's training made such pseudo-confessional soundbites second nature.

At that time, you could get a hearing for the view that no serious person went into politics to make money. There wasn't a senior person on either side, Lloyd George said, 'who would not in business make ten times as much as he makes in politics. The men who go into politics to make money are not politicians. Men go in, if you like, for fame ... for ambition ... from a sense of duty. But for mere cupidity, never!' And so he was forgiven. It was just as well.

He later became a great Prime Minister and war leader. 'Perhaps the public reaction, or lack of it, reflected a true sense of the national interest,' his biographer, John Grigg, writes, 'as well as a shrewd

· understanding of the frailty of politicians.' Alongside his financial peccadilloes, Lloyd George was the first Prime Minister openly to keep a mistress. But the British then did not damn political leaders to oblivion for their failure to be perfect human beings. Nor, a little later, did the Americans. President Kennedy was allowed, by the spacious class that knew about it, to be a serial adulterer, in which condition he none the less managed the Cuban missile crisis to a peaceful end, as well as inspiring multitudes of young idealists all over the world. His successor, LBJ, owner of a formidable array of private vices, was indicted for nothing except the prosecution of the Vietnam War.

Large figures of the past, in other words, have been beset by human failings which were not relevant to their public performance. Their job description was different in those days. While seeking to be admired, they didn't think much about being loved. While needing to be trusted for their public judgement, they weren't required to lay bare their private transactions, from bedroom to bank account, to prove it. Their public conduct was just about all that mattered, for better or for worse. This was a framework which helped the attractions of public life to outweigh its penalties, and resulted for most of this century, in these two· countries at least, in a fair proportion of the brightest and the best opting to become politicians.

That's no longer so. What do I mean by best? Among other things, risk-takers, and people of bold, category-shifting vision: people who can live at the edge of the possible: ruthless as well as decent people, adventurous as well as honest, and revisionist not conformist. People with the brains to be inventive, and the guts to be unpopular. Borrowing a lot of money, or sleeping with more than one woman, doesn't disqualify a man from any of those claims on our support. It may even show he has what it takes. Just so long as we don't look to him to do everything, public and private, according to rules laid down by ... by whom? Far from raising standards of government, the year of the serial Icarus seems far more likely to push politics towards the lowest common nullity.

Visit to a focus group

BEFORE COMING TO the Labour Party conference, it made sense to touch the real seat of popular power in modern government. The conference used to be something like that place, where the masses made their impact on what the great figures in the party did and said. They may have been a pain, but they had to be listened to. Now they are supplanted. The 3,000 people in the hall to hear Gordon Brown yesterday – let alone the 20,000 said to be buying, selling and otherwise leeching on the back of the conference this week – are stage extras, beside the seven voters I heard in north London before the conference began.

The seven are not present at the trade fair the conference has become. Their ghosts, however, permeate the speeches of the leadership. They are, in a certain sense, the arbiters of modern politics. Judged by the leaders' relative responsiveness, the focus group cuts more ice than the conference these days: helps determine what is said to it, and matters far more than a local ovation as the measure of whether the words worked. Scores of groups are commissioned by the parties every month. Eavesdropping on a focus group set up for the *Guardian* by our pollsters, ICM, I learned that coming to the conference may be redundant – or worse.

For the mass of sensible citizens have no fiery interest in politics whatever. That was the first message. Not new, but at this season salutary. My north London seven were gender-balanced and middle-aged, and their interest in talking about politics at all was heavily stimulated by the £30 a head they got for ninety minutes of problematic chat, searching their heads for anything to say. The stipulation was that they had voted Labour or Lib Dem in 1997, and might possibly consider going Tory next time.

But the overwhelming conclusion was that they had trouble

caring either way. Opinion polls show the same dilute fascination. Bournemouth is on another planet. Conference, for all the weeks of preparation, emerges as a totally solipsistic activity. Not that the focus group were hostile to Mr Blair. Far from it. The striking impression they gave was of quiet tolerance, founded on low expectations. They hadn't expected much of Blair, and he hadn't delivered much, but it was too early to say whether he would do better, and there certainly wasn't any alternative.

There were niggles about health and education, and apparently complete obliviousness about the famous 'extra' £21 billion that Brown is pumping in. But nothing really caught them. They had better things to think about. In this muted company, any anxiety about Europe and the euro, which wasn't much volunteered, was effaced by the universally expressed certainty that 'it will happen'. On all matters, the end of ideology is perfectly reflected by focus-group indifference to arguments about policy.

Second, though, here is undoubtedly the nerve-centre of feel-good politics. This is really why focus groups matter. Mine came at least half alive when asked to think about leaders and their images. In three of six *Guardian* groups around the country, the baseball hat was the first thing that sprang to anyone's mind about William Hague. Sometimes the only thing.

This research tool – pseudo-scientific substitute for contact with real voters – has made political leaders intensely aware of what buttons might push a near-soporific nation into a mildly positive response. Mr Blair's speech this afternoon, we may be sure, has been checked out with his group-meister, Philip Gould, to gain a sense of the few things people do care about. When he attacked public-sector workers in July, with much harrumphing from John Prescott, he was speaking with calculation into a feeling picked up as the mood of the moment. When he got into trouble last February, for sitting on Richard and Judy's sofa and talking about Glenn Hoddle, an aide told me next day that he had been quite right to do so, because the focus groups, consulted the same evening, had said as much.

It is wrong to say that focus groups determine policy, but they're allowed to set its limits. They don't necessarily presume a follow-up – nothing worse has yet actually happened to public-sector workers. But as the glass of fashion and mould of form, they can efface the largest Commons majority. They instruct leaders about tone. Gould's groups, like ICM's, will have picked up Phoney Tony as one prevailing response to Blair – his mistrusted smile, his apparent switches from an Old Labour past, the equivalent of the baseball hat – which may be why his family, the guarantor of Real Tony, is often in the pictures, and the smile is now less present than the furrowed brow. How to handle things, rather than what to do, is the question focus groups are summoned to answer, though they never know it.

This puts them in the middle of a paradox, the third and least comforting conclusion for a politician. The only theme trenchantly shared by each member of the group I watched was impatience with dithering indecision. 'He's not leadership' was the verdict on Hague, still hopelessly compromised in their minds by the presence of that otherwise forgotten figure, Hezza. They sounded far more concerned that leaders should lead – Thatcher-nostalgia lives – than that leadership might be in the wrong direction. Thus, the focus group, whose inarticulate instincts the politician applies himself to studying in the quest for the lowest common factor, turns out to be asking the political leader, above all else, to have a clear conviction and stick to it.

The conference is designed to respect all these truths, except the last. Many categoric policy positions, *à la* Thatcher, require the making of enemies as well as friends, a talent which, to her credit, she never tried to shed. Here, instead, we have assertions and promises that nobody – certainly no Labour voter who remains even half-supportive – could disagree with. This is what Mr Brown, at his booming best, was offering yesterday. Privilege, cartels, monopolies, overcharging: fairness, newness, employment, children. These were the Brown buzz-words, positive and negative, and they're as recognizable in focus-group country, which is barely listening, as in a party conference that seems very keen to feel good about itself.

Asked to put a word each to the Tory and Labour houses, the focus group went for 'crumbling' and 'unfinished'. For Hague, it could offer not a chink of light in the darkened ruin. On Blair, the verdict can be summarized as patient acquiescence. He has *carte blanche* to finish the house pretty much as he wants, because, for overall credibility in an unexcited land, there is no contest. But what does he want, especially about the euro? Who speaks first, the leader – or the led, whose most coherent desire is, apparently, to hear?

The convenience of the Lords

NO ONE, AT LAST, is born to rule. Or only a rump of ninety-two. The moment is rightly savoured. Within a year it will seem, even in a country much deformed by its reverence for history, incredible that peers-by-birth survived as legislators into the dying months of the twentieth century. The tearful farewells are those of privilege weeping for itself.

It is a perfect New Labour moment, abolishing the past, declaring for the future, signalling what an old country made young should be about. The cosmetics are unforgettable. So brilliant, I guess, that they will be enough. Everything henceforth can only be messy. So messy that it will not happen. A column that normally shrinks from prophecy today risks exercising that faculty. Let me sketch the critical path that leads straight back to the benches where the Lords will continue ensconced, after this millennial gesture, unchanged for many years.

It begins with Lord Wakeham's Commission, where affability endures. The members are getting on well, though they may not agree on a single scheme for the second chamber. They are under the cosh of a Christmas deadline, but realize that extended debate is unlikely to settle any differences they have over choices which have been well known and thoroughly deliberated for much of the century. They will or won't write an agreed report.

What they understand, however, is that it matters little if they do. For sophisticated operators who know the decision won't be theirs, the last ditch is singularly absent. They were set up to buy time and clear the ground. Even if they came out for an all-elected, or an all-nominated, or a something-in-between, assembly, this would count for nothing beside the collective will of the government, or the individual will of the Prime Minister, both of which will be drawn to the inexorable conclusion that no further change is necessary.

Ministers do not say this now. They may not even think it. Good faith has not vanished from the scene. But three factors, I predict, will bear down irresistibly against reform.

First, it is, by any standards, difficult. Though the options are easily describable, the choice is hard to make. The formation of a second chamber, in a democracy steeped in the juices of existing power-relationships, is a genuinely complex task. Its measure is ably spelled out by Professor Vernon Bogdanor in *Political Quarterly*, who makes an enticing case for doing nothing more.

An elected chamber? Intolerable rivalry with the Commons. Indirectly elected? Just about the same. Regionally based? But there are no English regions. A new political class? This would merely replicate the already threadbare benches of the Commons. A chamber operating on different time-lines from the Commons? The clash of legitimacies with a house part-elected more recently would only enrage the lower house. And so on. Bogdanor's negativism, a serious argument persuasively put, will be found compelling by ministers who have bigger things on their agenda.

Second, the New Labour project has never made a case for the constructive side of Lords reform. It had no idea what it wanted to do except abolish birthright legislators. Any illusion to the contrary is based on a misunderstanding, indeed, of the party's wider constitutional programme which, though very big, was not fashioned from a reforming blueprint.

Scottish devolution predates New Labour. Inherited by Mr Blair from John Smith, it became a necessity, not a choice. There was no alternative to devolution, which Blair has rationalized with decentralizing pieties while he harbours much irritation about its consequences. Incorporation of the European Human Rights Convention likewise derived, in substantial part, from outside pressure: the desire to release ourselves from the anomalous exclusivity, in this field, of the Strasbourg court. It had its own inevitability. Besides, though momentous, it raised the power of judges more than it was seen to threaten that of politicians. It was not a conscious sacrifice of political power.

The next stage of the agenda is quite different. It is wholly optional. We see the first signals of the constraint this causes, in the dilute version of freedom of information which Mr Straw and Mr Blair are determined to settle for. Lords reform comes into the same category. It asks a potent question about what further legitimacy, if any, should be given to a legislative chamber that might make life more difficult for the executive.

But, third, in answering that question, New Labour has no ideology to guide it, other than that of control. To pick its way through the forest of obstacles and obscurities, it has no reformist principle to help it. There is nothing in his bones that might compel the master of the New Labour universe to engage in the reformist struggle, with a view to creating a second chamber worthy of such an effort, which, by definition, would be one that diminished the power of the government, in command of a Commons majority, to get its way on all occasions.

Quite the opposite. In the new and much updated edition of his invaluable book, *The Progressive Dilemma*, David Marquand asks whether Blair is really a pluralist, and comes to a discouraging conclusion. 'The logic of the whole ensemble is pluralistic,' writes Professor Marquand of the constitutional project. But the factual evidence raises questions about New Labour. 'Will it outgrow the dream of hegemony and renounce its *dirigiste* statecraft? Is it prepared for a politics of dialogue and negotiation?' Blair, Marquand suggests, seems 'determined to ensure that the channels of communication between the people and their elective dictator are not clogged by Cabinet colleagues or awkward intermediate institutions'.

The second chamber could be one such institution. What its proper reform must surmount is not only the passion for control but the constitutional exhaustion that is already setting in. We have done plenty, I hear ministers say. The people do not want yet more upheaval. With the descendants of the centuries now departed, and the last youthful anachronism jumping on the Woolsack crying treason, the comedy is over, which is all that anybody ever knew they wanted anyway.

The countervailing case against this requires energy and belief. I predict it will not be decisively made. The peers will soldier on. Those progressives who joined the Lords under the impression that they would soon cease to be there will be, poor fellows, disappointed. An irony will engulf them. The only elected bottoms on the red benches will be the rump of ninety-two, who will have the merit, at least, of being chosen by a group somewhat larger than the Prime Minister's patronage committee. Lineage and selection will, in their persons, be weirdly fused. Such will be the tenuous legitimacy of a place called new.

The gap in the market for serious radicalism

IN PARLIAMENT SQUARE on May Day, there was nobody on the grass as the big clock struck ten thirty. The guerrilla gardening was due to start, but decorum still kept hundreds of people to the paved edges of the target zone. A very British sight. An hour later, a couple of thousand had gathered, muddying up the turf. A bit of symbolic planting began, followed by the relaying of some sods on the car-infested tarmac.

These seemed nice people, herbivores to a man and woman, seasoned by a few dressy exhibitionists. They didn't threaten anybody, least of all the bastions of British politics or capitalism. They were caught both ways. They were always going to be either ridiculed or hated. More likely the former. Be violent, and you get noticed. Be peaceful, and be patronized or ignored. As many knowledgeable observers predicted, a minority of May Day exploiters were bent on violence. They duly carried out their assaults on McDonald's, beating up some bits of central London despite a police presence so massive that it acted as a challenge to the anarchist hard core, which swiftly succeeded in breaching the uniformed cohorts. This wasn't wanted by the herbivores, many of whom, suspecting it was coming, apparently stayed away. But it makes one think a little harder about their hopeless way of taking on the system.

Reclaim the Streets (RTS), the herbivores in question, is proud to be a 'non-hierarchical, leaderless, openly organized, public group', in which, according to its website, no individual 'plans or masterminds anything'. Many of its self-directed people are idealists, if not utopians. Most have an environmental agenda, which they believe organized politics is refusing to address. So they make a virtue out of being disorganized. They're proud to be inchoate, delighted to expose opponents who can't handle the fact that a leaderless entity is non-negotiable.

But they face enemies who are not inchoate. They're innocents who have been given a profile of menace they do not merit. The state and the corporations can see off events like feel-good occupying and digging without the slightest trouble. The anarchists exploit it as perfect cover for violence that will lose every shred of public sympathy. Meanwhile, some crippling defects in the British system of politics and power are stubbornly unaddressed, and will remain so as long as the shambles that took place yesterday is held to be state-of-the-art rebellion, the last word in revolutionary democracy.

No mainstream party dares have a truly radical idea about any environmental question. All confine themselves within a frightened consensus that refuses to challenge the philosophy of economic growth, however it touches on the non-economic aspects of society. None is capable of applying to the future of traffic a creativity that measures up to the coming crisis. But then nor does RTS, for whom the sincere, even romantic lunge, despairing of conventional politics, is supposed to make a decisive statement. A more serious political radicalism would engage with the economic complexities, and find a better way of pressing the case than supplying a backdrop for anarchist destruction.

More glaring is the absence of a coherent political challenge to large corporations. Corporate power is the prime beneficiary of Labour's evolution into a party of capitalism. A necessary development, perhaps. But its place of reverence in the British scheme of things was more awesomely asserted last week, when the chairman of BP, Sir John Browne, was permitted to deliver one of the Reith Lectures. These used to be the apex of the BBC's contribution to serious British life, an occasion for original thesis-building to challenge received opinion. How far have we sunk that a corporate boss should be offered the assignment to talk about global environmental challenges, which he duly seized for his company, providing no insight that was other than self-serving and no research that did not originate in BP propaganda.

No part of the political system contests such degeneration. Yet corporations are not popular. Their judgement of self-interest seldom extends to making people approve. Barclays Bank may be an extreme case, but its recent conduct revealed an indifference to public concerns which showed, more luridly than any recent episode, what corporate power will do when its short-term financial interest is threatened. Barclays' mix of brutality and complacency over branch closures could not, you might have thought, be surpassed – until you heard its chief executive's seigneurially contemptuous response to any notion that his £5 million personal package might be open to debate.

Such attitudes do not attract public support. Yet few elected politicians are prepared to attack them. Like democracy, capitalism, for all its defects, is the best system anyone can think of. But it needs constant criticism. And the downside of capitalism and its perversions has no spokesman. A gap in the political market opens up. Segments of the electorate await it. There's space for forceful attack, rooted in ideas not gestures.

The political system does respond to force. Arguably it responds to nothing else. Not violence, which is easily seen off by the superior violence of the state, but the force of a competing political reality which threatens the power of those who control the system. The herbivore world itself has sometimes proved this. Targeted campaigns, based on rational arguments, diligent planning and accountable leadership, have changed the political and economic landscape. No more major bypasses will be built in a hurry, after the trouble direct action caused at Newbury and the fulfilment of the protesters' predictions that the bypass would merely relocate congestion. Though ministers won't admit it, past protest has shifted the limits of future policy. It did more with Monsanto and its terminator seeds, which aspired to change modern agriculture.

Consumer resistance, marshalled and informed by campaigns of popular protest, put paid to a product which Monsanto expended vast sums on developing and trying to push through. Seattle and Washington, from which the London event was supposed to be drawing inspiration, connected with a different sort of reality. Much to the herbivores' distress, violence was not absent from the efforts to disrupt the meetings of the World Trade Organization and International Monetary Fund. But Seattle worked by amplifying real political forces already at large, especially in the Third World. Direct action was the ally not the enemy of political reality. Greenpeace and Friends of the Earth try to do the same. In the end, they make their effect by argument and action – very old operating principles – not by a bogus romance with anti-politics.

William Hague calls Britain
a foreign land

LET ME TAKE YOU on a journey to a foreign party. The party is called the Conservative Party. It used to belong to Britain as much as Britain belonged to it. For seventy years of the twentieth century it owned the politics and government of its country. The voters saw it as the party of the nation. But now it is a foreign party. It has become something altogether other. This means that anyone who votes for it next time may be doing so for the last time. People should understand this. Unless they do so very soon, an independent and sovereign Conservative Party will become nothing more than an offshore pimple on the British body politic.

Its transformation has been extraordinarily sudden. So much history was sacrificed so fast, burned on the pyres of zealotry and desperation. The philistines, who remember nothing, are now in charge. Insofar as they know history, they despise its compromises. Like the Taliban, they seem bent on smashing every memorable idol, above all the claim they once had to be the party of the British people.

This claim goes back longer than seventy years. Throughout the nineteenth century, Conservatives adapted to the society around them. That's why they enjoyed a longer continuous history than any other European party. From Peel to Disraeli, they became the party of one English nation. From Baldwin to Macmillan, they rode the tides of peacetime Britain, banishing ideology, speaking for the people, sucking up the votes. From Edward Heath to Margaret Thatcher, they remained at the centre of the centre ground, wherever that came to be defined. They were, in fact, its definers. Mrs Thatcher became an ideologue, but she was not foreign. She knew what the British people wanted. From this position she won three elections.

Now, something important has changed. The state of society is no longer the Conservatives' guide to political survival. For society, they say, is mistaken. Instead of listening to the people, the Tories want to fight them. The people have made some big mistakes. They gave Labour a landslide victory in 1997. From there the people have gone downhill all the way. After four years, they continue to reward Mr Blair with a fifteen-point lead in the opinion polls. Something must be wrong. It isn't, of course, the Conservative Party. The party is in denial about all that.

The people, for example, have watched their country being parcelled up and given away. Scottish devolution was agreed by the Scots and accepted by the English, and is working in conformity with a promise made at the last election. But the Conservatives cannot credit that. By raving against its iniquities, they announce their distance from the people. They are stepping away from being fully British. This is only the beginning of a hallucination that Disraeli and Macmillan and even the pre-retirement Thatcher strove always to discourage: the belief that the people cannot be right.

That judgement reaches into every cranny of what Labour has done. The government's persistent popularity is simply, we learn, an error. The British people are prepared to pay their taxes, they want better public services, and support the Chancellor and Prime Minister who have been in charge of the modest social democratic progress of the last four years. But in Tory eyes, this is an aberration. The government's anti-progressive side, also popular, is another fraud. Having been even more reactionary than the Tories on issues of liberty and law, asylum and immigration, Blair and Straw may have gained votes, but this is all part of a package designed to take the country from the 'decent, plain-speaking people', as the Tory leader called them this weekend.

Only a party that has become foreign − alien − could seriously believe that. Conservatism, we discover from William Hague and Michael Ancram, is alienated from reality. It doesn't merely believe that Blair, the people's choice by a mile, is wrong. It says that he is not, at a deeper level, entitled to be Prime Minister. That was the message from Harrogate, with its references to the 'stench' of Blairism, as compared with the simon-pure days of John Major. It has become the seigneurial presumption of Mr Ancram, a mild man now evincing apocalyptic rage at the presence of these filthy upstarts in the seats of power, stealing the very birthright of the British – the same British people who are about to cast the Tories once again into electoral darkness.

There are those who believe the latest Conservative synthesis is a pose, and that the party is not really accelerating towards the fringe. Forgive them their madness, they have nothing else to say. Wait until they get back to power, we are assured. They'll sober up, regain their balance. In particular, wait for this moment to see the return of realism on the issue where, at present, they are most obsessed with the image of the theft of a nation: Europe.

The chances of this happening seem slight. For a start, until they remake contact with the centre ground, they will never get back. But leave that small point aside, and observe the depth of their unrepentance. Call them extreme, and they reach further towards xenophobia, sneering at foreign doctors. Call them racist, and they plumb the richer subtexts of political incorrectness, vowing to lock up all asylum seekers, implying that foreigners are not welcome, suggesting that Britain will soon no longer be Britain because of them.

Call Hague reactionary, and he plunges deeper into promises of more prisons than Mr Straw. Call him a nationalist, and he exposes hostility for the European Union of a breadth he's never shown before. He promises to march into the EU demanding a new agriculture policy, a new fishing policy and a torn-up treaty of Nice. These statements do not connect with reality. They say nothing about the fourteen member-states whose agreement would be needed, nor about the consequences of their refusing it. But we learn what there is to know about the modern viscera of the party Hague leads: its virulent passions, its deluded fixations, the myopia that prevents it focusing on a world beyond itself, its belief in the defiant journey up its own backside.

This is not the posture that kept the Conservatives alive for two centuries. Nor will it do so now. The party is becoming a foreign body. Instead of being in touch with the people, Hague describes a country they do not recognize. When he says they're living in a place that no longer belongs to them, they look at him as though he's crazy. Far from pointing to the broad uplands, he plunges deeper into the fetid cave that offers very temporary security.

Fearful and disgusted, Michael Heseltine even contemplates not voting Conservative. Habit called him back, but he thought about it publicly. Disraeli would have seen such a danger coming. Macmillan would have learned the lesson. Thatcher spent a decade keeping the broad church together. But modern Conservatism neither understands nor respects the people. Let me take you on a journey to the party that is leaving its country behind.

The one-party state

ON THE SURFACE, Britain is a country politically doing what it should. The government has a big mandate. It continues to be tolerated by an unecstatic but untroubled public. The Prime Minister is better regarded than any of his predecessors at a similar point in their second term. The polity is evidently working. Yet in reality it is diseased. It lacks conflict. Britain has evolved into a mental as well as political one-party state. There's a uniformity of allegiance, under which the absence of organized disagreement legitimizes, or at any rate readily accepts, a culture of easy opportunism.

The government rejoices in this, but the Tory disintegration is just as responsible for it. We see that the failure of the Tories stretches far beyond the party. It taints the entire quality of British life. For there is no alternative magnet of power, no competition for Blairism, and this means that contention is mostly futile. The establishment, whether in politics, in business or in intellectual life, is all of one colour. There is little point in being anything else.

There's no more telling place to watch this than in the BBC, nor could there be more revealing textual evidence of its evolution than the memoirs of John Birt, the former director-general. Has any man ever been more certain that he was right in everything he did? More staggeringly vain in his recitations of success? More biliously scornful of the efforts of every colleague who challenged him? More blindly aggrandizing of every particle of credit for anything good his organization did in the last decade? More serenely obtuse as to the effect such a chronicle of perfection might have on even a sympathetic reader?

But this is not why Birt is an emblem of Blairite Britain. By comparison with his lordship, Tony Blair is a model of decent and human self-doubt. Where Birt personifies what Britain has become is in his creepy opportunism, culminating in his accurate perception that backing Blair is the only stance any sensible modern man could take. He began as a bit of a lefty, he tells us, sucking up in those days to Jim Callaghan. He became a Thatcherite at just the right moment, getting as close as he could. Power was all that drew him, cresting, with Blair, in an era, the present one, when almost all challenge to the reigning orthodoxy had anyway ceased.

The BBC's engagement in this culture was completed with the appointment of Greg Dyke as Birt's successor. It was shocking that Dyke could get the job despite having paid £50,000 to the Labour Party, and I wrote about that at the time. Much more shocking was that so few people were shocked – but now one better understands why that was. The Birt memoirs are not ashamed – are proud, indeed – to describe the author coaching candidate Dyke, at the instigation of his chairman, Christopher Bland, for the interview at which this awkward political detail might be raised. But in the wake of the memoirs we learn that the training was otiose. The BBC vice-chairwoman at the time, Baroness Young of Old Scone, wrote to *The Times*, innocence and indignation perfectly matched, to say: 'The question of political neutrality hardly figured in the process.'

In other words, the £50,000 didn't matter. There was no issue. It wasn't even worth considering. Could there be a more resonant sentence about the ethos of this time? For it is absolutely true. The governors did not have to bother about the money because, in the absence of political conflict, it now had no meaning. The body that once cherished manifest impartiality as the central plank of its credo could effortlessly overlook what, not long ago, would have been an absolute bar to the appointment: and could deploy Bland's Tory past as cover to show its political objectivity to those few people who might still slightly wonder whether it existed.

Bland, indeed, makes his own emblematic point. Like many once-Tory businessmen, he has become, in all that counts, a Blairite. With regulatory arguments to win and favours to seek, how could a BT chairman be anything else? How could any mainstream capitalist, whose business would tend to profit from amicable relations with the powers that be? It requires heroic weirdness these days for anyone with any ambition in any field, save perhaps the *Daily*

Telegraph and the Tory Party itself, actually to declare themselves a personal opponent of the government.

There may be occasional blips in the process. The Audit Commission has been resistant to the sliding of one Blairite, and perhaps a second, into its chairmanship. But who else would do? Where would you find one? Maybe the live-in partner of the arts minister, which is the status of the second candidate, is rather too flagrant a connection for a post peculiarly dependent on distance from government for its credibility. But the broad penumbra of public life, from which all such appointments are drawn, is now peopled exclusively by those who have made their number with the only orthodoxy they can see prevailing for many years ahead. Allegiance, in these days of apathy and opportunism, may not be strong. But it is all-pervasive.

This is an unhealthy, ultimately repellent, national condition, not found in any other Western democracy. The one-party state of mind as well as politics doesn't seem to be making the country happier, or better governed. It is a direct, pernicious consequence of the collapse of the Tories as a political force. It has pretty well the entire establishment, for reasons of opportunism or comfort or idleness, in its grip.

But it is more an offence against, than an endorsement of, the British way of politics, and perhaps that is a reason why, below establishment level, something is stirring. The Tories may have nothing to say, and offer no magnetic pole round which alternative approaches to power may gather, but some trade unions can. The extremity of the firemen's original claim was insupportable, but their assertion of a countervailing power against Blairite minimalism and control has come not before time. Still more enlivening would be the breakout from consensual apathy that seems likely to follow a decision by President Bush to attack Iraq without the support of the UN, a decision Mr Blair has left himself no option but to support. That might mark a conclusive moment for the single-track conformism that otherwise defines the Blairite era.

I pray devoutly this does not happen. A unilateralist invasion of Iraq poses dangers that are more credibly terrible than anything Saddam Hussein has an interest in perpetrating. But there's also a need to blow apart the coterie politics of compliance into which

Britain has descended and the post-Beeb Birt has formally migrated, and which nobody has the nerve or the means or the anger fundamentally to challenge. There are pinpricks and problems, but no sense of an alternative power centre: which means no guarantor of serious challenge, on which the health of democracy depends.

OFFSHORE

The undeniable French connection

THE ISLES: A HISTORY
by Norman Davies

The main island, the Great Isle, of what became known, centuries later, as the British Isles had a peculiar geography. It was ideally proportioned for the division that was eventually made of it. No inland location lay more than two days' march from the coast, which gave a marked advantage to maritime invaders. The position of the main estuaries – the Solway, the Clyde, the Forth, the Dee, the Severn, the Thames and the Humber – made it possible for each of the more mountainous parts of the island to be isolated by invaders and guarded by them. When they lost the towns and forts commanding these estuaries, the resident Celts were pushed back into their mountain fastnesses. The inhabitants at this time mostly were Celts, of the British rather than Southern European variety – we're speaking of the turn of the fifth and sixth centuries. The invaders were Angles, or rather Germanic peoples, and they created a chaotic patchwork of statelets which took half a millennium to evolve into larger political and cultural units.

This did not have to happen. It wasn't inevitable. But about two hundred years later, after countless battles, marriages, mergers and chance occurrences, a dozen rival kingdoms emerged, followed, in another two hundred, by settlement in two distinct zones, one mainly Celtic – behind those mountains, and on the Green Isle to the west – the other exclusively Germanic. Thus, Norman Davies writes, 'the conditions had been created where England, Ireland, Scotland and Wales could begin the initial and most tentative phase of their crystallization'.

The Isles' deep history, therefore, was Celtic and, before that, genetically Continental. These were lands of migration from the east, which the Celtic strain came to dominate long before the later wave of Germanics. 'Britain' has been Britain, in the sense of a unified island, in only two brief phases of geological time, first when, with the exception of Scotland, it was under Roman occupation (55 BC – AD 407) and known as Britannia, and then since the Act of Union between England and Scotland in 1707. Otherwise there has been no such place as Britain, and therefore no proper repository for the kind of British nationalism, imbued with the sanctity of ages, that now excites so much political interest. Britain is a brief artefact, not a continuous entity, and it is a profound falsehood that generation after generation should have grown up imagining the opposite. This is Davies's ferocious contention, the error that has driven a notable scholar of the history of Central Europe – he has devoted less time to this new terrain, he grandly announces, than an undergraduate would normally spend on a history degree – to write the saga of the islands he belongs to.

Historians, Davies says, have a lot to answer for. They have misread, and more important, ideologically miswritten these islands' past. He sets himself the task of reconstructing it, from a perspective which refuses to be merely English. The Englishing of history, Davies believes, has been a betrayal of scholarship and a serious disservice to understanding, not least about the nature of the country and civilization that is now being asked to make an irreversible commitment to the European Union. Though the euro, he happens also to insist, is the wrong project at the wrong time, his book rises from the vastness of the centuries to a quotidian conclusion about current events which he regards as irresistible. He thinks 'Britain' cannot last. As an internally united entity, the Great Isle is finished, and ready to recede back into the shape it held at roughly the mid-term of its broken past. He also makes it seem incomprehensible that the divided bits of the former Britain – and England above all – should imagine they either have, or need to lust after, a future separated from the Continent, all in the name of a precious British identity that faces imminent liquidation. This is certainly a book it was surprising to see serialized in *The Times*.

The Englishness of received history, Davies says, has produced not only falsehood but massive intellectual aggrandizement. 'The English have been taught for centuries that their civilization is superior to that of the Celts ... the weight of popular admiration, and indeed a strong sense of identification, has been attached to the Roman occupiers of Britain rather than to the native British.' The Romans, though invaders, had the merit of not being Celts. The Roman Empire worked as a psychic forebear to the British Empire: a noble legitimation, which accounted for a whole literary genre, epitomized by Kipling, stressing the bond of identity between imperial Britons and ancient Romans. Rome provided the model for the civilizing mission of a multinational empire, and the precursor of centuries of English leaders who suppressed or ignored the Celts while still, at any rate latterly, grandly proclaiming Britain's rulership of the waves. In conventional histories, Davies writes, 'it is as if Anglo-Saxon England were bordered by an ocean to the north and the west as well as by a channel to the south. The mental planet that is peopled by Alfred and the Danes and Harold and the Conquerer has no place whatsoever for Hywell Dda, for Brian Boru, for Kenneth Mac Alpin or Macbeth.'

The culprits here were the Victorian historians, writing from and into their imperial time, as if all previous events had led up to the glorious present. Some famous names come under the Davies hammer, as he destroys not only the Whig interpretation of history, but the Protestant prejudice and narrow nationalism of most of its exponents. An exception, gratifyingly, is Macaulay, whose brilliant narratives are freer than most of blindness to the Celts. But Henry Hallam, F. W. Maitland and, above all, William Stubbs are presented as the high priests of inveterate Englishness. 'Despite their immense erudition, and their enormous services to the subject, all these scholars positively crowed with nationalistic self-satisfaction.' Moreover, the multicultural Davies crows, none of them gained a reputation outside the English-speaking world. They were mired in a mental framework that simply could not conceive of a world that did not place the greatest country, occupying a fourth of the globe, at its centre – and this held true even when they were writing about the Plantagenets and the Tudors. Moreover, not only was their work not read elsewhere, they were unaware of the existence of such a subject as comparative history. Thus, 'England in the period when its Continental connections were most intense was effectively (and damagingly) divorced from its essential Continental context.' J. A. Froude, A. F. Pollard and J. E. Neale, hagiographers of Henry VIII and Elizabeth I, are demolished with equal relish. The pillars of the English historical tradition, whom A-level history students were urged to read uncritically a generation ago, receive a vigorous kicking. Only one merits Norman Davies's unqualified approval. It is an arresting retrieval from oblivion. John Lingard's eight-volume *History of England* (1819) has been thinly, if ever, read during the last hundred years. But, written by a Catholic priest, it escaped the grip of both nationalism and Protestantism. It gave, uniquely, something like a global perspective. 'Lingard never gets anything wrong,' Lord Acton wrote. For Davies he is a solitary hero, his achievement 'colossal'.

Can the same be said of Davies? His book is at least colossally long, and shows signs of the short time its author proudly says it took him to write, from sources that are avowedly all secondary. It is not a measured book, with an even spread of interest, nor is the space allocated with any care for proportion. It won't supply the first-time reader, who has resolved at last to digest the whole of these islands' history, with a comprehensive text. On the other hand, it is moved by corrective passion and insatiable curiosity. General histories with argumentative themes are often more accessible than grand pseudo-objective tomes, and this one makes very clear what it is knocking down. It doesn't have the confusing omniscience which is to be found, for example, in the brilliant work of Norman Davies's own tutor at Oxford, A. J. P. Taylor, or give the reader the same tiresome sense that he is being got at in ways he cannot contest. Instead, the record of two millennia and more is bound together by an important and forgotten thesis. Celtic history, together with the sometimes over-copious richness of Celtic poetry, literature and myth, is accorded an equal place with the English line of kings and the English appropriation of Britain's imperial identity. Liberated from the ineffable Stubbsian stereotype of England/ Britain as the source of most good things in this world, we are forced to reconsider much we were never taught to think about.

Some of the myths left by the wayside have a sharp contemporary relevance. Two drive with special piquancy to the heart of the present obsession with British/English identity. First, this was for many centuries a country dominated and peopled by the French. The Norman and Plantagenet kings never fully distanced themselves from their French roots. In Crusader times, England was a part of the French empire. Its kings were Guillaume and Edouard and Jean. With the monarchs came many French settlers and a French ruling class; French was the language of the court and élite, and the insistent reach of French influence prevented the formation of a true national identity on the part of the natives. This mongrel country, after a century as a dependency of Denmark, became little more than an extension of France. The period of the Crusades, indeed, saw the beginning of something more than the Continent's genetic aggrandizement: the reach of its culture overcame anything that could be called typically English. This happened elsewhere. 'England, Sicily and Jerusalem,' Davies spaciously suggests, 'all formed part of what some historians have seen as the first experiment in the overseas export of European civilization.' The first year the Lord Chancellor opened a parliamentary session using the English language was 1362. This was the session in which a statute was passed allowing English to stand alongside Latin in legal pleadings. But French remained the professional language of lawyers until 1600.

All in all we have to conclude that even the English, let alone the British, have a very different national essence from the one which has penetrated so deep into their modern psyche that it may never be successfully extracted. Maybe the uncomfortable truth will always be resisted. But a nationalism did emerge, thanks mainly to the Reformation. Until then, the Isles remained intimately bonded with the mainland. Davies elaborates for this earlier period the demystification performed by Linda Colley's *Britons* (1992) for later centuries. He makes clear, as she does, the association of Englishness, and later Britishness, with self-preservation against Catholicism. The Reformation cut the Isles off from a connection that had lasted a millennium. 'This spiritual isolation,' Davies writes, with typical but stimulating hyperbole, 'was arguably more profound than anything that resulted from all the political invasions and geographical changes since the Ice Age.' The religious break didn't just have political and religious effects. The definitive severance of the previously interwoven relationships with the people on the other side of twenty-two miles of Channel determined the only identity available: the Channel, by the way, far from being the defensive moat or sea-girt wall, was for many centuries the facilitator of the contacts that made the Isles the multi-tribal place they were. Since the Reformation, however, 'the English have had little choice but to take pride in their isolation and eccentricity. Indeed they have recruited it as a virtue.'

This leads to a second undeceiving for modern British nationalists, whoever and whatever, exactly, they may be. The sacred date of 1066, since when the Isles have legendarily survived without foreign invasion, becomes a moment of reduced importance. Cultural if not military links with the Continent reached a peak in the era of Erasmus and Thomas More: 1534 was the year of greater truth, when Henry VIII's Act of Supremacy created an independent Church of England with him as its head.

This jarring adjustment of an iconic constitutional moment is one of several that Davies proposes or recalls. Simon de Montfort, conventionally presented as the originator of English parliamentary freedom, may well, it now seems (the matter is under much scholarly debate), have been following French ideas. The very idea of Parliament's Englishness, in fact, is one of the myths which the European Davies seeks to wrest from the Anglocentric Victorians, who regarded the imperial triumphs of Westminster as requiring an inexorable narrative to lead up to them: the story that parliamentarianism was a uniquely local invention. Davies debunks it. Though absolutism came to grip the Continent in later centuries in a way that Britain escaped, parliaments, diets and assemblies were thick on the ground in late medieval and early modern Europe. Poland and Lithuania developed a legal and parliamentary tradition which 'in several respects – such as the principles of habeas corpus and "no taxation without representation" – foreshadowed later developments in England'. In any case, the Mother of Parliaments harbours within her past the Court of Star Chamber which, for most of a century from 1540, mattered more than any Parliament, in a society that permitted no independence for judges, no immunity for jurors, no free press, no freedom of speech even for parliamentarians.

This land of the uniquely free, in short, is not and never has been quite so unique or quite so free as its mythologists have contended, especially its modern ones. Today's equivalent of Bishop Stubbs is the editor of the *Daily Telegraph*, relentlessly committed to a view of Britishness that does not account for Scotland, a view of Ireland that excludes Ulster, and a view of England that, regardless of history, depicts it as a place on which any European influence can work only as a contaminant. Brushing over the historic truth is a habit by no means confined to the Victorians. Into this situation, which becomes more fervidly ahistorical by the year, no more disturbing intellectual projectile than Norman Davies's could have been launched.

His book divides into two rather different halves. The first, which has a genuine originality for the non-scholarly reader, opens up a period whose dimensions – indeed, whose very existence – have remained for the most part obscured. His discussion of the beginnings of the Islands, the migrations that made them, the blank periods, whether of prehistory at the beginning or the so-called Dark Ages at the end, becomes an absorbing inquiry into the connections between past and present. Periods that the Victorians simply left untouched – as if they were undiscoverable or, if unearthed, likely to be uncongenial to progressive English history – are exposed, and become part of a whole. The fact that much of this new material concerns the Celts is a rebuke to history teachers in schools for many generations – and not only English ones. David Hume's eight-volume *History of England* was as unsympathetic and diminishing to his native Scots as the work of Stubbs and Hallam.

The modern scholar, by contrast, makes his own journey into fields he has never penetrated. This is not a handing-down from on high, but an investigation of new territory by someone who wanted to explore hypotheses he apprehends but is not sure of. We can therefore share his own fascination at what he finds. He is especially good on the sheer emptiness of ancient pre-Britain. Dealing with these early centuries, his powerful imagination fuses with tireless reading of the sources to construct a gripping picture of people who had little sense of who they were or where they were going. If they thought about where they lived, as the Romans were departing, 'they continued to think of Britannia'. But there was no glimmering of an idea of national unity, much less ultimate destiny. Davies fiercely resists the shaping of history, even up to the Glorious Revolution of 1688, as it has generally come down to us. The heroes he fills out are not Henry VIII and William Shakespeare, but James VI of Scotland (and I of England) and Herbert Butterfield, the first iconoclast of Whig interpretations.

The second half of the book, from, say, 1688, is swifter and sketchier. There are numerous excursions out of narrative into set-piece essays on topics ranging from the eighteenth-century monarchy to the imperial growths of the English language, from Scotland's own imperialism to a potted history of the Royal Navy. What emerges is something of an omnium gatherum from the teeming mind of Norman Davies. His reflections on modern as well as pre-modern times sometimes cast the light of new prejudices on familiar material, and do not shrink from bold assertions. Illumination flows from brilliant summary. One such encapsulates the thesis of the book: 'Scotland may have united with England in 1707; and Ireland may have united with England and Scotland in 1800. But England has never united with anyone.'

Sprawling widely, *The Isles* in its later part conveys the impression of a hell-for-leather chase to meet the deadline for a work that ends up, given its enormous ambition, too short at a thousand pages. But its modern significance is the point. It is a history of, but not for, the ages. It is even more for the here and now than was the work of Macaulay. It speaks to one of the most potent beliefs of this age: that the Britain we know is a place whose timeless history has composed a nation which now owes to that history a mighty struggle to preserve itself against enemies within and without.

Davies shows how much of this is bunk. The fact that it is bunk may not alter the perceptions of several million people, goaded to a different view by mass-media propaganda that simply does not want to inquire into the truth. The myths of the nation-state are perhaps what they incorrigibly like to believe. But the demythologizer – half-Welsh, half-English, larded with Lancastrian and European – deserves his own place in the annals of whatever nation he chooses to call his own.

The summary is this. There has been no long-lasting British nation. It came into brief existence as a product of, and accessory to, the making of an empire. When the empire broke up, it had served its purpose. Such as it is, it will not last. All its foundations are in an advanced state of decay. The so-called United Kingdom is not and never has been a nation-state. It has no single Established Church, no single legal system, no centralized education system, no common cultural policy, no common history – 'none of the things, in other words, on which nation-states are built'. These were replaced by an invented belief system, which made people die for Britain, but can no longer hold out against the centrifugal experience of the nations that were suppressed by it, and are now regaining their ascendancy in the larger context of a European community of nations that can give each of them succour and protection.

That, however, requires the nation that dominates the anachronism called Britain to abandon its attachment to the vestiges of superior status and national domination. Davies doesn't explain how this is going to happen. He concedes that both the break-up and the absorption may be some way off. He also describes himself, with perhaps an exaggerated sense of his near-uniqueness, as part of a 'tiny minority' who sense they are standing on the edge of a volcano, or alternatively of a 'quietly gathering avalanche that could strike out of the blue in the best of weather' to overturn the British state as we know it. On the contrary, the history he explores yields, in its fullness, little other conclusion. Messy and subjective though it is, and unwilling to allow merit to the perspective of almost any other historian, *The Isles* is a key book for its time. It seizes the conventional wisdom of the moment, and destroys most of its foundations. Might Britain last until its 300th birthday in 2007? Out of full communion with 'Europe'? There will be a massive struggle, although the former is marginally more likely than the latter. But it would be a repudiation of history, either way.

A Maastricht referendum

THE CLOSER WE GET to Maastricht, the more obviously it crystallizes the failure of the British political system. On the mountain-climb towards European economic and political union, this summit is hardly at the top. But it marks a high plateau, en route no doubt to another assault. Each part of our system, however, conspires to ensure that it takes place enshrouded in dense mists of obscurity.

The government is the first culprit. Having grown accustomed over many years to pretending that the project has never moved out of the foothills, it is not about to change its strategy now. Its negotiations, it insists, concern little more than another natural step forward, preordained by the numerous earlier steps. There are difficulties, it concedes. Every EC country has interests to protect. But EMU is no big deal, especially now that another Parliament will make the decision. And modest steps towards more unified political action do not constitute union anyway. Trust Mr Major and Mr Hurd, they say, and don't ask too many questions yet.

Alongside this understandable government posture is a graver dereliction by Parliament. The House of Commons excludes itself from being the arena in which the government's furtive tactic, and the lack of debate that accompanies it, is put to serious challenge. This is mainly because of the Labour Party. Labour has become a 'European' party, which means that it snipes at ministers for not being European enough, without displaying anything more than the shallow Euro-vision to be expected of a party so recently committed to getting Britain out of the Common Market. The last thing Labour wants is to articulate, let alone contest, what economic and political union might really mean.

Any 'debate', therefore, is left to the Thatcherite wing of the

Conservative Party, abetted by a tiny handful of Labour MPs. The Thatcherites oppose going any further. They cope with the awkward fact that Mrs Thatcher presided over every advance, including arrival at the cloud-bedecked halfway camp of the single market, by saying that this is where the line should be drawn. Enough is enough. Some of them seem determined to ask awkward questions and create, if they can, an explosion.

The debate they are trying to initiate, however, is badly flawed. For a start, some of them, looking to their seats and the need for leader-loyalty, are inhibited from saying what they think. For another thing, they are as disarmed as anyone else by the calculated elusiveness of what ministers really believe they are doing. But most of all, their contribution depends for almost all its impact on an unverified phantom: namely, the apprehension that the British people, unconsulted through all these years of deceiving conduct by successive governments, would actually oppose what is happening, if they did but know what it meant. Although the anti-Union cause has some rational argument behind it, its clout depends on the proposition that the absence of debate conceals an absence of popular assent.

This might not matter much if Parliament was doing its job. When working properly, the Commons could be credibly seen as the furnace in which popular opinion was forged. Nor would it matter so greatly if the Prime Minister were not making calculations of what the people would accept on the basis of what the Thatcherites were telling him. But what is happening is that Parliament forges nothing but counterfeit debate, and Mr Major is in a lather of anxiety deriving from the much-touted suspicion that the British are the most anti-European people in Europe.

In one respect I believe the Thatcherites are correct. What happens at Maastricht is intended, whatever the reassurances, to produce a step-change in the EC's development. All present will be negotiating towards more union, and less national independence. That is the deep essence of the matter – understood and accepted by most of the political and all the business élite, but not really understood by the people, who find their ignorance and perhaps agnosticism manipulated by politicians who have been on the losing end of the Westminster argument for twenty years.

The only escape from this travesty, it seems to me, is to hold a national referendum to discover what the nation thinks about economic and political union. Not only is the Commons disqualified from representing any answer to that question clear enough to settle it, but the coming election will be no better. On the core issue, the main parties will be couching the same answer in the same sneaky language. Each would be able to claim a bogus mandate, only to face yet another trial of legitimacy when the next advance up the mountain begins.

The referendum, of course, is customarily the expedient of the antis. The 1975 referendum was devised by Harold Wilson under pressure from his anti-EC majority. In 1990, Mrs Thatcher briefly canvassed a referendum as the way to save her skin after her calamitous performance at the Rome summit. So deep and narrow is her vision of sovereignty – pound sterling, mother of parliaments, etc. – that she cannot imagine anyone, from public bar to 19th hole, disagreeing with her.

One final, definitive scotching of this canard is necessary, and now is the time for it. I think that would be the result. When the evidence of public opinion is collected, it already seems a great deal less fired up about Europe than it was in 1975 – when it gave an overwhelming verdict against what the referendum-mongers expected. The polls now show that the EC is seen as an uncontroversial issue, where most people, especially young people, are unmoved by the dreadful prospects summoned up by Mrs Thatcher and Mr Tebbit.

The value of the exercise, however, would not just be in the result I anticipate it would bring. It would unfold the argument which not enough politicians are now honest enough to have. The chosen question need not be a problem. On a general question to measure the endorsement for economic and political union, it would be impossible to avoid a grand national argument on what kind of Europe now heads the agenda of the people and their would-be leaders. I would see the debate as something between a seminar and an exorcism.

It could not, of course, answer all the questions. A Yes result would be unable to say anything about the myriad absurdities rife in some notions of political union. The politicians would loathe it. But one forum whose crudity it could not exceed is Westminster. Elsewhere in Europe, maybe, this debate is not necessary. But in Britain its absence is, I contend, poisoning the environment in which this critical branch of foreign policy is conducted. A referendum after Maastricht and before the election could solve several of Mr Major's problems at a stroke. Not only could he bury Mrs Thatcher but show, more than all his famous charters put together, that he cares what the people think.

A sad case of political cowardice

THE DEFINING THEME of Gordon Brown's statement yesterday, ruling out entry into the euro for the rest of this Parliament, was its stunning insularity. Here was a momentous statement of policy about Europe, which made the great question sound as though it were nothing but a British political and economic problem. In that, it did make one thing clear: perhaps by inadvertence, but certainly beyond doubt, Britain has abandoned any chance of becoming the leader of Europe, the goal Tony Blair once set as a prime objective.

Mr Brown showed no particle of awareness of what Europe, as opposed to Britain, might feel about his posture of indecision. Indecisive he certainly was, behind the rumbling pretence that he was making hard decisions, establishing clear national purposes. To Europeans this will look neither hard nor clear, but an attitude of such neurotic caution, laced with largely bogus pieties, as to amount to a sad case of political cowardice.

This may be defensible in British terms. It lies down in front of the heaviest guns in the British media. It will make life easier in the short term for a government that has its sights set unwaveringly on a second term. But to suppose this stance is cost-free – enabling Britain to stroll into EMU five years on, maybe, or then again maybe not, at any moment of the government's and the people's choosing – is an illusion which shows offshore-islanderism as alive and sick as ever.

Let us grant a few credit points. There is a certain value in hearing the Chancellor say formally from the despatch box that Labour sees no constitutional bar to British membership of EMU. Though EMU will involve a large pooling of national sovereignty, Mr Blair and Mr Brown could carry that through their party with ease. Since the Tories, through Peter Lilley's first bumbling intervention, made clear their inability to stake themselves in unity to the opposite proposition, some progress has possibly been made.

It is also hard to argue with the need for preparation. After years of officially sanctioned Euro-scepticism, public opinion has a one-sided view of the issues that will confront them in a referendum. Likewise, business and the City have not lived with the same pro-EMU assumptions as their French and German counterparts have for a long time. The divergence of economic cycles is another problem, which almost nobody any longer argues could be sensibly addressed by entry in January 1999.

But then the illusions start. The first is that there is no certainty of these cycles converging with any more decisive conviction in 2002–3 than they do now. It is just as plausible that divergence will remain, the difference being that as the EMU economies are recovering, Britain's has entered a cyclical downturn.

Mr Brown will be struggling with might and main to avoid this, but he can offer no guarantees. Certainty in a wider sense is also, therefore, absent. There is negative certainty, but positive certainty – of the kind needed by business and the wider world – is absolutely missing. On what basis are practical people meant to be preparing for something that might or might not happen five years from now?

The politics, at that stage, are as likely to have gone wrong as they are to go right. If European economies have started to do better than the British, we may be sure every setback will be laid at the EU's door, further stoking anti-EU opinion. The idea of a natural convergence, progressing on all fronts towards the right conclusion under the hand of a government that has made the decision of principle, is the merest speculation. I would call it thoroughly fanciful.

The second illusion is that Europe will meanwhile have stood still. For the candidate members of EMU, the venture is a journey into an unknown land. They are as aware of the risks as they are of the benefits, and will exact a price from those who seek the latter without the former.

The construction of EMU is work that will exclude the non-members. The British interest, even as an outsider, will be less easily defended; for a putative insider, it will have been progressively over-ridden by the member-states. Five years down the line, the conditions of membership will have hardened, in particular the need for prior membership of the ERM, also laid down at Maastricht. Mr Brown's dismissive assertion that 'it is not our intention to join the ERM' is something on which EMU members will have plenty to say.

Mr Blair seems to be relying on slow convergence, massive preparations, big business's de facto adoption of the euro, free-wheeling delay, painless negotiation, and the continuing enfeeblement of the Tory Party. But one can write an alternative scenario: an economic reverse, preparations on a five-year hold, big business unconvinced, a stronger Tory Party, weaker government, and Europe writing Britain out of the script.

To most Europeans, the British position is incredible. They see a government with a majority none of them can match, hugely popular, charismatically led, presiding over Europe's strongest economy – the envy of the Continent it says it wants to lead – yet willing, with all solemnity, to miss a moment that may never be repeated to hold a referendum it would have a maximum chance of winning.

They cannot but look upon this with jaundiced eyes. As for the British, they may look back on late October 1997 as the moment when, far from leading Europe, Britain began the process of an undesired but inexorable removal to the fringes of the game.

Why I'm glad to be European

AS A BOY, I was entirely English. There was nothing else to be. This was true even though an education by Catholic monks offered alternative possibilities. Henry VIII, we learned, was a very bad man, and the heretics burned at the stake by Mary Tudor deserved their fate, whereas the victims of Elizabeth were martyrs and saints. The arrival from Holland of William of Orange, displacing the Catholic Stuarts in 1688, far from inaugurating the Glorious Revolution from which, as I now believe, most British constitutional freedom flowed, was a disaster for the one true faith.

This bias in the teaching of history didn't touch our real allegiances in everything that mattered: cricket, soccer, rugby, the ubiquitous redness of the map, the naturally British order of things. Allegiance, with victory as its quest, was the habit that school instilled in me: gangs, cliques, houses, teams, Sheffield United Football Club, the Yorkshire County Cricket Club and all who played in it. There had to be something to support, and on the international plane Britain, or England, had to win.

This tendency stayed with me for many years. It has never really gone. When Brits do well, it still gives me a warm glow. Cricket continues to matter, especially when Darren Gough plays a blinder, and partisanship defeated all temptations (those swilling lager louts, the Union Jack as offensive weapon) to forget the World Cup was going on. I'm obscurely glad that Simon Rattle is British. When a great British movie, like *Secrets and Lies*, captures the world, its national origin matters. When the SAS took the first Serbian war criminals, I remember feeling quietly pleased it was us.

My esteem for Britishness also stretches into professional fields. We do some governmental things better than other people, and should want to keep it that way. Our public life is relatively honest, our judges are straight, almost all our politicians selflessly industrious. Our Parliament is a living thing. As for our history, it's a wonderment, reaching out from this tiny island, producer of a language and a literature and a record of power that the people of pretty well every other nation must regard with awe.

So I can confess to being disgracefully congruent with a typical reader of the *Daily Telegraph*. And in the early days of 'Europe', this collection of awarenesses sheltered me from the new cause. Voting Yes in the 1975 referendum was a routine orthodoxy, shared with two-thirds of the British people, including quite a number who now seem to have changed their minds. For years, I never felt zeal for either side. But now I do, and I wonder why. What has happened, while the majority allegiance appears to have gone into reverse, to push me effortlessly the other way?

The initiation began with a book I wrote about the history of these matters. I started work on *This Blessed Plot* as a Euro-agnostic, but completed it a few years later in a state of struggling incredulity at the demons and panics I had uncovered: the British exceptionalism that has seduced generations of our politicians into believing that 'Europe' is somewhere to escape from: the hallucinations, both positive and negative, that have driven so much of the British debate for so long. Having begun with the idea of writing a history that might call itself detached, I found myself in a process of self-instruction that now concludes, as the new currency gets under way, with the great simplicity of describing why I am a European.

The most obvious but least relevant part of this is cultural. It's easy to say how keenly I adore Schubert, and wallow in Proust, and am anticipating my next journey to consort with the shades of Virgil in the Roman Forum. But this is almost completely beside the point. European culture is the world's inheritance, absorbed on every continent, and the ability to appreciate the works of Johann Sebastian Bach, or even to speak his language, says nothing important about anyone's sense of 'being' a European.

Even Peter Lilley loves Michelangelo, as he and his colleagues never cease to explain, by way of proving that they are not anti-Europe, merely anti-'Europe': the European Union, the artefact of federalists, the dismal construct that has illicitly purloined the received identity of what Europe is held to mean these days. Lilley has a house in France, and Michael Portillo has roots in Spain, and there's a cross-party agreement that Umbro-Tuscany is where the British political classes most like to take their holidays. Does this not show their un-insular engagement with the Continent, and expose the calumny that they might be Europhobic?

But the test cannot be who has heard more versions of *The Ring* between Bayreuth and Covent Garden. As the boy becomes a man, the discovery that Shakespeare has a peer group who write in different tongues may begin to broaden the mind. It is helpful to learn that these are not rival cultures, a zero-sum game of allegiance, but that they mingled and grew together. This discovery makes no demand on anyone's sense of belonging. Though the Conservative government proposed a ban on Beethoven's Ninth as the theme music for Euro '96, a football competition staged in England, it's safest to say that a taste for the Renaissance and Enlightenment is too universal to be significant. Like the travel, it proves nothing.

Very soon, therefore, what raises itself is the political question. About the culture, there is no issue. It may be important to many Eurosceptics to be able to say that because they love Mozart, they love Europe, but this isn't what the argument is about. The division between the pro- and anti-Europeans is, in the real world, about nothing more or less than the European Union. Everything else is sand in your eyes, an evasion. The EU, enlarged, or not: reformed, or not: with or without all its multiple imperfections, is the only item on the agenda.

It is not possible to be a European, in any meaningful sense, while opposing the EU. And it is not possible to support the EU without also supporting the success of the euro, and the belonging to the euro of every country that wants to call itself European.

I can think of many points which, added together, make a formidable critique of the EU. Its bureaucracy is strong, its democracy is weak, its accountability is seriously underdeveloped. The complexity of its tasks is always in danger of overwhelming the consensus needed to carry them out. Getting it to act demands formidable energy and patience and will-power from national leaders. Ensuring the singleness of the market it purports to be is work that is far from completed.

Equally, I can make the case against the euro, a project which fills those who support it with almost as much anxiety as it does excitement. Will this risk, which includes a repudiation of nationhood as traditionally understood, pay off? Will its hazards be sustainable? Is the closer political integration, which it undoubtedly foretells, something that the members, with or without Britain, have the wit, will and wisdom to express in acceptable forms?

These questions don't fill me with horror. Their terrain awaits a long unfolding. They assume a process not voluntarily attempted anywhere in history: tampering, by common agreement, with aspects of national identity, and working to create, in limited but significant aspects, a new kind of consciousness. To modify the nation-state throughout Europe is an extraordinary ambition, full of risks and difficulties. Yet if I'm ever tempted to despair of it, I need only remind myself of the alternative world summoned up by those, most ferociously in Britain, who devote passion to dismantling it. They've had a long time to describe this non-European Britain, and the picture, where it is clear, is not persuasive. I conclude it is not meant to be. Portillo wrote not long ago that even to ask the question was 'extraordinary'. All the future has to satisfy, in the minds of many Eurosceptics, is the need not to be 'European'. As long as it meets that test, the details hardly matter.

Thus, Little England (Scotland will be long gone from this) is, incorrigibly, a straitened place. Striving to define it, David Willetts, a Tory front-bencher, wrote a pamphlet, *Who Do We Think We Are?*, which, as well as saying our politics and economics were different from Europe, made much of the Changing of the Guard and Wensleydale cheese, calling in support some ancient paragraphs from T. S. Eliot and George Orwell to exalt the eternal time-warp in which England must be lodged. In all these tracts, the mystic chords of memory echo. Betraying history is most unimaginable, while predicting the future is subsumed into fantasy: the dream of an independent Britain, freed to assert her famous sovereignty, throwing herself on the mercy and markets of the non-European world.

So the anti-Europe cave is claustrophobic. It is also being refilled (for we've been here before) with futile arrogance, making it obligatory not merely to criticize Brussels but abominate the Germans, laugh about the French, find nothing good to say about another European country, lest this betray our beleaguered sense of Britishness. A smart-ass headline writer in the *Sun* can get attention when the BBC finds an item of punning xenophobia so funny as to be worth a mention in the news.

At the heart of this is an impenetrable contradiction in the anti-Europe British mind. It cannot decide between terror and disdain. Britain is apparently so great, as well as so different, a place that she can afford to do without her Continental hinterland. But she is so puny, so endangered, so destined to lose every argument with the Continentals that she must fear for her identity if and when she makes the final commitment to belong among them. Studying the movements of sceptic thought, I see in their inability to provide a clear answer on this fundamental point a mirror of the vacillations, pro- and anti-Europe, that mark the personal histories of so many of the characters in the story. Either way, the conclusion points in the anti-Europe direction.

The same axiomatic outcome has penetrated every stage of Conservative Party thinking about the euro. While often purporting to be technical, the discussion has in fact been wholly political. First they said the euro wouldn't happen: 'a rain-dance', Major called it. Then they said it wouldn't work. Then they said it might well work. Now they say that even if it does work, it cannot work for Britain, as they edge into a position that bets their entire political future on its failure.

As each prediction is falsified, the threshold for the euro's acceptance is raised. Shamelessly, the playing-field is tilted to make the game unwinnable, though most Tories still shrink from saying what they so plainly believe: that, as far as they're concerned, the British national identity as we know it can *never* coexist with membership of the European single currency. Thus the party that took Britain into Europe prepares to fight to the last in favour of excluding Britain from what 'Europe' any longer means.

My own odyssey has been quite different. The euro presents massive political challenges, but there seems no point in being outside it, since our future – the only future anyone has been able, with any respect for realism, to describe – is entirely bound up with its success or failure. Far from the development of 'Europe' being a conceptual barrier to belonging, it's the very reason why belonging ought soon to be seen as essential. I know the snags, and will argue for some radical political reform, but the European-ness of the euro is what makes it an exciting and benign adventure. We need to be a part. It should be Britain's own millennial leap, away from the century of nation-statehood, into a new time. All our neighbours are seeking a different way of bringing a better life to the Continent and its regions.

What is so strange about Britain – so particular, so fearful, so other-worldly – that she should decide to withhold her unique wisdom from the enterprise? I can reject the premise of the question because I've grown up. Allegiance, to me, no longer has to be so exclusive. I still need it, as a psychic prop, a way of belonging. But the threat to the national identity now strikes me as bogus. This categorizing is what anti-Europe people insist on, but the best evidence of its falsity is to be found in the places that have been part of the new Europe for forty years, as against our twenty-five. Would anyone claim that Germany is less German as a result of the experience? We are all invaded by America. If cultural defences are needed, it's against transatlantic domination. But do I hear a single soul, on either side of the Channel, contend that France is less French than it ever was because of the EU?

So it will be with Britain. This reality won't come easy. Decades of propaganda defining national identity in the language of scorn for other nations can't be wiped out at a stroke. Persuading the British that they are allowed to be European should be the simplest task, yet the accretions of history, manipulated by frightened politicians, make it difficult. Though the Queen in Parliament already looks like a bejewelled dot on the ocean of the global economy, there are voices that insist the only way of being British is by proclaiming her supremacy.

Redefining identity is not a task for the furtive. It cannot be done by the back door: another lesson of history. Nor will it be easily done by political leaders who still feel obliged to stand aside from the project they think they eventually want to join. But neither should the work be too alarming. In the twenty-first century, it will be exciting to escape from history into geography: from the prison of the past into a future that permits us at last the luxury of having it both ways: British *and* European.

The curse of British symbols

SVEN-GORAN ERIKSSON is the latest evidence that there's a limit to English nationalism. Could there be richer proof? In the absence of war, no British activity generates nationalistic feelings more ferocious, more bloodily visceral, than football. Opera, where the resident maestro at Covent Garden is Dutch, is everywhere a haven for globalists. Cricket, now in the hands of a Zimbabwean, is a Commonwealth club. But to put a Swede in charge of the modern substitute for battle is a startling tribute to the broadmindedness of the English. It signifies a neglected but contradictory truth about national character, a resonant paradox of our time.

In some respects, the British care little about nationality. They're extraordinarily unexcited by questions of ownership or control. They seem unlike any other people, even Americans, in their indifference to the economic consequences of globalization. A benchmark moment was 1994, when Rolls-Royce agreed to sell itself to BMW. The most potently British industrial brand passed into the hands of the Germans with hardly a murmur of regret. Among both politicians and the public, disinterested maturity prevailed.

This persisted down the decade. Most big players in the City of London are now foreign-owned. The famous merchant banks, many of which came from the Continent, have gone back there, or to America. Hambros, Warburgs, Schroders, Lazards, Barings, all these pillars of what makes up financial London have been ceded to foreigners. The Stock Exchange itself is ripe for plucking by a Swedish group. Some people in the City don't like that, but only on financial grounds. They just think Germans or the French or the New York Nasdaq might give them a better deal.

At no stage has there been national angst about this. Neither Conservative nor Labour governments took much interest, and outside the financial community such developments are barely noticed. Britain sits at the top of the UN list of national businesses investing overseas, but also shows an inexorable increase in foreign ownership of British enterprises, 10 per cent of it, last year, being German. Around 9,000 UK companies are owned by Americans. The British accept this with nonchalance. When BMW swallowed Rover, the only political concern was about preserving jobs. The idea that the nation is a lesser place if foreigners own major slices of the means of production, distribution and exchange never seems to cross anyone's mind. In France or Germany it would be as unimaginable for Brits to buy the motor industry as for an Italian to coach the national team.

This pragmatic indifference reaches wider. Not long ago a survey found that only 27 per cent of British consumers thought British products excellent or good, compared with 38 per cent who thought that of German products. Contrast that with Japan, where 75 per cent think domestically produced goods are excellent or very good, and France where that figure is 45 per cent. Likewise, Chelsea don't lose support for fielding a team of Continentals, and the English Football Association is run by a Scotsman. So there are zones where the English and/or British seem capable of taking a realistic view of their own limitations. We have the mentality to be the world's aptest globalizers. Unresentful and unalarmed, we watch the old citadels crumble in the interest of a better result.

But wait. Something is wrong here. All this clear-sighted realism, this stoical self-confidence, also has its limits. Our character is strangely split. Alongside such exceptional breadth goes a neurotic narrowness, a panicky phobia. Confident enough to let Germany have Rolls-Royce, we regard the geopolitics of Europe as filled with menace not opportunity. Superbly contemptuous of the notion that a Europe-owned City could diminish our national identity, we think Brussels will destroy it. Glad to put a Swede in charge of our peacetime proxy army, we're urged by many politicians and most newspapers to curl a quivering lip at the damage a European defence organization might do to that fragile, tottering construct, the selfhood of Britain.

How to explain this personality disorder? It is not a madness. There are sane reasons to object to the way the European Union is going. It is rational, if contentious, to see Brussels as a malign bureaucracy against which we should be ever watchful. There are cool, defensible, logical arguments against further integration. But these do not fully encompass the emotional turbulence of British opinion, which has as much to do with heart as mind, with viscera as neurones. The insouciance that enables Brits to ride over every assault on their economic heartland seems entirely to desert them in face of any adjustment, however minor, resulting from our twenty-seven-year membership of the EU.

The contrast, I suggest, is between substance and symbol. Substance we can evidently sign away, as long as the economics add up. This is not always a reliable test, by the way. The BMW takeover of Rover ended in tears, and foreign-owned banks may survive a recession less readily than if British interests still controlled them. But we blithely swallow that. Symbol, on the other hand, must be defended at all costs. The parts of Britain/England the EU mainly threatens are her symbols not her substance.

Passports are a symbol. The half-baked idea for an EU passport is silly and gratuitous, but in a hard-headed world not worth the hysteria vented on it. The pound sterling is another item that's more symbol than substance: icon of nation much more, in a borderless trading world, than unique guarantor of economic success. Parliament itself, while capable of its historic tasks, now seldom performs them. Under all parties it is a tool of executive government, just as all countries face interlinked complexities of politics and economics that none can alone control. Though Parliament can't be destroyed by the EU, it is in truth as much symbol as reality. The British condition – the preoccupation of an old country – is to be moved more by challenges to its symbols than anything else.

One question now is where in the British mind football is allocated. If Mr Eriksson wins the World Cup he will become an English hero. He'll be seamlessly received. The pragmatic decision to dispense with the national symbol of a native-born coach will be no more worth discussing than the sale of Rolls-Royce. Along the way, even some of the self-aggrandizing thuggery that passes for English soccer nationalism could be dispersed. If he fails, on the other hand, football will go back to the place where defeatism is endemic, and nationalism the only haven from chronic insecurity. The empty symbols that the English really care about will resume their thrall.

A more serious question is whether the British can be persuaded to reconsider the sterile absurdity of their political passions. Uniquely adult in disclaiming the nationalism of ownership, they are uniquely puerile in their fearful attachment to symbols that impede rather than advance the state of their nation.

It's the politics, stupid

OVER THE PAST twelve months I've been conducting a modest personal survey. Each time I meet ministers I've asked them whether they believe politics rather than economics might prevent them from holding a referendum on the euro in this Parliament. If the economic tests are passed, but the opinion polls show only 30 per cent of the voters ready to vote Yes to ditching the pound, would they decide not to ask the question? Each one of them – and they include all the senior people involved in making the judgement – has emphatically denied any such possibility.

Tomorrow's Queen's Speech will not reflect the imminence of this commitment being put to the test. Supposedly a dossier on the politics of the year ahead, it will do no justice to the truth, which is that the decision on the euro, whichever way it goes, will dwarf everything else that happens, with the possible exception of the fate of Iraq. Actually, the euro probably matters more than Iraq to the future of Britain. But the Speech will do little except allude to the five tests being made in June. It will reek not of commitment but the usual hesitation. It will thereby pretend that time is not running out.

This reflects the mood in a wider world than Labour politics. Taking the temperature of the politico-business class, you'd have to say that expectations are quietly on the wane. Irrespective of their preferences, more people than six months ago seem pretty sure the referendum will not take place. The familiar old inertia is taking over. Comfortable illusion once again beckons us towards another day, and another, and another, down the decade.

Seigneurial demands are made: that Europe must reform; that the growth and stability pact, pending the vitally necessary reshaping of its rules, must not be compromised; that the Giscard d'Estaing convention must be seen to favour British answers to questions of federation. And so on. We must wait and see. And besides, isn't our economy stronger than the Continentals'? We do want to go in one day. But not just yet. This is the warm bath of righteous caution in which the government is being pushed to wallow, perhaps until just one more election is out of the way – when all the arguments will resume, so goes the illusion, in a different and more decisive spirit. The position of this column has always been that the 2002 Queen's Speech would be a decisive moment for the euro. If by this time Mr Blair hadn't shown his hand, the odds against a referendum would grow. It's commonly agreed, though won't be publicly admitted, that 2003 represents the first and last date the referendum could take place, and I believe public opinion needs to be prepared over a long period, starting now. We can now see this isn't going to happen, so my judgement holds. A referendum is still possible. But it's becoming less likely, and reversing that balance of probabilities will require an ever more galvanic burst of political energy as time goes on.

The material for such a campaign is there. It lies in a political argument that the inertia-mongers – the believers in another day, and another – never adequately address. Right now, Mr Blair can claim to have a big influence on the EU. Britain has a loud voice in the convention. Even Gordon Brown's more suspect voice is taken seriously by those who want to reshape the stability pact and the operations of the central bank. But these lines of influence are contingent. They assume Britain intends to join the euro next year, as do the Japanese manufacturers taking decisions on where to locate in the eurozone.

The spectacle of the strongest government in Europe deciding, after all, that it was going to postpone the matter once more would have a devastating effect on all that. It would be comprehended by these political and business partners only as a statement of political cowardice. It would imperil the influence we hope to have on the post-Giscard constitutional shape of Europe, a decision that will be taken at an intergovernmental conference a year from now, months after our euro die has been cast – or cast away. As for shaping the euro, we would have said in the starkest possible manner that we were ready to be heard only *sotto voce*. A decision of the greatest possible magnitude would have been taken, of self-exclusion from the centre of the EU for at least the next five years.

If that happens, it will be defended in economic terms. You can hear the arguments now. The eurozone is economically sluggish. Its rules are deflationary. It needs reform. Its chief central banker isn't fit for his job. We do things much better in the City. The interest rate that suits Germany doesn't entirely suit Ireland. Cyclical convergence, even now, isn't quite what we need.

There are three things to be said about these arguments. First, they are all true. Second, there's an answer to every one of them. But third, the answers will never convince people who don't want to be convinced. There will always be room for doubt. There's no such thing as absolute proof of economic correctness. If one ECB chief is defective in 2002, we may be sure his successor will be, for different reasons, in 2006. If one set of rules is bad now, another will disclose its defects later, especially if Britain has opted out of the task of reform. An eternity of debate lies ahead, for those who want never to decide.

Mr Blair and Mr Brown know all this better than I do. For one of them the euro-glass may be half-full and for the other half-empty, but they share a desire, ultimately, to make the historic change. Knowing all that, if they run away from a referendum, we'll know what their reasons are. These will all be to do with the fear of losing. The polls, far from being beneath the consideration of leaders engrossed by national destiny, will have pushed them into ignominious retreat, with untold consequences for Britain's interest.

Losing is a risk. But let's be clear about the risks of not trying. These will echo down the years when crime bills, and twenty-four-hour drinking, and Section 28, and the rest of tomorrow's stunning legislative repertoire are deservedly forgotten.

ANGLO-AMERICAN
COUNTRY

Let's hope the lecher survives

HIS PERFORMANCE was astonishing. Has there ever been such nerve in face of the world? This was a man in absolute command of his public faculties, matching with awful symmetry his inability to control his private parts. All right, it wasn't a press conference. Free from questioning, he milked the ceremonial that gave him an hour's immunity. And since the State of the Union is on the up, there was nothing his message had to explain away. It was easy to make the people feel good about his public works. None the less, the control was something altogether special.

President Clinton, as the truism goes, is a divided being. Never was it clearer than on Tuesday night that his inner frontiers are not abstract Chinese walls but concrete barricades reaching to the sky. He lives in more impermeable compartments than any politician I've ever been aware of. Robin Cook, for example. Mr Cook is plainly not compartmentalized. His private troubles have reached into his public life. Always liable to inner turbulence over his marriage breakup, even though he provoked it, he then behaved with irascible folly about his personal staff. The Tory press and party, which he once often tore apart, is bent on vengeance, and the experience is getting to him. To be honest, he hasn't seemed the same man from the moment all this got into the press. There has been seepage from the public to the private and back again.

In Clinton's case, the lack of seepage is awesome to behold. There's something inhuman about it. That a leader can behave in public with such utter coldness to what is happening in private resembles the psychopath's indifference to the consequences of his actions. Are no connections anywhere to be made? Is every act confined to the pigeonhole where it serves its own purpose, like the state slaughter of Rickey Ray Rector, the half-demented killer whose execution had to be approved because the Governor of Arkansas wanted to be President? Or like the serial sex acts? Sometimes the compartments, far from shoring up the public mandate, suggest an emotional, even intellectual, lobotomy.

For the truly ruthless man, however, they're also a strength. They may yet see Clinton through. They may see his presidency survive and – who knows? – flourish. If he escapes the irrefutable edge of guilt this time, he will last the course of the next three years, and need not necessarily be a paralysed laughing-stock, which is currently defined as the best fate he can hope for. Such is the strength of the compartmentalized politician. It may even prove triumphant in this case.

Some charges are unsurvivable. Having raised the stakes to the greatest height, the Clintons have put their jobs on the table. They're backing their own credibility against any competing account his latest lover comes up with, gambling on linguistic games. What, for example, does a denial of 'sexual relations' deny? That term may not be understood with the same biblical exactitude outside the White House as it plainly is, by special dispensation, within.

Every particle of the Clinton apologia will be examined with the utmost harshness, and there are things Ms Lewinsky might say that are so explicit as to defeat all attempts to prearrange her lack of credence. If the test can plausibly be made a legal not a political one – lying under oath, or suborning others to do the same – not even Clinton can survive.

But if this test can't be set, or if Prosecutor Starr is tarnished, or if the testimonies leave enough that's grey and moot, the President will live on. He could even recover strength. He would have seen off the charges, having blackened them, with pretty outrageous hyperbole, as a rightist conspiracy. Back from the near-dead, he need not be the whispered joke that's commonly predicted. He might have lost moral authority, but it's a long time since he has been strong in that department anyway. His political authority, on the other hand, need be no lower than it already is. Having consigned the charges against him to the compartment labelled not proven, he would still be a viable President.

The world has good reason, I believe, to hope this is what happens: to see a deeply flawed character survive rather than a criminal expelled. If Clinton can't be destroyed, we must hope he is partially vindicated. This objective may be hard to reach, but if it can be met, it would satisfy two necessities.

The first is global. The world needs America's leader to be strong enough. Clinton's record as a foreign-policy President is mixed. Very late into Bosnia, he has at least managed to insist on the US staying there. In the Middle East, he has been close to disastrous, refusing to use the massive leverage he has available against an Israeli leader who is doing more than anyone except Saddam Hussein to deepen the region's instability. But even in the sordid depths of Fornigate, the President was still being offered bipartisan Congressional support for a firm stand against Saddam. The politics of the personal are, even now, not entirely disabling him.

Clinton has never shown much desire to engage with foreign affairs, or bring a critical mass of effort to bear upon the international complexities that America is uniquely placed to address. He's far from a proactive map-maker in the new world, which is a grave deficiency. But hesitant and inattentive though he is, ever watchful for the next opinion poll, his expulsion from office would produce a worse result.

This is because of the second thing that makes one hope an impeachable charge is not convincingly raised against him. The presidency, when all is said and done, matters to the world. It's a mundane office, but exists within an aura of treasurable solemnity. There's usually a certain bipartisan desire, alongside the virulence of Washington, for its incumbent to succeed, a sense of it being in some ways above politics, even containing traces of the monarchical. The forced eviction of another President before his natural time is up would be a happening of the utmost gravity: a destabilizing moment: an enormity which, save on a quite inescapable pretext, would diminish rather than restore faith in the American system.

With a brilliant lecher in the White House and an incompetent drunk in the Kremlin, this is not an era of Olympians. I hope the lecher finds a way of persuading America his offence is not terminal.

Heading for estrangement

NEARLY FORTY YEARS AGO, it was unforgettably said that Britain had lost an empire and not found a role. Dean Acheson's jibe was prophetic as well as painful. Its truth abided longer than he could ever know. But now Tony Blair believes it can be laid to rest. The British role, he says, at last is clear: to be the pivot at the axis of a large range of international force relationships. This is our uniqueness. Above all we're now ready, thanks to economic recovery and new political self-confidence, to be the key player in the choice we must never have to make – between the US and Europe.

As one way of countering Europhobia at home, while even-handedly reassuring everyone abroad, this formula has its value. The Prime Minister's speech on Monday to the Lord Mayor's banquet was a level-headed plea for internationalism. Like Robin Cook's, next day, it contrasted magisterially with the paranoia that passes for the Tories' policy of deluded independent nationhood.

The facts, however, are changing and the argument is moving on. The way Mr Blair put it, while superficially attractive in its catholicity of allegiance, ignored some jarring developments. Is it any longer enough to be the pivot, a Blairite image which carries the sense of being above a contest in which Britain is similarly linked to, yet similarly distant from, both sides? A balance with equal weights on the end? Umpire and facilitator, jockeying one special relationship based on geography against the other based on history? Consider what is happening to challenge the formulation Mr Blair hopes to retreat painlessly behind.

The Washington that gave birth to the special relationship with the Brits has gone. Most of the midwives are in their graves. These internationalists – Acheson, Lovett, Harriman, Rusk, McNamara, another generation – have been replaced as the determinants of US foreign policy, now that the Cold War is over, by a gang of unilateralists and isolationists. This group exert an ever more suffocating influence from Congress, with the object, quite openly, of destroying the internationalist consensus.

Their heresies are as startling as they are righteous. They see treaties as a threat to US sovereignty. Merely by being a treaty, such an obscenity involves the possible influence of other countries over US policy, and thus, like the nuclear test ban treaty, must be dismantled. The UN is an affront to isolationist unilateralism, so Congress withholds the funds America owes for peacekeeping and war prevention, as well as its share of basic UN costs. US military intervention, to stop conflict spreading, is intolerable to this new *Zeitgeist*. Foreign affairs, as a function of state in the greatest state in the world, was curtailed this year by the brutal excision of $2 billion from the budget the President requested.

Sandy Berger, head of Clinton's National Security Council, recently berated the narrow betrayers of the past who've been doing all this. 'They believe in a survivalist foreign policy – build a fortified fence around America, and retreat behind it,' was how he characterized their project. But the State Department itself is not immune from the infection.

For decades it has been urging the Europeans to take more responsibility for their own defence. Now that they're trying to do so, with their own defence and security initiative, Washington is panicking. What began as evenly divided councils over the evolution of the Anglo–French St Malo agreement has degenerated into pervasive scepticism, mainly in the face of the usual French word-play over relationships within Nato. Instead of leaving the French to be seen off by the British, Germans, Dutch and Italians – in an initiative which, in any case, will remain little more than words for years – the State Department joins the Pentagon in promoting a relentlessly carping attitude.

There is, in short, a crisis brewing in US–European relations. Some would say it's already under way, and nobody is confident that future events have much chance of recalibrating the diplomatic weaponry. The arrival of George W. Bush in the White House in a year's time would, on most evidence, give these trends another fillip. If the Republicans keep both houses of Congress, that will certainly be so: Bush's faltering approach to foreign policy has exposed some pretty hard-right instincts. Even if they keep only the Senate, the ascendancy of isolationist attitudes, punctuated by unilateralist abrasion, will become more rooted as the US philosophy of the early twenty-first century.

The question for pivotal Britain is whether this prospect seriously offers a relationship she should still insist on regarding as special. The issue is no longer whether Britain deserves to be special, but whether the US remains worth being special with. Will a US teetering between isolationism and unilateralism be worth the congruence with Europe, in the British scale of priorities, that Mr Blair still pleads for? Leaving aside all sentiment about the Anglo–American past, and all preferences concerning the future of the EU, is the British interest really best served by the finely balanced pivotry that is supposed at last to answer Acheson's derisive complaint?

For a time, it will do. Mr Blair's proposition is not empty, and is certainly an advance on the Thatcherite tendency to measure foreign policy by the enemies who could be routed from the field, rather than the allies that were assembled. The old adage lives. We speak better than anyone for Europe in Washington, and for Washington in Europe. A Prime Minister trusted by both sides, and in the fullness of his unmatched domestic power, has a special role to play.

But the pivot pays a price. Tied to US unilateralism, Blair supported and still helps carry out, alone in the EU, the disgraceful bombing of Iraq. Though he has taken a critical line on the UN-dues scandal, the old instincts make for too much fealty. This can't last unrevised without, at some stage, weakening the other side of these pivotal relationships. If aggressive isolationism under a Republican hegemony is now to become the Washington orthodoxy, sweet Florentine discourse on the 'third way' won't be the only current transatlantic undertaking that starts being gradually confined to the European side of the water.

In that event, the choice Blair insists mustn't be made will begin to loom. It won't necessarily be harsh and obvious, still less sudden – the military imbalance will remain for decades. Nor does it mean a zero-sum, black-and-white exclusion of the American connection. But it does imply a change of tendency, a willingness to face the fact that these two continents, in certain respects, have vitally different attitudes. Part of the growing-up of Britain will be to reach beyond the search for elusive balance and, without shame or terror, be ready sometimes to choose, very clearly, geography not history.

The millennial past, and future

BRITAIN APPROACHES the millennium moment standing still. There has been a huge build-up to an essentially static moment, marked by a lot of sententious reflection and a structure that roots this moment in time and place. America, by contrast, hardly notices it. Americans are approaching the double zero without a pause. They crash through it glancing neither left nor right, and certainly not behind.

In Britain, you can't get away from the mania, the excuse for every kind of reckoning with the past: every list of the best, every rehash of history, every marking that anyone can dream up. It is as if we really need to make sense of it as a nation – no doubt because it catches us in a state of some self-doubt as to what this nation of ours amounts to. This makes for a very big moment. But a stationary moment: at the heart of which is a big Dome.

The Dome has unfortunately been made the entire British point of the millennium. Mr Blair calls it the biggest thing anyone anywhere in the world has done to mark the moment, and he is right. But that is a wretched not a beautiful truth. Via the Dome, located where New Labour politicians reverently announce that Time Began, Blairism has taken over the orchestration of the millennium, and with it the responsibility for saying what it means. The exercise has been disastrous. The meaning may have been sought, but, as the Dome's emptiness shows, has not been found. A sponsored groping for significance was assembled, as a grand national performance. All we have at the end of it are politicians petulantly telling us we have a national duty, at £750 million, to admire what they have done.

A lot of committees sat. They looked back, and looked forward, and struggled to agree, as regards the past, on what would be politically correct and, as regards the future, what would be commercially acceptable. You could say that, all in all, this was an apt expression of the times. Maybe the Dome, in its soiled and commercialized vacuity, is as telling a monument to its period as was the cathedral at Chartres, whose builders never doubted for a moment the faith they were exalting. But that hardly justifies a national preoccupation with the millennium on a scale no other country in the world has shown.

In America there is no Dome, nor anything resembling one. There will be few monuments of any kind, scattered through the states. The twentieth century is the maximum span anyone seems inclined to address with lists and reckonings. It is already established, beyond demur, as the American Century. Stopping for millennial agonizings would only dampen the insouciant energy with which the US seems well placed to see off all contenders for ownership of the next one too. What Americans approach is not a moment worth stopping for, but a landmark whose prime interest concerns the chance of Y2K glitches interrupting the economic cataract, or auto-dealers pushing their millennial special deals under the wire before 1/1/00.

Normalcy, in other words, is not disturbed. This is just another year in the thundering onward march of USA Inc. Big numbers interest people far more than the biggest plastic building in the world. Next February will mark the longest period of continuous economic expansion in American history, at eight years eleven months. Unemployment approaches a thirty-year low. All forecasts of the economic future guarantee still more unchallengeable hegemony for the continent that bestrides the Internet, which generated business worth $20 billion this year, rising to $60 billion next.

No wonder that when you land in New York, the surging electronic economy immediately seems to have effaced the chance borderline between millennia, in the larger part of the American psyche. Nowhere could memories of a thousand years be less relevant than in a country engulfed by transactions completed in a nanosecond.

It follows from this that political leaders are not millennially preoccupied either. They don't try to take possession of this moment, with or without the help of the public's money. Still less do they seek to explain what it means for America. The forces of the economy, as they know, are greater than they are. As the presidential campaign accelerates, and the great champions present themselves for Clinton's seat, what emerges is not their potency but their puniness before these tides of uncontrollable circumstance. They do not clothe themselves in millennial rhetoric, and, if they did so, would strike a jarring chord.

More of the right sort of millennium awareness would be to democracy's advantage. For there are problems which are truly millennial in scale, the product of this American century now segueing into another one. Consider two. America has 4 per cent of the world's population, yet generates 25 per cent of its greenhouse gases. America holds in jail 25 per cent of all the jailed people in the world: there are eight million prisoners worldwide, two million of them in the US.

These two dismal quarters of the global whole speak for social problems unaddressed, and social challenges not met, on a scale that can decently be termed millennial. Yet we may be certain that neither Al Gore nor Bill Bradley nor George W. Bush nor John McCain will propose the smallest gesture, on the part of the 2000 presidency, that would offend the American preference for unbridled car use, or American blindness to the possibility that drug-users are not best treated by social removal. Likewise the staggering inequities that underlie American triumphs: the fact that every 1 per cent growth in US per capita income requires an 80 per cent growth in Indian per capita income if India is not to fall further behind: or that, as Kofe Annan mordantly remarked of the Internet's global possibilities, it is as well to remember half the people in the world have never made a phone call.

The concession these American leaders do make to the times is to talk, more than usual, about religion. There has been an indecent vying between the presidential candidates for their proximity to God. Only Bill Bradley has tried to insist it is a private matter. The others lay claim, with differing degrees of mawkishness, to belief. It is a squirm-inducing performance, not because belief is bad but because there is no way to check whether it arrived via the ministrations of a focus group.

It is not, however, millennial. It does not have such pretensions. It does not make an expensive journey down a blind alley in the mistaken view that the people will be pleased to pay for an empty exercise in triumphalism. Serious countries don't need to invent a millennium they must somehow own.

On the day after 9/11

AT ITS FOUNDING, the United States never wanted to run the world. George Washington decreed that commerce not politics was what mattered, and Thomas Jefferson warned against the danger of 'entangling alliances'. The treachery and slaughter endemic to the great powers, France and Britain, in their seven years war for European and colonial supremacy, were anathema to the builders of the shining city on a hill. The economic domination the founders envisaged need never, they thought, bring imperial responsibility.

Much later, a word was coined for this: isolationism. It has come and gone in the American soul ever since. Theodore Roosevelt challenged it, desiring to control the Western Hemisphere, and deriding an electorate 'which screamed with anguish over the loss of a couple of thousand men'. Two world wars changed the national stance utterly. But the psyche of the heartlands, and their hunger to be left alone, remained. It was intensified by the Vietnam experience. In many Americans, a certain innocence, the very opposite of power neurosis, has survived all these events. They are not warlike people. America was secure behind the stockade – and that was all that mattered. This is the instinct that George W. Bush, unlike any President since 1930, has tried to make the linchpin of his foreign policy, by defiant unilateralism and rejection of any international treaty that might burden his voters.

What happened on 11 September 2001 changed the course of human history. We cannot yet grasp, by any stretch, all that this means. But already we start to imagine how it will poison trust, wreck relationships, challenge the world order, and vastly magnify the divide between the enemies and friends of what we call democracy. It will harden the last vestiges of tolerance for compromise, and further reverse the presumptions of freedom – of travel, speech, politics, everything. It calls into question what power any longer is, or means. But most of all it has punctured the dream of American isolation.

This presents a great challenge to America, but also to her allies. It calls for an internationalism that neither side fully understands: a solidarity that requires both America and Europe to be clearer than they've been about their roles.

For America, disengagement of any kind is now more plainly not an option. To pretend that the Middle East could benefit from Washington's withdrawal of mediation might have been honourably meant, but it was disastrous. It helped only to stoke the Arab–Israeli conflict. Flaunting one's national entitlement to abandon the global struggle for environmental, nuclear, biological, or missile treaties was a way of showing two fingers to the world: fulfilling the worst suspicions that, under a new President, the Great Satan was becoming a parody of itself. This may have been an unfair reading of Bush, but it is a perception widely held, which Washington cannot allow to survive 11 September.

Europe, however, is not guiltless. Europe, especially the Europe of the Left, has been deeply confused about what it wants America to be and do. For three decades, the Left was the chief critic of American power and influence. France led the charge against the hegemon, and she wasn't alone. Yet, faced with a President who showed signs of withdrawal from global influence and responsibility, what have the social democratic governments of Europe done? Taken fright at American retrenchment, and pleaded with the US to stay in the Balkans. The critique that used to tell America to go away now worries about America withdrawing into herself.

No more, I think, will that siren song be heard. There must be less rivalry and no confusion. The cataclysmic abominations inflicted on New York and Washington are bound to mark the end of Bush's excursion towards unilateral disengagement, but also the end of Europe's double-talk about the excesses of American power. The truths that emerge from the infamous day point without ambiguity in the same collaborative direction.

The first truth is that there are severe limits to American power. Its supremacy exists only in certain circumstances. In crucial ways, we discover, America is very weak. Built to defend herself against a structured threat from visible enemies, she turns out to be powerless against other kinds of attack. Indeed, she is more vulnerable against them than other countries, for the very reason that her ostensible power is so invitingly colossal: the most alluring target for a force capable of savaging any society on earth by the suicidal ordinances of Allah.

The greatest military power there has ever been cannot defend itself against terrorists who have no respect for human lives including their own. All the wire-tapping in the world could not save it. All the intelligence it could muster, all the fire-power, all the planes, all the subs, all the nukes, all the missiles, all proved worthless against a gang of fanatics with a cause that breaks the bounds of normal human discourse. This is not a reason to deride America, still less rejoice in her impotence. It simply discloses a new and hideous fact about the world order, which it's hard to see being changed by any upgrading of the missiles. Only better intelligence has a chance of equalizing the struggle between good and evil.

But secondly, this needs to be a collaborative enterprise in all the directions it takes. There's a contradiction between saying that the assault was not just on America but on the entire civilized world, while also insisting that America must be supported in making whatever response she chooses. Tony Blair and Gerhard Schröder quickly echoed Colin Powell in declaring that. They're right to depict the suicide bombers as striking at the free world: this was an attack on the political system of democracy, not just on one enemy state. But if that is so, then the free world at large is entitled to some sort of voice on how its values are now best to be defended.

The temptation is to wait and watch while America gears up for a response. Who could blame the American people for demanding some kind of recompense, which might even be termed constructive vengeance, for the hitherto unimaginable crime committed against them? Who could deny the greatest power on earth the right, in all honour and dignity, to determine alone what it will do to demonstrate that it cannot be defeated?

Yet one must hope its leadership does not see things so simply, and that its allies, led by Britain, can do better than offer fatalistic support for unilateral and undebated retaliation. There must be solidarity, yes. No equivocation about 'understanding' the grievances that are supposed to justify what is unconscionable. But retaliation against precisely whom? And defence against what? By what future means? With what appreciation of the hold the weak now have over the strong? These are questions to which the democratic world as a whole needs most urgently to direct itself, if freedom is not to perish from the earth.

Christmas in war-torn Vermont

I'VE BEEN COMING TO the United States for many years, and thought I knew it. I studied here, reported here, and have kept the fruit of those connections. I married an American, which surely took me closer to this place, and even more affectionately into its heart. So I possessed most of the materials necessary to read America. Yet it turns out I did not know it. This may be for a simple reason. Until 9/11 and the Afghan War, perhaps America did not fully know itself.

What's most striking to a frequent visitor, holed up for a white Christmas in Vermont, is not that America has changed. Everything about the place may remain much as you suspected. But it is all more so. Each virtue and each vice, if vices they can be called, declares itself without the ambiguities of before. I dare to generalize from a small corner. But the shock of this war, I'm guessing, has forced America, all across the continent, to think about itself more urgently: to show itself: to say without complication what it is.

Americans always were considerate. They're now super-caring for friends and neighbours. Wherever they lived, they shared the attack for which history had left them totally unprepared. Three months later, not one iota of the memory has been stoically sloughed off. The shock reached the depths of the national psyche, and continues to reverberate there. The people still blunder about, unsure why it happened. Their response is to care and share more tenderly, more generously even than they used to.

Americans always were self-confident. The events of 9/11 summon them to greater displays than ever of this singular faculty. There's no whining, no trace of self-pity. Self-sufficiency is second nature. American certainties, so maddening to Osama bin Laden, are redoubled. All that three months have done, after the due period of solemnity, is to liberate the humorous dimension, allowing Garrison

Keillor, the great radio raconteur, to make innumerable funny jihad jokes, which show that Islam has been de-listed from the scope of political correctness.

Americans always were patriotic. Flags hung in many yards on the dirt roads throughout the ten peaceful years I've been coming here. But now patriotism is a far more intense experience. Vermont sends to Washington the only congressman who calls himself a socialist, and has more than the usual quota of plain-speaking residents who retain a low regard for President George Bush. But their patriotic response to 9/11 is unquestioning. This is a locality with no tourists, and very local local papers. Yet it has discovered the world. When Hamid Karzai was sworn in as head of the interim council to govern Afghanistan, it made the lead in the *Valley News*, White River Junction, which also had a down-page item on Yasser Arafat's pledge to pay a Christmas Eve visit to Bethlehem.

But I don't take this as evidence of a new internationalism reaching into the obscurest byways of America. It shows, though, that when the patria is under threat, Americans can shed their indifference to the world the threat is coming from. In another part of the polity, Washington as much as Vermont, they lose their angst about America's role. America's role is to protect America against all-comers. That's what patriotism means, and it's nothing to be ashamed of. It is all remarkably simple, the more so for never having been made so forcibly clear before.

Americans, however, as well as being patriots, were also always constitutionalists. And here the change is marked. Even my liberal Vermont acquaintances have only modest dislike for the military tribunals and other weapons against due process that Bush has assembled. They're not rising up against them. Aware of their sensitivities, the government cites Abraham Lincoln and Franklin Roosevelt as precedents to show that great men are allowed to abolish habeas corpus and free speech when the Republic is threatened. It seems to be enough, in this hour of crisis when Americans see themselves facing a danger their ancestors did not experience.

I don't say that politics has ceased, in this new America. There are familiar arguments about the budget. There is a Left and a Right, just as there is in Europe, and they argue about roughly similar things, namely the size of the state and the level of taxation and the finer ideological points concerning how best to stimulate a flagging economy. There are big elections in 2002, and each side is manoeuvring for position in the great game of modern politics, which is less about claiming credit for success than disclaiming the blame for damage wreaked by forces beyond politicians' control.

But in the great abroad, politics virtually has ceased. Over that terrain, America has become easy to lead. Alarmingly so. Even Vermonters who detest Bush are prepared to put their trust in him, because the situation seems to offer them no other course. He vows to get the job done, that archetypal American phrase, and it is clearer than it has ever been, at least since 1945, exactly what the job is.

They talk jestingly about seeing us next year, 'as long as we haven't been blown to pieces'. The implication is that Armageddon could come from either side. But Fate, they seem to think, has taken over. America must do what America must do, which is to extinguish al-Qa'ida from the face of the earth. American idealism, that fickle jade of post-war diplomacy, at last has a purpose everyone can agree on: the saving of America itself. It is not clear what this will mean for the world.

But it's clearer than it has been since Jefferson what the world means for America: safety from sea to shining sea, and maybe not beyond.

Blair the intervener

WHAT TONY BLAIR SEES when he looks at Iraq is a country that has the ingredients to be a good and happy one. It has 22 million people and 9 per cent of the world's oil reserves. It could be one of the world's attractions rather than its principal pariah, and would be so if only it weren't ruled by a murderous psychopath, the worst villain in contemporary history. The world needs protection from this evil maniac but, just as important, Iraq and Iraqis need help. Here is the moral challenge of the hour, and perhaps the supreme task facing political leaders in 2002.

Occupying this place in Mr Blair's mind, Iraq exemplifies the most extraordinary change in British life since he was elected Prime Minister five years ago tomorrow. You can keep class sizes, hospital waiting-lists, cuts in car crime or the fine-tuning of economic progress. These are tasks all governments take on with variable success, and any shifts, though important, are at the margin. What's new is Britain's evolution, entirely at the personal hand of the PM, into an eager player anywhere in the world where there is work, usually moral work, to do: whether with a handful of retired security men in Israel/Palestine, a few hundred troops camped permanently in Sierra Leone, a couple of thousand in Afghanistan or, potentially, any number of thousands one day in Iraq.

For Mr Blair is a driven intervener. He believes in that role for Britain, and defines the national interest more broadly than any leader since Gladstone. Mrs Thatcher's sense of the national interest confined it to the defence of Britain's shores and possessions. Mr Blair reaches beyond that, beyond our local continent, into the far blue yonder, anywhere the world might be made a better place by the benign intervention of a good, stable, rich and militarily capable country like Britain. Iraq is the place where this philosophy looks like next being tested.

Such zeal for intervention, as a way of making the world better rather than the nation stronger, is unique in modern Europe. You never find it among French or German leaders. Even de Gaulle didn't really fit the category, being more of a pallid Metternich than a pious Gladstone. But the comparison also stands against contemporary America. The Bush administration's performance since 11 September has been driven not by a desire to improve the world but to make American territory safe from the world, and the world safe for American domination. The world will get some benefit. But those non-travelling Republicans on the Hill, like Bush himself, do not have a developed concept of disinterested idealism. If they go into Iraq, they will leave when the business is done. The only business that matters is to kill off Saddam and thus protect Americans, coupled with the name of Israel.

Mr Blair's impulse is different. Several conversations with high officials persuade me that we misunderstand what, from his viewpoint, the Iraq option is really about. London tends to be seen as a restraining force on Washington, a wise tactical adviser on the side of caution. In the early tactics against al-Qa'ida – notably the ultimatum to the Taliban and the binding in of Putin and Russia – Mr Blair did, I can believe, have an influential voice.

But over Iraq, the dynamic is to some extent reversed. Rather than being a restrainer, Mr Blair is quite eager for action. His catalogue of infamy against Saddam and the Iraqi arsenal of mass-destruction weapons, including Saddam's imminent nuclear capacity, is not qualified by doubt. The moral crusader offers a clarity of vision that makes some, though not all, officials in Washington tremble. Sometimes it almost seems as though the US is helping the UK rather than vice versa. If America can help the great intervener, so much the better. Here we have a leader delighted to have at his disposal the greatest power on earth, abetting any moral cause in which he believes.

Another consideration pushes him the same way. He believes it is Britain's duty to ensure that the US is not isolated in its great geopolitical campaign against terrorism. He hears America accused of unilateralism, and counts it as a virtue on Britain's part to stand as the visible guarantor that this is not the case. On trade issues, abrasiveness is permissible. But on global security, irrespective of the substance, Britain's gift to America is to demonstrate, by standing shoulder-to-shoulder or flying wing-to-wing, that the unilateralist calumnies emanating from the Middle East and Europe are false.

This Blairite attitude has a public history. Kosovo prompted him to articulate a doctrine of moral interventionism, and 11 September drew a great oration to the Labour Party conference. But these impulses have deepened and spread. He would think nothing, if he could persuade the Americans to go along, of organizing an Anglo-American expeditionary force to move round Africa, training local police and armies *à la* Sierra Leone, and thus at modest cost shoring up the democracies that could be the basis of African economic recovery. The vision of the moralist demands nothing less. An Iraq left in peace to prosper on its oil and educate its citizens in democratic values naturally belongs there too.

However worthy this vision may seem – to some inspiring, maybe – its insouciance strikes me as terrifyingly naive. Brazen words to say to a five-year Prime Minister, but two reasons support them.

First, the interventionist compulsion is producing policies that have been little discussed. Nobody minds sending a few retired officers to detain Palestinian terrorists. Even Sierra Leone is paying virtuous dividends. But an army, or an air force, against Iraq? Where are the frontiers of this moral vision, and how much are we prepared to pay to make it come to pass? How does it relate to Mr Blair's other driving priority, his alleged intimacy with his European partners? Romano Prodi will doubtless be scorned on many sides for his reproving words yesterday, asking Britain where she stands on the EU. But the point was correctly made. It may be true, as Blair insists, that Britain must remain in good odour with both Americans and Europeans. History and geography still allow that possibility. But dreams of wiping out Saddam Hussein smack more of a mesmerized attachment to American power than any serious attention to what Europe needs and wants.

Second, what leverage does Gladstonian ambition retain for a country that lost Gladstonian power a century ago? The danger Blair faces is that, when the time comes, he will have none. Britain will turn out to have been the useful idiot for the Pentagon's big project, supporting it in the name of a virtuous imperialism for which Washington has no stomach, and dragged into battle according to timetables that suit America's domestic needs not Europe's or Britain's – which most other EU countries will possibly oppose. Blair is deciding, if not saying, where he stands, because of a singularly personal idea about the purpose of politics in the modern world. Some day soon, Washington will eat him for breakfast, along with the morality it then spits out.

Dissenting is not anti-American

BETWEEN 11 SEPTEMBER and 4 July, this Independence Day in America, I find I've written twenty-two *Guardian* columns devoted one way or another to what grew out of that infamous September moment. Perhaps it was too many. For sure, these pieces contained their share of mis-spoken words and fragile judgements. But here was the big subject. It raised so many issues of global concern, from Euro-American relations, through all the Blair–Bush encounters, into the Middle East process, on to civil liberties. How to forestall and suppress global terrorism is the greatest of all contemporary challenges, subsuming many others about economic and territorial justice on a grand scale. I've tried to address them as a reporter and analyst, as much as an opinionated columnist.

Independence Day, however, is the moment to note an unhappy trend. Discourse and relationships have narrowed not broadened in ten months. There's a hardening of tone between Europe and America. I sense trenches being dug. In particular, it becomes ever more difficult to discuss these colossal problems, rife with potential for prudent scepticism, in words that don't call forth instant labelling as to their categoric loyalty or treason. At the beginning, President Bush stared at the world and said: You are either with us or against us. Time hasn't worked any refinement of his message, rather the reverse. We are all anti-Americans now, unless we happen to be pro.

Each side has made its contribution to this starkness. The Europeans began it, with the voices that refused to address what had happened. A seam of vindictiveness exposed itself. Anti-American paranoia enjoyed its finest hour, in some quarters, at the hands of Mohammed Atta, the leader of the plane-bombers.

This lack of empathy, though no longer so pitiless, is still apparent in Europe. Despite the best efforts of some reporters, the European mind – which includes the British mind – recoils from what America has embraced. It does not understand the enormity of what happened not only to New York and Washington but to the psyche of a once invulnerable nation. Most of Europe still tends to take its own experience of terrorism as a reason to disdain Americans' overreaction to their own taste of it, and I'm speaking of the citizens at least as much as the political leaders. Ultimately, there's a difference of caring and a want of rage.

This has led Europeans into some amnesiac generalizations. They speak about Americans without remembering history, or distinguishing between the people and the Bush regime. They over-look American generosity, both as a world power – which nation was it that saved the world from German and Soviet tyranny? – and as a nation of open doors and open hearts. Though the government, even one with a mandate as doubtful as George Bush's, can be said to be acting for the people, it seems important to be as careful in vaporizing about Americans as about, say, Jewish or black people. Ethnic monoliths are a curse at every level of humanity.

But some Americans are moving down the same slope. Europeans too are generalised into infamy by the East Coast *Zeitgeist*. Europe has been smeared as generally anti-Semitic, on the basis of a microscopic number of voters in two or three countries. Europe is stigmatized as wimpish if not cowardly, because it does not place the same faith as America in the military response to terrorism.

To some extent, each continent is reacting according to the facts of geopolitics. Lesser powers have always sparred with great ones, as jealousies collide. No formerly lesser power knows this better than America. In 1795, John Adams, on the brink of the presidency of a new country still suffering under the transatlantic yoke, wrote to his wife Abigail: 'I wish that misfortune and adversity could soften the temper and humiliate the insolence of John Bull. But he is not yet sufficiently humble. If I mistake not, it is the destiny of America one day to beat down his pride.'

Now that the beating is long done, Europeans have a problem that's acutely visible at this time. They may never be sufficiently humble, but they should at least be clear. Neither the most pro- nor the most anti-American European governments, including this one,

are unambiguous about what they want America to do or be. Sometimes, as in the Middle East and Afghanistan, they want intervention of a certain kind. Other times, they rail against American
interventionism as if it were an ideological disease. There is justice
in the Pentagon's scorn for a continent that wants America to do the
heavy lifting against terror, while it dithers on the side.

Americans also need to consider some unlearned lessons. In
power politics, the present period cannot be characterized as one of
their magnanimous phases. Donald Rumsfeld is as insolent as John
Bull used to be. At the grass roots, the soil is even more acidulous
than it was a little while ago. I judge from the email responses I've
had, often in massive quantities, to some of those twenty-two
columns, almost entirely from the US, where the *Guardian* website
seems to be a must-read. While it's true that more anti-Bush voices
are starting to surface, the vocal majority have become more
inflexible, more righteous and more harshly scathing of European
critics than they were at the turn of the year.

And now we hear their British echoes, from people drawn towards
the same stark analysis. Iraq is being prepared for its role as this
generation's Vietnam. Long before an invasion happens, adamancy is
beginning to prevail. Positions about pre-emption are being pre-
emptively demanded: Will you be with us or against us, whatever we
choose to do? The question is asked at dinner as well as at Camp
David. To give the wrong answer is to face certain ignominy from
one side or the other, for failing or passing a simplistic loyalty test on
an issue no longer to be treated as amenable to honest argument.

It would be another simplistic error to think these attitudes can
be reconciled. Goodwill is not enough to bury such visceral
differences as exist on a familiar and lengthening list of issues. The
continents are without doubt drifting apart. They have interests in
common, but also interests around which America, as now led, has
the power and the hardness to insist on non-negotiable policies that
we can take or leave. There are few cosy solutions to anything
much, which the allies in the old Western alliance will any longer
unanimously sign up to.

But it only demeans things further to pre-stigmatize all debate
with the mark of 'anti-American'. Some Europeans deserve the
label, but very few. Most want to share in a dialogue where they are

listened to, especially when they disagree. The crisis is far, far too serious for its terms to be entirely coloured by that convenient, thought-killing smear. The US, I think, will do what it wants anyway. But I don't think it's anti-American to say so. The real anti-Americans – anti-worlders, in fact – are those who don't want a serious discussion.

The special anachronism

THE RELATIONSHIP THAT now dominates, perhaps fatefully, the life of Tony Blair has a tortuous history. Anglo-Americanism is not as seamless as those who fervently live by it make it appear. It has been messy and contradictory, with moments of disaster as well as triumph. But at the bottom of it has always been the democratic principle of consent, for a special relationship that has often affected the lives of the ruling class in both countries more acutely than those of the people. This is the problem that neither history nor sentiment allows Mr Blair to avoid.

The founders of the US were, naturally, anti-British. Thomas Jefferson said he would happily 'lend my hand to sink the whole island in the ocean', and Benjamin Franklin rejoiced that every nation in Europe 'wishes to see Britain humbled, having all in their time been offended by her insolence'. According to a recent biographer: 'Jefferson's palpable hatred of all things English (except perhaps their gardens) coloured his entire performance.'

But the relationship survived. Ultimately it was all, as it still is, about power: power desired, power attained, power regretted. Sensible statesmen were realists. America's growth to prosperity depended on the protection of the British fleet. Through the second half of the nineteenth century great swellings of sentiment either way were expressed on both sides, as the balance of power was seen to be shifting. The British especially could hardly contain their effusion. 'I refuse to think or speak of the United States as a foreign nation,' said Joseph Chamberlain. Such has been the attitude of many successors in all parties, as they watched their own eclipse.

There was a brief period of true balance, before the US converted its economic dominance into political responsibility. For the first decades of the twentieth century, until Franklin Roosevelt entered the war, there were two great powers, and for the two following years the specialness of their relationship lay in the evenness of what they brought to victory. But in 1943 the equipoise ended. Churchill went to the Tehran conference to find that Roosevelt, observing the realities of power, cosied closer to Stalin than to him. Britain was cut out of the triangle. Forever after, she became the lesser power, the supplicant in Washington, which set the terms of business, as it has always continued to do.

Three things should strike anyone who examines the contemporary crisis through the prism of history.

First, the unique relationship became long ago not just about power but, exclusively, military power. It doesn't invade the whole of life. Blair can deliver a blast against steel tariffs without penalty, though the US concessions last week came, of course, in response to EU not British pressure. He can stand on his African podium and send out the message of a free and environmentally aware nation that the US got it wrong at Kyoto. This kind of thing is not seen as a breach of trust. In matters of tax, trade and economics it has happened under all governments. What is sacrosanct is security, along with geopolitics. Here Britain will never criticize. This rule is epitomized in the Ministry of Defence, but found invariably in Downing Street, and is always one-sided. When the UK goes to war, as at Suez, the US is undependable, thank goodness. When the UK declines to make a military commitment, as in Bosnia, the US pressures a change of line. When the US goes to war, the UK will never dissent and often joins the effort. It would have been inconceivable for any British Prime Minister since the war to emulate Chancellor Schröder's verbal violence last week when he withdrew his country from a future Iraq conflict.

Second, the price of this military intimacy has not always exceeded the reward. Historic trust as much as immediate material from Washington helped Britain take back the Falklands. There is no harm, and may sometimes be national advantage, in being the special ally of the most powerful nation on earth. Not long ago, in the after-shadow of 11 September, I heard one of our top spymasters questioned about the new collaborations supposedly taking place between the intelligence agencies of all right-thinking countries. Did this portend a new sharing, a new sense of trust across the wide alliance? The curl of his incredulous lip and jocular raise of the eyebrows said that, however bad the world scene, the Americans trusted only the old ally they had made in war. In the age of the terrorist, when knowledge is power, this cannot be bad for Britain.

But much of the specialness is more pretentious. It's enjoyed by the political class, not by the public or, arguably, the nation. For public servants, top tables are irresistible. Who could resist the delectations of discussing high strategy with Americans, or the illusion that the British input matters? What politician, aware of how pale a shadow he casts by comparison with any predecessor of fifty or a hundred years ago, does not thirst for the kind of engagement with power that Washington offers? This is what they were surely born to do. So who will fail to warm to the convenient rationale, now much heard in Whitehall, that Britain has a selfless duty to act alongside the US in its military ventures precisely in order to show the world that Washington is not alone? Is that what we have come to? To be America's badge of multilateralist pretence? As the price of access to the Pentagon, it appears to important people worth paying.

But third, there's the public. The truth is that most voters are indifferent to life in this stratosphere. They're not particularly pro- or anti-American, or ditto European. They're sort of pro-British, with a strong desire to be left alone. So the leaders can play their games – as long as the voters aren't roused to take an interest.

Edward Heath, one of the only two Prime Ministers to break the post-war mould, cared little about public reaction as he studiously worked to show that Washington was second to Europe; but the miners, not foreign policy, put him out of power. His predecessor, Harold Wilson, was the telling case. Wilson, though as seducible as anyone by top-table posturing, wasn't a crusader. He drew the line at sending troops to Vietnam. He understood the voters would never wear it. Their tolerance of a relationship they barely knew about would expire when they confronted what it meant. So Wilson said no to Lyndon Johnson.

Mr Blair faces the same predicament, with the burden of being a moral imperialist. He doesn't like to see a wrong without trying to right it. And Saddam is plainly a wrong, against which George Bush may seem to offer the means of correction. Bush has the muscle to bring about the vision Blair articulates. Anglo-Americanism saves the world! The trouble is that the British voters, for once, show no sign of remaining asleep and offering their customary acquiescence, to a project steeped in multiple risks and probable miscalculations. Let it never be forgotten, they may say: America is a foreign nation after all.

It's just not cricket

IT'S HARD TO SAY how the addiction began, but I think it had something to do with the decline of cricket. In my youth I was passionate about cricket, especially Yorkshire cricket. Len Hutton was god: restrained, flawless, uncanny, beyond human. The Yorkshire of the fifties and sixties were heroes every one. I still see with perfect clarity the presence of Willie Watson and Johnny Wardle, Phillip Sharpe and Ken Taylor and F. S. Trueman – their movements, stance, action, foibles, character – planted for ever in my memory during those summer days at Bramall Lane in Sheffield.

Yorkshire still matters. During a writing career that turns out to have been spent, in part, hoping to persuade the British that there's life beyond the nation-state, I still really care about England only insofar as Darren Gough is taking wickets and Michael Vaughan making runs. But somewhere along the line, cricket lost its hold. The game has been on the wane for twenty years. The characters are less alluring, the results less important, and economic circumstances forced changes in the ambience and rules that only intensified cricket's aura of desperation. From being at the core of England's emotional existence, it has moved inexorably to the edge. It just doesn't matter what's going on at some patch of urban greensward in Essex or Northants before an audience of fifty old men. Besides, Yorkshire won almost nothing in those twenty years. And the Bramall Lane wicket was long since buried under a football stand.

Is this just the dyspepsia of someone who has grown up, and perhaps grown out of sport altogether? Far from it. A long time later, when introduced to Sir Leonard Hutton, standing on the very same level as I was, I could not look him in the eye or find a single word to say. My reverence rendered me as speechless as the day when, lurking behind the pavilion, I acquired his autograph. In any case, I can't give up on a certain kind of game. It seems I needed a replacement.

I had always been aware of baseball. In my time as a student in America, cricket was still in its sixties pomp, from which a young Englishman looked down on what appeared to be a version of rounders, raised incomprehensibly to sporting hegemony in the American way of life. But I began to penetrate its significance. Along with the Constitution and jazz, it was, somebody once said, 'one of the three most beautifully designed things this culture has ever produced'. Although I was closer to seeing the point of Thomas Jefferson and Jelly Roll Morton than Babe Ruth, I couldn't dismiss baseball's connection with the country that came to enthral me.

But I never actually saw baseball. My interest advanced only from the negligible to the quiescent. It was a few decades, 1995 to be exact, before I made my first visit to a game. By that time, however, I'd become an obsessive student, an armchair fan whose emerging passion was whetted by daily study of the back pages of the *International Herald Tribune*, where the scores of the thirty Major League teams can be found, and the raw material that was always part of cricket's appeal – batting averages, pitching records, stats of every kind – can be pored over, though without the density of detail that appears daily in the *New York Times*. Full immersion, into material that makes *Wisden* seem the sketchiest of statistical compendia, awaited irregular trips across the water.

There's also, I found, a copious baseball literature, much superior to the general run of cricket books. Whether or not baseball was a metaphor for deeper aspects of American life, it had been chronicled by writers from well beyond the diamond. US political journalists seem to regard it as obligatory to take time off from their columns to engage with baseball. I plunged into the sporting works of David Halberstam and George F. Will, emerging each time with a bit more of the sediment of other people's memories beginning to cling to my own.

But I had to find a team. Following a sport is nothing without allegiance. I needed a Yorkshire, and I found it, by some homing instinct, in a team with the same inner arrogance, the same historic superiority, the same hate-object status among all opponents, as the club that had once, of course, been the finest county cricket team in England.

The New York Yankees, I admit, was opportunism. But at least it was the team I had the best chance of seeing, because New York is a regular transit point to our house in Vermont. The Yankees also have history draped around them. They were world champions twenty-five times in the twentieth century. They were the team of the only ball players Brits have ever heard of – Babe Ruth and Joe DiMaggio (the latter for his marriage to a movie star rather than his loping stride and incomparable hitting). The famous pinstriped uniform they still wear was selected in the 1920s as the way to make least of Ruth's formidable girth. Lacking any other reason for allegiance, I reckoned, why not start at the top?

So a new Yankees fan was born. He had, moreover, connections. A friend in the NYPD had access to tickets. Police chiefs have friends in all the best boxes, so one day in every August for some years has been spent with a perfect view of Yankees baseball, sitting behind home plate, slowly discovering that what I thought was my formidable theoretical knowledge of the game had, in practice, its limitations.

Home, I learned, was certainly the place to see it from. The pitcher, from his mound, hurls to the batter at the plate, and only from behind the plate can you see where, exactly, the ball is passing, how close to the plate's edge, how far wide, how it moves, why the batter hits or doesn't hit. From there too you see the game as the batter sees it: the 90-foot square (called a diamond because it rests on one of the corners) round which he must manoeuvre, via three bases, from home plate and back again. Also how the fielders range: what ground the shortstop covers, what intimacy there is between pitcher and catcher (the equivalent of wicket-keeper), what signals pass between the dugouts where managers call most of the shots. And then how the batter scores his run, by arriving back at that symbolic place called home.

'Coming home', former baseball commissioner A. Bartlett Giamatti once said, was a pregnant phrase. For a nation that set much store by home and family, he thought it resonated far beyond the field. Sven-Goran Eriksson may be the first English football coach to list Tibetan poetry as his prime leisure interest, but Giamatti was the first baseball boss to have taught Renaissance literature at Yale. He's reputed to have been the best of all commissioners, and what he said is one of 10,000 meditations over the years, that have sought, more convincingly than anyone has done for football, to link baseball to the larger things of life.

Then, miraculously, I was able to do so, in a smaller way, myself. For baseball has its grand finale, the World Series between the champions of the American League and the National League. The Yankees, winners of the past two Series, were in the frame for the American League. Nobody could know who finally, after climbing the weary ladder of play-offs, would reach the peak. What was certain, though, was the coincidence of timing between this epic contest and the final days of the presidential election.

As Al Gore and George W. Bush reached the climax of their struggle, I prepared to witness the parallel battle. The years of waiting would be over. When I told American friends I'd be getting a press pass for the World Series, reproach as well as envy crossed their eyes. Why should a Brit, especially one whose track record as a fan they had to take entirely on faith, secure an easy ticket to the most sought-after collection of sporting occasions ever invented: a seven-match series, crammed into nine days, split between two cities, neither of which might be known until a few days before the start. Undeterred, I made my preparations, reasoning that a political columnist could as well cover the election from the randomly selected Series cities as from Tennessee, Texas, or Washington DC. I arranged air tickets and hotels to cover every possible shuttle between Seattle, St Louis, Atlanta, Chicago, Oakland, San Francisco, some of them tight political as well as baseball cities, all in with a chance. And, of course, New York. The Yankees were where this obsession started. Though they lost fifteen of the last seventeen games of the regular season, they surely had to make it.

They duly did. It would be the Yankees against someone, and the someone turned out, for better or worse, to be the other New York team, the Mets. After all that preparatory coast-to-coast network-ing, the only travelling would be by subway. It was a World Series, but also a Subway Series, the first for forty-four years. 'World', already a grandiloquence bestowed by baseball on America pure and simple, would be limited to New York, New York.

There could, I realized, be worse places.

You can know plenty of big things about baseball without actually seeing it. One concerns economics. While cricket struggles near the poverty line, eking out a life from the fickle pocket of Sky TV, baseball, in the biggest cities, flourishes colossally. The Yankees' highest-paid player, the pitcher Roger Clemens, on $15.45 million for a season, takes home three times more than the entire turnover of Durham CCC with its twenty-seven contracted cricketers. At $114 million, the Yankee payroll, not counting any of the club's other activities, is close to the entire turnover of the English Cricket Board.

These sports exist not in different countries but on different planets.

For their money, the players work unimaginably hard: 162 games in the regular season, five days or nights a week and sometimes both. Yankee Stadium in the Bronx, when I paid this year's August visit, had a full house of 55,000 for a three-game series against the Seattle Mariners. You can't say they were unremarkable games. Much of the thrill in baseball is that every game may turn on a single hit, a single out, a single error. One defining moment might always unleash a cataract to turn an 8–0 deficit into victory. Nobody in their senses departs before the ninth inning is done. But this was mid-season. Lose this game, and there are still another seventy to go. Yet the stadium was full of happy, roaring, hollering families, as it is for many of its ninety games. Lord's cricket ground, a piece of prime real estate without Bronxian deterrents of distance or crime, is lucky to be full six times a season.

But then baseball is business as much as it is sentiment. Whereas the life's ambition of our previous Prime Minister was to become president of Surrey CCC – a pastoral presence at the Oval, where the run-stealers flicker to and fro and there's doubtless honey still for tea – much of the fortune as well as fame of George W. Bush was based on his part-ownership of a ball club, the Texas Rangers, and his ability to arrange for the taxpayer to subsidize the building of its stadium.

Ownership has its trials. In every financial or social struggle in baseball's history, the owners have sought to hold a line and been defeated. Essentially, the post-war history of the game is one of player-power, at first slow to work but now aptly evidenced by the fact that no regular major leaguer earns less than a million bucks a year – which, for the *major* major players is peanuts. Even the fourth-ranked pitcher at the Yankees, Denny Neagle, was looking for $9 million to keep him there next year.

Before 1947, owners colluded to ensure no Negro played in the major leagues. Their defeat was not entirely painless. Hundreds of blacks have played major league baseball since 1947. But as recently as 1973, when Hank Aaron, then the most famous black player ever, was about to break Ruth's career record of 714 home runs, he received scores of death threats. 'Dear Nigger Henry,' read one. 'It has come to my attention that you are going to break Babe Ruth's record. I will be going to the rest of your games and if you hit one more home run it will be your last. My gun will be watching your every black move.' Now, with a majority of the biggest stars being black or Latino, the melting-pot has reached fully from the streets into the stadium. Last season, when John Rocker, a redneck relief pitcher from Atlanta, made ugly, racist remarks about New Yorkers, on a visit to New York, he was derided on the mound and hundreds of cops were needed to protect him when he came to the city.

In 1975, the owners lost a different sort of battle, whose resolution, in my opinion, continues to reveal something still more evocative about the place of this game in the American mind. Until that year, the clubs owned the players. Even the biggest stars weren't free agents, able to offer their services to the highest bidders. The legal battle to end this produced the salary regime that pays Roger Clemens his $15 million. But it also means that there's massive player-trading all the time, especially as the season reaches its climax, and the Boston Red Sox feel they could use another left-handed pitcher. As the Yankees moved through the 2000 season, and their hitting looked weak, they bought David Justice from the Cleveland Indians, in exchange for a couple of minor leaguers and an outfielder, Ricky Ledee.

Such negotiations are like a meat market. Lesser players can be turned over at a moment's notice. 'About half an hour before tonight's game,' reported the *New York Times*, 'Joe Torre [the Yankees manager] summoned Ledee into his office and told the outfielder that he was being traded. Ledee said goodbye. His eyes were puffy and welled with tears when he spoke to reporters.' The team the Yankees collected for the Series included four players specially purchased for the occasion. Yet, despite player power, the team's the thing. Allegiance seems to survive every change of personnel. Some stars are obviously untouchable. If Derek Jeter or Bernie Williams, the Yankees' biggest hitters, left the club, it would be seen as a death in the family. But in the end it's around the club, the name, the team, that the bonds of loyalty gather, and the mystic chords of memory echo down the years. All these huge stars are somehow subservient, in the minds of tribal fans, to the accumulations from the past that give their team its character.

For baseball, I began to appreciate from my armchair, is a game that revolves entirely around different kinds of memory.

One kind is scientific. You could call it the measurement and recording of failure. Every hit a batter ever makes is added to his stats, and it's a very great hitter who can lay a bat meaningfully on more than thirty per cent of the balls he faces. The 'strike zone' – the area in which, if he doesn't swing at a pitch, it counts against him – stretches across the 17-inch plate, and vertically between his chest and his knees. His record in that zone collects over a month, a season, a lifetime, and is subdivided into many categories.

Every batter's strike-out rate against every pitcher is recorded. Each one's form against right-handers and left-handers is separately considered. The data are all there. Every pitch pitched in a Major League game this year has been logged somewhere for speed, curve, strike-rate, hit-rate, high hit, low hit, no hit. When the pitcher returns to the dugout between innings, likely as not he'll be scanning what the computer printout says about the next man up at bat. Simultaneously, the other manager will be judging whether to replace that man, just because, according to the stats, the pitcher in question has got on top of him before.

So percentages rule. Every decision is set against the laws of probability. Neither pitcher nor batter, once taken out of the game, can return, which means that the stakes for an opportunistic exit are high. Juggling the team is the manager's prerogative – his skill, his meal-ticket, the very basis of his reputation, for he gets measured too – and it is science as much as art. Baseball, like American football, reflects the national yearning for precision, for numbers, logic and reason. Memory also has its artful side, its poetry, its human factor. We think cricket has that, and it does. I know how Hutton stood, how Trueman ran, how Taylor fielded, how Sharpe caught. I see them before me. With a little help from *Wisden*, I can recall Roses matches as if they happened yesterday. Some cricket fans have memories of particular innings in particular tests that brought the Ashes home, or the day Dexter hammered Wesley Hall.

But baseball memories are in the blood, tended lovingly by every class of person. 'I saw my first home run in 1946, a towering fly ball over the Alpen Bräu beer sign in left field hit by Whitey Kurowski,' writes Robert B. Semple Jr in the *New York Times*, one of many outpourings of reminiscence in October 2000. George Will is an encyclopaedia of remembered moments. Collective memories are celebrated everywhere baseball is played, forever raked over, whether good or bad.

There's a man called Bill Buckner, for example, first baseman for the Red Sox in the 1986 Series against the Mets. In Game Six, with the Red Sox ahead, he let a ground ball trickle through his legs, allowing the Mets to win the game and eventually the Series. Every Boston fan knows where he was when Buckner fumbled. Shortly after that, Buckner emigrated to Idaho, where there is no baseball team.

At the opposite pole stands Kirk Gibson, best hitter for the LA Dodgers in 1988, but so badly crippled with a torn hamstring when the Series against the Oakland Athletics began that he didn't even dress for the first game. In the bottom of the ninth inning, with Oakland 4–3 up, the Dodgers manager sent to find him. Perhaps he had one good swing in him. After being almost carried to the plate, Gibson watched five pitches go by, his bat never leaving his shoulder. One more good pitch, and it would be all over. But he hurled himself at the sixth pitch and put it into the tenth row of the bleachers. It was Gibson's only appearance. The Dodgers took the Series in five games.

Both Buckner and Gibson appeared in effigy this year too. Their stories featured on the screen or in the programmes, rejoiced in, chewed over, raged at once again. For these were decisive moments. They won and lost the Series. Baseball is a game of moments more than phases, of sudden explosions rather than dying falls, of absolute results and never tame, dreary draws while the light fails or time runs out. In baseball, time never runs out. There's always that possibility of a terminally dramatic moment. So it was in the 2000 World Series.

Roger Clemens produced such a moment in Game Two, the one he'd been reserved for. Pitchers can't pitch too often, the arm needs a four-day rest. The percentages told Joe Torre that Clemens would be better in the second game, and then if necessary the sixth, rather than the first.

Some reckon Clemens, though old at thirty-eight, is the most fearsome pitcher in the Major Leagues, the hardest, fastest, meanest thrower of them all. He certainly looks it. Preparing to pitch, he scrutinizes his prey from behind the glove on his other hand. The eyes, barely visible by the batter from behind this medieval shield of leather, stare him down for longer than any other pitcher I have watched. Clemens, by some accounts a pleasant, private Texan, reeks of menace and seems to boil with rage. Many of his pitches cross the 60 feet 6 inches from mound to plate at 100 m.p.h.

Game One had been a slow, tortuous beginning. At 4 hours 51 minutes, it was gleefully logged as the longest in Series history, an early record in the stats. The winning of it, by the Yankees 4–3, depended on some crucial errors by the Mets, none worse than the failure of one batter to run hard round the bases, rather than gaze at what looked as though it might be a home run. It failed to clear the fence by six inches, and as a result of dawdling, Timo Perez, who had been on first base, failed to make it home. Ahead in all the innings from second to sixth, the Mets couldn't make their position pay. But neither could the Yankees. Three times they had men on base, positioned to score, only to be thrown or struck out. It was twelve innings, as against the statutory nine, before, with the bases loaded once more, they drove home the winning run.

But something was established in Game One that I hadn't expected. The New York crowd was raucous but civil. For all those hours, beginning at 8.30 p.m. (to catch West Coast television viewers – who turned out not to care about an all-New York series as much as Fox TV hoped) until 1.15 a.m., they kept roaring. Cross-town rivalries, often touted as hatred, proved little more than jocular. The subway up to Yankee Stadium was packed with loud talk and some derisive chanting. The crowd experience includes a constant stoking-up by bellowing announcers, exploding score-boards and brazen one-sided cheerleading.

But nobody runs on to the fenceless field. The crowds accept the limits of commitment. So do the players. As games mount to the end, there never was more tension in any sport I've watched: every game could still go either way: those defining little moments again. When Paul O'Neill, one of the oldest Yankee stars, who had a brilliant Series after a lousy late-season, missed balls, his shaking head was interpreted as a shocking display of exasperation. But the baseball man makes few displays. After hitting a home run, he circles the bases coolly, with the bearing of an Athenian hero, mildly touching fists in the dugout, disdaining utterly to milk applause. No mid-wicket hugging, no ecstatic chest-beating to a goal-mouth crowd. These sportsmen have a lot of class.

The Clemens game, though, was different. There was needle between two men, Clemens and the Mets' star batter, Mike Piazza. The pitcher carries a lethal weapon, and, in an incident this summer, the Mets thought Clemens used it intentionally to fell Piazza. Pitchers do that kind of thing. It's the other side of the batter's Olympian dignity. It's called 'going inside': hurling well inside the inner edge of the plate, as a way of scaring the batter out of reach of the next ball which will shave the other side. Piazza was knocked out of baseball for a week, recovering from concussion. The memory was fresh in the head of every person in Yankee Stadium.

No memory could match what now happened in Game Two. There was no precedent. When Piazza swung at one of Clemens's pitches, the crack of ball on bat snapped it clean apart. The largest piece of the bat bounced back towards Clemens, who flung it towards Piazza, as he ran towards first base, nearly hitting him – and prompting incessant analysis of this mystifying scene throughout the night and into next day. What had Clemens meant? a hundred pundits asked. The great man's only utterance was to say that, being hyped-up by his zeal to win, he 'mistook the bat for the ball'. The incident assuredly entered the baseball hall of famous memories, and led to Clemens being fined a measly $50,000 by the commissioner.

'Roger Clemens has not intimidated our ball club,' said Piazza. But everything else about the game got buried under this incident, and the Mets still lost again, another close one, 6–5. Good. My boys seemed to be digging deep into their legend of superiority.

Game Three was another game again, on the Mets home turf this time. Crossing by subway on a balmy autumn evening to Shea

Stadium in the borough of Queen's with another amiable crowd, I did not longingly regret the alternative, the true Series experience, of hacking to St Louis or Atlanta. But the result did not appeal: the Mets took a game back, 4–2. It was notable, though, for another record-breaking moment. Second in fame only to Clemens on the Yankees' pitching roster is Orlando Hernandez, who arrived by small boat from Cuba in 1996, and turned out to have the most stupendous arm. Where Clemens's arm is high and hard, Hernandez's is often low, delivering curvy slingshots in every kind of variety. The unheralded refugee from Fidel Castro graduated in months to heroic megastar of Manhattan. Until this night, he had never lost a post-season game. It had been a long time since the Yankees had either. In sudden-death, post-season ball, Yankee experience in depth had produced, over three seasons, fourteen successive winning Series games. But now they were downed by a flash of hitter's brilliance in the bottom of the eighth.

Game Four was another close one, 3–2 to the Yankees, on the strength of a home run by Derek Jeter off the first pitch of the game: like someone hitting Gough for six in a five-day test match before the crowd had time to clear its throat and settle in its seats. We came to Game Five with my team on the verge of its third successive Series.

It, too, was very close. Every one of these games was poised on a fine edge as the ninth inning began, and the last one was no exception. After eight innings, the score stood at 2–2, through a mixture of errors, smart base-running and a single home run by a Yankee champion, Bernie Williams, who until that moment had hardly hit a single ball.

As the ninth began, the Mets, unusually, stayed with the pitcher they'd begun with, the lefty Al Leiter. He had already thrown 121 pitches, and would normally have been replaced. Still, he was doing well. He struck out two of the three batters he needed to get rid of to close the inning – but then he stumbled. The Yankees eased two men on to base. Their most recent purchase in the trading market, a pudgy journeyman called Luis Sojo, bought in August from Pittsburgh, had the indelible pleasure of hitting a ground ball into centre field, far enough for both the base runners to make it home. On came the specialist closing pitcher – a fast-ball hurler, Mariano

Rivera, employed most playing days to keep his nerve and sharpness and protect Yankees' leads for a single final inning or two – and the Mets were finished.

I felt as pleased as when Yorkshire won all those Roses games a few decades ago. There's nothing quite so sweet as beating the nearest neighbours. But eighteen hours of baseball left many mysteries. The more I watched, the more I realized how little I understood. In particular, I didn't get near the heart of the game, the complicated inwardness of the contest between pitcher and batter, either its science or its art.

This is a relationship full of mind-games, as well as brutal speed and lethal cunning, matched by batters who think they know what's coming, and apply a speed of eye–hand co-ordination that might have taxed even the great Len. It takes years of watching, probably begun at the age I first went to Bramall Lane, to be able to gauge instinctively what's going through each man's mind as the missile is about to be launched: what he wants to happen, what pitches are meant to be hit, why some are aimed to miss etc. etc. and many more etceteras. I got nowhere near it. I did get as far as grappling with the paradox that the hard, fast ball across the middle of the plate, in theory heading for the middle-stump strike-out, is also the very worst to pitch because it's the easiest to hit. But that's just the beginning of the story. The rest has to be left for another Series. I'm much more of a novice, I see, than when I began this strange fascination.

On the other hand, I saw my team win. I tasted baseball's particular excitement, since every game was close and needed only the smallest deflection for it to have changed hands in the last innings. I saw the elegance of it, the perfection of the fielding, the mighty arm of every fielder, the loping, easeful way they make their catches, the faultless speed with which they pick off the base-runners, sometimes two in one play. I sat behind these batters, as they faced balls coming at their heads and yet contrived to hit them over the fence. I breathed the air of Yankee Stadium, the head-quarters of my dream. I saw a World Series in all its phases from start to finish.

And I got a result. Which was more than could be said about the presidential election.

OLD EMPIRE, NEW WARS

Agonizing into the Gulf War

THE WAR WILL BE unimaginably hellish. Even though the fire-power has been the object of the utmost voyeuristic fascination, its use will extend the range of human experience. Appallingly so. Never has so much weaponry been assembled in one place, or promised such technological proficiency in killing and destruction. So horrific is the product of this slow-motion build-up that it is quite hard, even now, to believe it will soon burst off the screens of fantasy into brutal truth.

Some people believe that anything which can be so described must be avoided at any cost. It would be comfortable to be among them. They argue that no modern infraction of the peace is worth a modern war. They might make an exception for the defence of the homeland, but as far as Kuwait goes they don't just say no war now but no war ever. They do not believe that in modern conditions, with the technology available especially to Western armies, the notion of collective security should ever be fulfilled by force of arms, even when the United Nations has endorsed it.

This is a coherent and honest position. It recognizes how frightful war is, and dismisses the contention that long-term good can come out of short-term suffering. In the case of Kuwait, its consequences might be vast. If Saddam Hussein were not evicted, the Middle East would become more unstable, in thrall to this tyrant, under nuclear threat from Israel and later Iraq, with all the environmental and political disasters which now seem implicit in war still indefinitely impending from peace. These are to my mind most menacing probabilities. But they could be called speculative risks not actual events: and given the imponderable future of the region anyway, they might be risks worth taking. Such is the respectable, if despairing, case against any war at any time, made with most fearless clarity by Mr Tam Dalyell MP.

Other people say no to war now, but apparently concede that it may be necessary some time. It would be even more comfortable to be among this faction. For they have it both ways. They assert that Saddam is a monster, and are outdone by no one in the rhetoric of disgust about Kuwait. But they believe, wish, hope against every hope that there is another way. Sanctions, they contend, will do the trick, or rather must be given time to do the trick: but if sanctions fail, this argument needs to add if its anathemas against Saddam are serious, war might at some stage have to follow.

Sanctions, in other words, are the all-round moralist's alternative. Caring, agonized citizens, deeply anxious not to appease Saddam, hang on to them as a golden promise, the perfect instrument of his painless destruction. But unfortunately this skirts too easily past aspects of the real world.

First, sanctions must at some stage yield a verdict. For how long would the sanctions school be prepared to carry on? They seldom say. One has the impression of people who, in the end, would rather see sanctions last for ever than make good their implied contention that at some stage Saddam must be evicted, whatever the price. The horrors of war would always be so great that the time would never be ripe for unleashing them.

It is already apparent that the decisive impact of sanctions has in any case been indefinitely postponed. What evidence in Saddam's recent conduct, in face of the massive sanction of the military threat, fortifies any belief that mere economic sanctions would bring him to surrender? What internal forces exist, as they did in Rhodesia and South Africa, to exploit the economic erosion and political discontent international sanctions are meant to bring about? Who can suppose that Saddam will care a toss if his people begin to starve? Who can be confident that sanctions would be maintained anyway?

Secondly, there are the realities of diplomacy and combat. These may be regrettable but they cannot be wished away. The mutual deterrence which kept the Cold War peaceful cannot instantly be replicated by armies on the move. The static and well-understood deployments in Europe have no parallel with the vast army shipped to the Gulf, which is not equipped politically, psychologically or militarily to sit and wait into a measureless future. Yet if it were to go home, what would be left of the sanctions? It is a horrible truth that military movements, perhaps necessary for instant deterrence, to some extent ordain their own future.

But if that is the case, it reflects a parallel diplomatic ordinance, another piece of the real world. For diplomacy too cannot preserve a kind of stasis for ever. To have secured the UN resolutions on the Gulf was a minor miracle of time and chance. But circumstances change. Each UN member has its own fluid history. Look what is happening in Moscow. It is hard to persuade oneself that the UN would hold to its resolve, any more than the allied forces could remain on the qui vive for battle, while a leader, who unless he is the ultimate brinkman shows not the slightest sign of surrendering Kuwait, ignores for uncounted months the sanctions that are supposed to bring him down.

When the war is done, this will be one of the many messages to try and unscramble from its origins. Can force be assembled and diplomacy be conducted in ways that might permit peaceful outcomes to be developed over an even longer period than the five months allowed to them this time? There will be a lot of other questions too. Did diplomacy fail disastrously at an early stage, as is argued elsewhere on this page? Did Washington send the wrong signals in July? Can foreign policy strive to cleave closer to principles which bear some resemblance to moral absolutes, the better to avoid the terrible outcome of war against a leader we first armed, then supported against Iran, then mollified despite his crimes against the Kurds?

But now, on 15 January 1991, the issue has become one in which both sides cannot win. The middle position is a fantasy: desirable, longed-for, infinitely preferable but unavailable. Whether today or next week, the choice lies between picking up the gauntlet Saddam has scornfully thrown down and permitting it to lie uncollected, gathering sand, while one little country – a very unattractive little country, which reinforces not weakens the principle – is annexed by passage of time as well as arms.

Two predictions can be made with confidence about what now seems all but certain to unfold. One is that pacifism will increase. The horrors will be so awful that, whether during or after the Gulf War, more people will cease their agonizing and simply state that in the modern age nothing is worth such carnage. The second is that more people, while showing no enthusiasm for the opposite position, will accept the painful lesson that life as well as war can be hell, and there are some situations in this imperfect world, populated by some leaders who do not believe in peace, which can be settled only by combat. This is a terrible realization, to be embraced only with fearful caution. But it will not be written off the agenda. The best one can hope is that the passage will be quick.

In denial about the Balkans

WE EUROPEANS KNOW more about the Balkan War than any other war of our time. Television pictures tell plenty, but this brand of knowing is more the biblical variety. We know the Serbs and the Croats because they are part of us. This is not an Asian war or an African war, bloody but a million miles the other side of the global village. It's happening where we go on holiday. It should be an intimately involving experience.

It is, moreover, a war that involves exactly what we swore would never happen again, here or anywhere else. That vow, against the special horror of genocide, was honoured in the breach when blind eyes were turned to faraway Pol Pot or what China has done to Tibet. But here, a day's march from Auschwitz, ethnic cleansing enters the language: a term once capable of shocking, but actually deployed as a euphemism, clinical and even purifying, to take the unspeakable heat out of mass racial torture and murder. Since Hitlerism of a kind is repeating itself in Central Europe, one might imagine that Europe as a whole would rouse itself against what, after all, the Second World War was fought to end for ever.

But nothing like that has happened. These terrible things occur, but neither the leaders nor the people are ready to make much sacrifice to stop them. Out of office, Lady Thatcher rails and castigates. But in the chancelleries, ambivalence reigns from top to bottom, north to south, east to west. A year ago, when military action would have been easier, the political will wasn't there. Now, when a political tide is inchoately perceptible for something to be done, the military complexities have become too great for anyone to know what. There is no consensus for action. So there is no action.

One may speculate about the reasons for this deadening failure of imagination. Television, the great homogenizer, is one of them. It tends to render everything equidistant from our consciences. Starving Sudanese child, tottering Kurdish refugee, necklaced innocent in Soweto, bereaved mother in Warrington, raped Muslim in Srebrenica: discrimination is hard to keep a hold of. A crisis needs to get very close in order not to seem very far away.

Connected with this is the capriciousness of the news. Former Yugoslavia ebbs and flows in the headlines. The editorials surge indignantly, then fade away, lost not merely in their own uncertainties but through their reluctance to accept that this, above all other problems, is at present the greatest. The political leaders cannot decide to act. But their hesitation puts them in large company. They know that the people, whether in Europe or the US, are not applying irresistible pressure on them to do so. Leaders and led are co-conspirators. They face a possible moral catastrophe, without the moral capacity to do anything about it.

At the heart of this vacillation is a more concrete failure. The people no longer know what to think about the purposes of military policy. For fifty years these have been very simple. The Cold War and the Soviet threat justified everything. Most people were comfortable with a strategy that required few awkward choices. Nuclear weapons and the level of defence spending were matters of only fringe debate. Governments could rely on passive consent for just about anything they did in that context, unless they entered a massive commitment, like the Americans in Vietnam, without a proper public debate about its objectives.

But this legitimizing basis for military policy has all but vanished. The comfortable certainties of the Cold War, which not only aided stability but pre-empted almost all public argument, are exchanged for a strategic quagmire, through which no map shows a clear route. The envisageable dangers to world peace, which are now far more likely to resemble the Bosnian disaster than the Soviet nuclear threat, have yet to produce an intellectual framework within which they can be handled.

In particular, they are not agreed to be truly urgent. It is as if, the nuclear menace having receded, the democracies sense that nothing merits the same attention. Nothing else attracts the same concerted opinion about what matters. Nothing, even on our Balkan doorstep, deserves more than a helpless shrug – and an emasculated soldiery put to the service of humanitarian relief which the combatants are determined to sabotage.

Maybe this is what ordinary Americans and Europeans want. Maybe their indifference will extend to other theatres. If Russia breaks up into civil war, maybe the agonized inertia of Western leaders will continue to be endorsed by the unwillingness of voters to support a policy that admits even the possibility of wanting to prevent other outbreaks of ethnic slaughter. Maybe, in Bosnia, we are content to say, with Douglas Hurd, that the horrors 'cannot, in fact, be ended from outside'.

If so, it seems important not to sleepwalk into that position – or, equally, to lurch towards the sudden use of force – without the honest debate that has so far not taken place. The debate in Britain has hardly touched the main issue. Labour, as usual in foreign policy, is relieved to bury itself in the same blurring ambiguities as the government. If there is anger, it seems to be directed against the injustice the arms embargo inflicts on the Muslims. Most *enragés* look no further than levelling the killing-field, the preferred Thatcher option.

But let the lady, not for the first time, be a catalyst. The real issue is military intervention by the West, under a UN mandate, perhaps after President Yeltsin has won his referendum on 25 April and therefore has less domestic reason for applying his veto in favour of the Serbs. The debate needs to be honestly conducted, without the hand-wringing bromides too often used to blank out all contention.

Are we prepared to let the genocidal slaughter continue? See the Serbs scoff at international law? Countenance their drive for total victory? Imagine this will have no consequences for the rest of Europe? Permit a precedent to be set for other destabilizers of world order? Tolerate the degradation of the UN? Accept the military impossibility of doing anything whatever to help? Live with the moral consequences of doing nothing?

Or is this the moment to start redefining by deed and word the security policy of the West? Reframing the purposes of a national standing army? Insisting that at least part of Bosnia and its inhabitants will be defended? Defining a world order that regards military intervention as a legitimate expedient through which the UN agrees to prevent a greater evil? Accepting that this is ground where leaders have to lead, or the people will never have the chance to follow?

Hypocrisy in defence of apartheid

SOUTH AFRICA WEAVES an ignominious path through modern British politics. Tomorrow's election is a miracle which no revanchist horror can destroy, but it's also something else: the delayed termination of the British Empire.

On 6 May Cape Town will witness the final handover from imperialists, or their proxies and beneficiaries, to the citizen majority. The moment asks a question about the British contribution to this process. The legacy is still great: half the foreign investment in South Africa is British based, and British exports were worth more than £2,000 million in 1993. But this huge commitment is now vulnerable. If history's judgement on politicians depends on their foresight in defending the national interest, the verdict in this case can only be harsh. In the post-imperial age, South Africa became a British obsession, but also a British disaster.

On the left, apartheid induced a rare solidarity. Vietnam was divisive and nationalization an embarrassing shibboleth, but for thirty years the case against white South Africa was the one cause enlisting the support of all men and women of the vaguest liberal sympathies. The anti-apartheid movement flourished in Britain, and so did many related pressure groups. The liberal conscience knew without effort where it stood.

In Labour governments, it was a different story. The sixties were when hypocrisy entered the record. Violently critical of Tory arms sales to the Republic, Labour found its commitment to end them hard to carry out. In 1967, much of the Cabinet, desperate for £100 million worth of sales and jobs, wanted to continue them, a policy from which George Brown and Denis Healey, with Jim Callaghan alongside, were diverted only by one of Harold Wilson's numerous threats to resign. Even Roy Jenkins spoke up for the economic value of arms sales, according to Barbara Castle's diaries.

But this was still the period of gesture politics. There was no possibility of toppling apartheid, and no serious global sanctions were adopted against it. Rhodesia was Wilson's great problem, and South African assistance in the deposing of Ian Smith his great illusion. As regards apartheid, the comforting capitalist analysis stated that economic growth would have the natural consequence of liquidating the evil system and, one distant unspecified day, enfranchizing the black majority.

This argument was especially beloved of British capital, now deeply entrenched in the white economy. Great was the shock administered to it by a series of exposés in this newspaper by Adam Raphael, who showed in 1974 that British companies, far from leading the field of benevolence, were paying starvation wages to many or most of their black workers. It was a seminal piece of journalism, and provoked a European response which eventually produced a code of business conduct. But it did not uproot the wisdom of the status quo, or the contention that, at the political level, South Africa could not be expected to change for years.

Actually, that was a false version of Pretoria's, and business's, position. Nobody seriously argued, as they did before earlier decolonizations, that the natives would have their freedom 'when they were ready for it'. The South African contest was a straight power struggle, in which it was obvious there would be no voluntary white surrender until circumstances made it inescapable. Behind the thin rhetoric of liberal concern, the British state operated a policy through the seventies and eighties calculated to do nothing that made surrender more likely.

All around it, meanwhile, the other approach began to gain ground. One of the most successful popular campaigns ever conducted in Britain, led by Peter Hain, achieved a sporting boycott in 1970 which hurt South Africa where it counted. Desegregation of SA sport, though painfully slow, began in three years. More crucially, economic sanctions, mobilized through the Commonwealth, entered the agenda, where they remained for two decades until this year, when the imposition of democracy was irreversibly guaranteed.

We now reach the period of maximum British folly. Unfortunately, the beginnings of white South Africa's collapse coincided with the presence in Downing Street of a Prime Minister whose ignorance of South Africa was alleviated only by her husband's opinion that the Cape, of all places in the world, was the most desirable to live, and whose scorn for the black men of the Commonwealth (not to mention their white fellow-travellers) was inextinguishable.

The Thatcher years were the peak not so much of hypocrisy as of catastrophic judgement. The lady, abetted by many supine colleagues, entertained two prejudices. The first was in favour of Chief Buthelezi, whose opposition to sanctions she parlayed into the delusion that he spoke for the majority of Africans. Many business people, not to mention the British Embassy in Pretoria, gave serious time to promoting the chief as the saviour of the day. But this was less serious than the second Thatcher prejudice, against Nelson Mandela and everything he stood for. The ANC, she told the Commonwealth in 1987, was a 'typical terrorist organization'. She added: 'Anyone who thinks that the ANC is going to run the government in South Africa is living in cloud-cuckoo-land.'

This was a fair sample of the Thatcher wisdom, less than three years before Mandela's release from prison. Far from stiffening white resistance, as the Tory mind routinely insisted, global pressure, led by the comprehensive economic sanctions finally imposed by the United States Congress, had shown President F. W. de Klerk the writing on the wall.

Some may still regret the sanctions, and all must concede that they were unevenly applied. A significant faction in the West continues to whore after white rule, and awaits with mordant anticipation the crises that will certainly beset majority rule. But no serious observer now doubts that sanctions – the world economic pressure the British always resisted – were a decisive agency of change.

As a postscript to empire, this record is more obtuse than anything that went before it. It makes its final mark all too suitably, with the presence of a famous Conservative PR man working all out for the white and losing side in the election. It is hard, even now, to find a British minister exulting in the triumphant birth of democratic politics over which De Klerk and Mandela have jointly presided. When Mandela takes his place as President, what gratitude will he have reason to show to South Africa's most tenacious investor and historic Western link, and what reason to heed the sensible economic advice London wants to offer? For perverse and reckless reasons, none.

The elders round on Governor Patten

A FREE COUNTRY was handed over to the only Communist super-power, with due and doleful ceremony, at the stroke of midnight, and nothing palpably changed. The British side looked bleak. Somewhere out in the territories, 4,000 Chinese troops were moving in, and armoured trucks were giving a profile to China's presence that the British Army was careful never to display. No decolonization has been longer in the making or more exactly timed. But then no decolonization has consisted of passing a people from freedom into bondage.

It was bound to be something like this, with the Prince of Wales doing the honours, and one lot of owners shaking hands with another as the lease falls in. The scenes on the ground were chaotic, as thousands of dignitaries sat in engulfing rain watching what an old nation does best: beating the retreat with wonderful military precision and playing all the old tunes. Tears were jerked from even the stoniest heart. But they weren't tears of pity or regret. All in all, the run-up to the due transfer of Hong Kong has been, against every prediction ten years ago, a triumph: economy booming, construction rocketing, people alerted, by late British insistence, to the meaning of democratic freedom.

Yet not everybody was pleased. Behind the ceremonial rituals, a chorus of elders was chanting the omens. This wasn't the Hong Kong Democrats, though they could be heard, and made their own gestures of rejection. The lamenting came from the people with whom all this began: British officials who got it under way in the 1980s, now standing watch over the final act and hating what they see. They tell one a lot about the peculiar *schadenfreude* of the official mind.

Plenty of them came. I didn't see Sir Percy Cradock, but Geoffrey Howe, the point man on the 1984 Joint Declaration, Sir Alan

Donald, a prime Foreign and Commonwealth Office sinologue, Lord Wilson, former Governor and the sinuous epitome of a British version of the Chinese mind, and quite a few others were here, all attending the obsequies not so much of Hong Kong as of their own delicate handiwork: the Ming vase they made, which Governor Patten, grandstanding for democracy, shattered.

Lord Howe thinks yesterday could have been quite different. It should, he told me, have been the Asian version of the Mandela–De Klerk handover. The analogy is, frankly, fatuous. A generous optimist might see one or two De Klerks skulking on the Chinese scene, C. H. Tung, the new local boss, possibly among them. But where is Mandela? Never mind: what some elders who crafted 1984 believe is that, handled as they had brilliantly arranged, this could have been the climax of a rapprochement between two cultures, instead of the perilous stand-off which, as they believe, is entirely Mr Patten's fault.

They think that, back then, they did something extraordinary. The Chinese could simply have walked in. Britain held no cards, yet the great FCO apparatus of sinological learning brought them to the table, patiently manoeuvred for years, agreed the procedures, fixed the timetables, and built a through-train carrying legislators elected in 1995 past 1997, with only occasional rebellious passengers flung out of the door if Beijing didn't like them. All this, they think, Patten recklessly put at risk, as only a barbarian could do.

The elders do not always chant in tune. For example, they say contradictory things about the Asian attitude to democracy. Much of the attack on Patten used to claim that Hong Kongers would never care about democracy anyway. The indictment has changed. It says, instead, that Patten has put democracy itself at risk. One former official told me that the downside of the Patten initiatives, which gave many people a fragment of a vote without Chinese permission, was that they would delay by many years the democracy the Joint Declaration provided for.

This contestable proposition is part of a wider conflict in these people, between optimism and pessimism concerning China's real intentions. Most of them, Cradock being the acme, have spent a lifetime kowtowing to a force they consider to be beyond challenge. Cradock's straight-faced verdict on the Tiananmen Square massacre, in a recent article in *Prospect*, was that 'it made the Chinese authorities even more resentful, sensitive and suspicious of British intentions in Hong Kong'. At the same time, other members of this chorus seem to have discovered new heights of lyricism, contemplating what might have been.

If only Chris had not been so honourably stubborn, Howe thinks, a glorious future stretched ahead. Patten had tried to secure by confrontation what had not been available by agreement. Telling the Chinese what to think about human rights constituted a kind of recidivist imperialism. Imagine how much more influence he would have carried, had he been in dialogue with Beijing for the past five years. Howe's dissent from Patten had apparently persuaded him that Deng Xiaoping was on the verge of conversion to Jeffersonian democracy, courtesy of the Joint Declaration, until the Governor reversed the process.

I can understand what the chorus is lamenting. What's at stake here is pride of authorship. Sitting in the audience at the handover they'd spent a decent part of their lives preparing for, they had been, to some extent, overtaken. Their version of how to deal with China had not prevailed, and Lord Howe chose to satisfy his vanity by proclaiming his attendance at China's own celebration. Lumbering alongside, Sir Edward Heath, the arch-exponent of Asia's negative attitudes to democracy, who not long ago on British television told Martin Lee, the brave leader of the Democrats here, that he had no business challenging what China wanted, cut a signal figure: the man who says, as most of them fundamentally believe, that the only proper way to close down the British Empire was by following the rule-book of the twenty-first-century imperialists.

So they were an unsettling presence, in their discontent. But they did not spoil the party. As yet, their prophecies have proved false. They thought things would get much nastier than they have, much sooner, as a result of Patten's unnecessary quarrel. But if anything, China eased up on its political threats and demands, as the handover got closer.

Nobody can foresee the future, but then nobody ever could. *Le tout* Hong Kong were there last night, when the British said goodbye, and few of them were mourning. The identical crowd will be there today, when the new chief executive of the Special

Administrative Region, Mr Tung, gives his own first party. In the end, most people needed neither Geoffrey Howe nor Chris Patten to teach them about reality.

Kosovo for the Kosovans

THE WAR DEBATE in Britain has been unusually free of political dishonesty. The absence of ulterior agendas should be a consolation at a hideous time. This is not Vietnam in sixties Washington, nor is it Europe in nineties London, with hatreds and histories obscuring the merits of the issue. Left and Right are divided, and permitted to be so without any of them having their throats torn out. Many participants do speak from their history, whether with the Serbs, or against all war, or as scholarly ideologues of air bombardment, or whatever. But serious people in and out of politics continue, I think, to struggle with anxieties that few pretend are the prerogative of one side.

Alongside this political straightness, however, comes an intellectual – one might even say a moral – confusion that gets more pressing by the day. Is the anti-war side really anti-war? Or are its members, at bottom, critics of the way this war has been run, rather than opponents of the pursuit against Milosevic? Their fury suggests one position, their reasoning another. Now that Nato has launched plans to take itself to the threshold of a very different operation from the one fought so far – making good, one might say, the errors of the past – the question is no longer an academic rattle-bag. It becomes intensely urgent.

The critics often sound hostile to the very fact of Nato's military action. Their loathing for its immorality is exceeded only by their contempt for its mismanagement. They make an eloquent case against every aspect of it: the ahistorical folly of its leaders, their malign incompetence as negotiators, their blindness as strategists, their cruelty as proxy bombardiers, the mendacity of their claim to good intentions, not to mention the geo-strategic price they will pay for stirring up the Chinese and the Russians.

This position takes its visceral strength from the appearance it gives of a wise and saintly detachment, which might otherwise be called pacifism. There should have been no Nato attack in March or at any other time, it says. Negotiation should have proceeded indefinitely. Rambouillet, the last throw towards a peace deal, was a sham, and by imposing an ultimatum on the Serbs, Nato never intended it to be anything else. There is never a time to stop talking. And so the seductive case is built.

The hell of the last two months in Kosovo has, apparently, been so appalling that any alternative was to be preferred. And looking at the devastation of the bombing – its failure yet to return the refugees, its ancillary role to the Serbs' slaughter – one might well think so.

But that doesn't seem to be all, or even the major part, of the anti-war case. Though a few people take that line, hardly any can resist slipping in a parallel and contradictory critique. Nobody wants to be tarred as a defender of Milosevic – which they aren't. The mass disbandments and cold-blooded official murders buried in the deodorized phrase 'ethnic cleansing' are beyond defending by any democratic politician. From honest, anxious Europeans, as they know, these crimes require better than burbling about the merits of perpetual negotiation.

So, many anti-war spokesmen insinuate smoothly into their discourse the notion that the case against the war is that it should have been fought differently. Behind the screams of disgust is a parenthesis to suggest that, of course, a proper strategist and sincere proponent of the global moral order would have marched into Kosovo the moment Milosevic's organized barbarities became apparent, a year ago or more.

This contradiction in the anti-war case was painfully exemplified, and never resolved, in Channel 4's big Kosovo debate last Sunday evening. Taken as a group, the critics seemed incapable of making up their mind whether they regarded the war as a disgrace because it had been undertaken at all, or because Nato had made a fool of itself by not immediately using every means to win it.

This was and is profoundly unsatisfactory. Is the Kosovo crisis merely a coconut shy, in which Nato's many frailties can be pot-shot to destruction? A theatre for disingenuous journalism and politics? Or did it always present a choice between intervention on the one hand and appeasement on the other: a choice in which the appeasers have no right to allow themselves the luxury of half-pretending that they weren't against a proper onslaught against Milosevic, only against the war as it has turned out?

Current developments put this school of anti-warriors to the question. They may be too dug in to answer it in the right way. But what is now being prepared is, at last, something better than the bombing. A serious Euro-American army begins to gather at the gates of Kosovo, not yet for certain use, but deployable if and when conditions arise where military intelligence and Nato's political leaders judge Kosovo ready to be reoccupied by its citizens, as long as they have military protection they can believe in.

Everyone agrees that the preparations for this from last autumn onwards were crassly negligent. But Nato is finally getting ready to be serious about restoring Kosovo to the Kosovans. It is doing what the interventionists and at least half the latter-day appeasers attacked it, explicitly or implicitly, for not doing. Merely assembling the troops will be hard, and will go on taxing Nato's unity. But are we to say that Nato's failure so far to do anything for the refugees except build camps continues to justify the adjectives of savagery and contempt, now the alliance has lumbered towards offering Kosovo more than bombing?

This shift requires something from the government too. Tony Blair has been big on moral suasion, and assertive in his promise that Nato will prevail. It has been the performance of a leader. But he hasn't levelled with the people about how Nato will get there, or the scale of the national sacrifice this international enterprise will demand. Getting ready for army operations now involves new risks; a military presence in Kosovo for decades ahead is a massive commitment. Blair has yet to look us in the eye with proper gravitas, and tell the country just what to expect.

The step-change in the war plan will surely make him do so. But it also asks the anti-war school to come clean. Should Kosovo be made safe for Kosovans? Should Milosevic be forced to stop his ethnic slaughter, never to resume it? Or should this war be altogether stopped?

The limits of moral consistency

POLITICAL LEADERS SPEND their lives making imperfect choices. Sometimes they have to choose between options that are all bad. They are driven to do a terrible thing, because the alternative was more terrible still. Yet, having made the choice, they think they must pretend it was not merely good but the only one a decent leader could possibly have adopted. An inverse ratio of truth to rhetoric invariably applies. The more agonizing and imperfect the decision, the richer the hyperbole that describes its incontestable rightness in every particular.

The most recent major example of this law at work was the bombing of Kosovo. Here was an extremely difficult decision for the members of Nato. They knew it was dubious in law and perilous in effect. Several of them wanted it not to happen, and even those who strongly supported it, like Britain, knew that it might never dislodge Milosevic, while inflicting a lot of damage on innocent Serbs and Kosovans. Once it started, however, there was no stopping the exuberance of Messrs Blair, Cook and Robertson in defending it. The bombing became a sacred duty. A task of utmost controversy and doubt was transformed into the humanitarianism of the new world order. The decision, from being a hideous choice, became a heroic enterprise.

Another seeming law of political conduct is that leaders must always be seen to be consistent. This is what the public has been taught to expect. Leaders lay down their principles, and stick to them. Everything must be seen to fit into a consistent framework.

But this can bring problems. Having made such a shining virtue of the decision to bomb Kosovo – the choice no man could avoid – the claimants to consistency have been put on the rack over the Russian siege of Grozny. If Kosovo could have been framed as merely a bloody mess, Robin Cook wouldn't have had to spend yesterday morning being knocked around the ring by John Humphrys, working from the premise that Grozny, where we have witnessed more frightful scenes than in Pristina, merited the same commitment from the good guys.

The grandeur that was spun around Kosovo, in other words, has caused much confusion. What's imperative in one place is surely not negligible in another. If Kosovo, why indeed not Grozny? Such contradiction isn't confined to backers of the Kosovo war. The opponents of it seem just as muddled.

They may be as appalled as anyone by the medieval behaviour of the Russian government, preparing with millennial weaponry to raze Grozny to the ground. But when they take derisive note of the West's inconsistency, what exactly are they saying? That Nato's military defence of Kosovo might be retrospectively justified if followed by similar mobilization to protect the Chechens? Or that the impossibility of intervening everywhere makes it a crime to intervene anywhere? Or perhaps the barbarities in Grozny some- how justify the do-nothing stance Tam Dalyell, Alice Mahon and others took when Kosovo was being bombed?

They can't really mean that. Yet they get close to saying it when they claim that Nato, in Kosovo, taught the Russians how to conduct aerial bombardment of a civilian population, and thereby sacrificed any authority to tell them to desist in Chechnya.

This is a facile argument. The Kosovo bombing was less precise than it should have been. Its outcome has had many of the bad consequences, along with some good ones, that made the decision-makers flinch before a desperate choice of evils. But Nato at least attempted to discriminate. It took some care with its targeting. It was supported by the Albanian nation on the ground.

The Russian onslaught against Grozny, by contrast, is an indiscriminately barbarous exercise in ethnic cleansing. Far from coming to the aid of a brutalized ethnic group, Moscow now claims to extinguish its remaining responsibilities by declaring that if the old, the lame and the starving are bombed to death next week, it will be their own fault.

The truth the Grozny–Kosovo parallelism illuminates is not that Nato's approach to Kosovo was good and its approach to Chechnya bad – or vice versa – but that politicians lay claim to the wrong models of leadership. The interventionist doctrine is as pernicious as the anti-interventionist anathema. The pretence to consistency is unsustainable, and the need to make it is a false requirement. The cement of moral principle that is supposed to bind together interventionism and consistency needs to be mixed with the greatest caution.

Tony Blair had a go at doing this in his Chicago speech at the height of the Kosovo bombing. In the small print, he suggested that any new doctrine must pay attention to practicalities as well as principles. There could not be intervention everywhere, and the world needed to think out the rules of the new game.

What was most arresting, however, was Mr Blair's assertion of the moral duty to intervene, within these conditions, wherever an ethnic group was being intolerably oppressed. This was the speech's emotional charge, designed to claim the high ground and secure domestic political support for bombing that had not yet achieved its purpose.

As moral obscenities, the fates of Chechens and Kosovans are on a par. But as political challenges to the West, they are quite different. In the new order, we learn, some very old rules continue to apply, the first of which is the supremacy of interest over morality. Though lauded by Blair (and in this space) as a humanitarian exercise, Kosovo was really worth fighting for because it abutted Nato-land: the Milosevic strategy threatened to destabilize Nato members: the deep military interest of the alliance was at stake: the enemy was puny: and success was therefore calculable, without too many uncomfortable repercussions.

Even then it was vastly expensive, and very slow to work. The choice had to be made, but was not heroic in anything except the propaganda of the moment. It could never be a model for much else, least of all a place as far away, as remote from ongoing assistance, as sensitive to another nuclear power, as unimportant to the interests of the alliance as the mountainous Muslim enclave of Chechnya.

This is a grim reckoning. Every picture out of Grozny grinds the conscience of those who watched Kosovo happening. It obliges Mr Cook and Mr Blair to stumble through a vocabulary of impotence that mocks the exultant rhetoric they produced when the Satanic

Serb had been forced back to Belgrade. On the whole, I remind myself, it will be better if we do not in future use the language of universal morality to raise too many expectations.

Seduced into Iraq

IF PRESIDENT GEORGE W. BUSH goes to war against Iraq, the ensuing conflict will be without a close modern precedent. Each of the main western wars of the last twenty years, however controversial, was perceivable as a response to manifest aggression. The Falklands War in 1982 was one such case, the 1991 Gulf War another. The military actions in Bosnia and Kosovo were conducted for the defence of ethnic groups facing aggression at the heart of Europe. Each had a measure of international approval.

A war to unseat Saddam Hussein would proceed on a different basis, encompassed in the seductive word 'pre-emptive'. The attack would be unleashed to stop Saddam doing something he has not yet started to do with weaponry whose configuration and global, or even regional, potency is hard to determine but might be serious. The Pentagon civilians pressing the case envisage a gratuitous attack – one not preceded by an act of aggression – by one sovereign country on another to get rid of a leader who happens to worry and enrage them.

Europeans who opposed all those earlier conflicts will certainly oppose this one. The usual suspects are already mobilizing for peace. But now we have something new. Many Europeans who supported the Balkan wars and the Gulf War, and even the Falklands absurdity, are getting ready to oppose a pre-emptive attack on Iraq. They suspect its political provenance. They reject its moral justification. They look in vain for the international support it needs. They see nothing predictably good in its practical outcome. And if they are British, they fear the prospect of being sucked into all these absences of reason, these diplomatic and moral black holes, at the behest of a different country, with different political impulses, three thousand miles away.

Nobody pretends that Saddam Hussein is other than a murderous tyrant. He has committed terrible crimes against his own people. He's a threat to his neighbours and a source of instability, one of many, in the region. There are signs he has restored some of the chemical and biological weapon-making capacity that was destroyed under the lengthy aegis of UN inspectors. It may well be the case that he is trying to acquire the capacity to build nuclear weapons.

But nobody is certain about the size of any of this. These ambitions, and some of these weapons, can be assumed to be there, but the advantage of the pre-emption doctrine is that its believers do not need to be specific. In Washington there's disagreement between the Pentagon civilians and both military and intelligence officials over how many, if any, ready-to-go missiles by which chemical and biological bombs could be delivered actually exist. No evidence has been published that begins to make the case for attack, as against the containment policy that has worked pretty well for eleven years. We're simply supposed to accept that it's there. Washington and London say airily that they have it. One begins to sense, in their reluctance to accompany the build-up to war with a display of evidence, the absence, in truth, of any justification enough to satisfy open-minded sceptics.

Until this is rectified, scepticism can only deepen. The moral case for pre-emptive attack needs to address issues of proportionality and collateral civilian damage. The protagonists have not even broached them. The legal case needs to take the UN seriously. So far, UN backing for an attack has been the object of casuistic evasion in both capitals. Conceivably this could be a negotiating tactic, winding Saddam up to concede. But nobody who has talked to any of the principals who are about to be involved in this decision can imagine them willing to risk losing in the Security Council as their juggernaut assembles at the gates of Baghdad.

The practical case hasn't been made either. What happens afterwards? Field Marshal Lord Bramall asked the question the other day. There are as many theories about this as there are operational plans for different modes of attack. A puppet regime of Westernised Iraqis? A different sort of military dictator? A government that includes the Kurds, the greatest victims of Saddam's brutality: or, more likely, one that's guaranteed to exclude

them in order to keep Turkey happy, and thus open Turkey as a base
for the attack? These and many other scenarios are on the table.
Washington is awash with them. There's a leak a day in the *New
York Times.* With each one that appears we become aware not just of
indecision, but of the colossal risks this speculative operation runs,
and the divided assessments made by serious military men.

One faction, however, is indifferent to the arguments. The
civilians driving the Pentagon have a less analytical agenda. They
seem ready to sweep through all objections. A group of hard,
obsessive officials, all much cleverer than the President, exploit the
instincts he shares, which include the instinct to secure vengeance
in a family feud after what Saddam did to his father. Their cocksure
certainty that they have a mightier military force than Saddam,
which of course is true, extends into a blithe assumption that the
solution to Palestine lies through a cleansed and puppetized
Baghdad. These are people who have shown many times how little
they respect international law, still less the spirit of international
collaboration. Having come to dominate the world, they tend to
despise it. Faced with allies they can ignore, they duly prepare to do
so. Tony Blair doesn't like to hear any of this, and is disposed to
deny it. He says that Bush is in charge in Washington, and Bush is a
sensible as well as an honourable man. Complaining that everyone
who asks a question is getting ahead of the action and should pipe
down, he asserts privately that he will not be pushed around by the
President but act, as always, in the national interest.

But his interpretation of this is disturbing. We read, from Bush's
aides, that Blair has already promised the President to commit
British troops to action in Iraq. In private he talks more of the
morality than the risks of doing this. Indeed, he sees so many
dangerous immoralists around that, in an ideal world, there would be
interventions against the lot of them. Very few of his closest
diplomatic advisers support a war against Iraq or the manoeuvres
now leading up to it, though the Ministry of Defence, with its frantic
Washingtonitis, may be slightly different. Yet Blair is in danger of
seeming helpless before the ferocious logic of Donald Rumsfeld.

I think he forgets the uniqueness of what is being prepared: its
gratuitous aggression, its idle optimism, its moral frailty, its
indifference to regional opinion, the extraordinary readiness of

those proposing it to court more anti-American terrorism as a result. Is Britain really destined to tag along uncomplaining, behind an extended act of war that few people outside America and Israel consider necessary, prudent or justified? Very many British, I surmise, more than Mr Blair would ever expect, will say no.

INSIDE THE LAW

Muffled by the Woolsack

LORD HAILSHAM IS an old and brilliant man who has occupied the Woolsack for almost twice as long as anyone this century. He has been a jewel of our post-war politics, gleaming with untarnished quality beside the bankers and bootboys who have come and gone from the table he has occupied for much of his political life. It must be said, however, that at the end of his years Lord Hailsham has become deformed by a single obsession.

That obsession is with what he calls the independence of the judiciary, and it is, on the face of it, commendable. He has been repulsing the challenges to it for many years, on occasions which nobody who cares for the law would cavil at. In particular, when Labour politicians, Michael Foot among them, launched the most unjustified attacks on the integrity of the bench under the Heath government, Hailsham retaliated with an eloquence that vanquished their odious insinuations.

Latterly, in his second term as Lord Chancellor, he has been just as vigilant. When MPs criticized particular sentences, he has pounced on them. He has railed against his predecessor, who denied preferment to Sir John Donaldson for a purely political reason. Altogether, he portrays the judiciary as men at bay, whose only protection, it appears, now lies in 'the courage, political experience and integrity of a man, and that man is the Lord Chancellor'.

An increasingly perfervid note has been creeping into these utterances in the last two years And however much one values judicial independence, it is time to wonder whether its chief and only guardian is not now extending his remit so far as to eliminate the very quality he imagines himself to be upholding. This is revealed by an incident trifling in itself but resonant in its gross presumption. BBC Radio Four decided to make a programme about the Bar and its present troubles, and approached a number of judges for contributions. There was nothing very novel about this, since senior judges had been interviewed about legal matters several times in the last decade.

The result this time was different. Almost all the judges approached said they could not appear. They consulted the Lord Chancellor first, and the Lord Chancellor said no. They were very apologetic, these eminent men, who have an unrivalled perspective on the Bar from which they had all come, but Lord Hailsham could not be defied.

A conversation ensued between the BBC and the Lord Chancellor's Office which disclosed that on today's Woolsack casuistry has become the first handmaiden of moral fervour. Any salaried judge, it was said, had to ask the Lord Chancellor before going on the air. This did not, however, amount to seeking his permission. A massive indignation overcame Lord Hailsham's senior official at the suggestion that the judges were being 'stopped' from broadcasting. They were not being stopped. They were merely consulting. On the other hand, there was no way, we were to infer (for I have written and presented the programme, which goes out tonight), that consultation would conclude with anything other than the Lord Chancellor stating that judges should not be interviewed.

Casuistry, you might think, could reach no more exquisite heights. But the cream of it is yet to come. For what is the general purpose underlying this position? The judges must not talk, it seems, because this is the only way 'to preserve their independence'.

Thus, the independence of the judiciary can apparently be protected only by removing the independence of individual judges. Several senior judges, among them past and present office-holders in the apparatus that invigilates the Bar, wanted to contribute to a serious public airing of its problems. But, although they are free men of whom it is proudly claimed that they owe nothing to anyone, they were told not to do so.

A passing aspersion must be cast on these characters themselves. The Lord Chancellor runs their lives only because they let him. Ultimately they have no obligation to bow to the rulings of him and his officials – as a law lord, Lord Templeman, and a circuit judge, Quentin Edwards, well showed by agreeing to take part, come what may.

But the principal culprit is the Lord Chancellor himself, now fired up by the interesting idea that independence means its opposite. Judges must be free from political criticism, but not from administrative control. They are the incorruptible beacons of independent justice, yet they cannot be trusted to come down from the bench into the market-place without imperilling that great function.

This is an insult to them, and surely does the cause of the law no good. For what particle of their independence, of justice, of the esteem in which judges are properly held is endangered if they occasionally contribute their wisdom to a debate they are directly concerned in? It is not as if they are being asked to attack the law lords' judgement on Victoria Gillick, or second-guess the Cyprus secrets jury, or enter into a discussion on the merits of Thatcherism. These are cautious men, trained not to let themselves go – but with, perhaps, a greater sense than Lord Hailsham that the law and its functioning needs a better-educated public constituency which they, as the men at the top of the tree, could help create. For one accompaniment to the cloistering of the law, and the preservation of the judiciary as a priesthood that surpasseth understanding, has certainly not been the expansion of the law as a popular public service. The law needs to be better valued. Lawyers need to shed their public image as grasping and expensive procrastinators.

Judges can contribute to this necessary process. They could with benefit descend on occasion from their pedestals and demonstrate the truth: which is that many of them, far from being toffee-nosed reactionaries, are ordinary men of the world, with matchless experience, first-class minds, judicious habits of speech, and a certain sagacity which they could impart without inviting the charge that they had compromised their position.

The Lord Chancellor, faithfully echoing his department, will have none of this. It is as if the privacy which surrounds all its processes must now reach as far as humanly possible even into the public role of judges. All judicial appointments are made without reason given or public scrutiny allowed. Sir Derek Oulton, the Lord Chancellor's permanent secretary, holds more patronage in his capable hands than any other official in Whitehall, and divides the elect from the damned with no explanation.

It's a system which, judged by results, has worked well; there are remarkably few disastrous appointments. But it fathers a philosophy that is terrified of any breach with the myth that judges are bloodless mediators, untouchables, inhuman magic-men.

They are, in fact, people who could do a lot to make the law more valued and respected, and therefore perhaps more available: a task in which successive Lord Chancellors have dismally failed. Legal aid, the key to availability, has not kept pace with the minimum demand for it, as today's annual report on it yet again reminds us. Government after government has declined to give the law more resources. Hailsham after Hailsham has failed to persuade the Cabinet that legal service deserves not to be bottom of the priorities. Declaiming about judges, they have fought a losing battle for law.

The Lord Chancellor may not agree that judges who went more public could help him to rescue the image of his profession. But he should at least not violate the language. Let him not pretend that it is for the good of their independence that he commands them to be silent.

Muttering judges

THE LORD CHIEF JUSTICE arrives with a message. Lord Taylor, taking office this week, wants the judiciary to shed the outward signs of priesthood by removing their wigs. He also wants them to come out of their secluded temples. They should be more accessible. 'I think the judiciary ought to be open to criticism,' Taylor said on the day he was appointed. In other words he would usher them into the real world, where all of them live but which they take pride in excluding from their professional lives. The real world is the political world. Implicit in what Taylor is proposing is a redefinition of the sacred cow, judicial independence.

Lord Lane, his predecessor, worshipped vigilantly at this altar. He had an admirable suspicion of the executive branch of government. He discontinued periodic contacts between civil servants and judges, and kept all ministers beyond his own arm's length. When he thought Home Secretary Whitelaw was getting at him in the early eighties, he declined to speak with him for months. Whitelaw found this rupture of normal establishment civilities incomprehensible.

But Lane was also an obsessive. While making serious efforts on his own part to secure a pattern of lower sentencing, he resisted formal dialogue with government about sentencing policy. When Lord Mackay published proposals to weaken the monopoly of the Bar, Lane made these sound like the biggest threat to our sovereign freedoms since Hitler. When criticized, he seldom stooped to reply. But his proxies suggested not only that the criticism was wrong but that, since the Lord Chief was too far above the battle to respond, the very act of criticizing was a dangerous challenge to judicial dignities.

No one would contest that judges should be free of party politics. To that extent, judicial independence is elementary. Everyone would agree that they must keep their distance from the government of the day, and not be subject to the kind of visits paid by Lord Chancellor Hailsham to Master of the Rolls Denning at the height of the industrial troubles of the Heath government. Judges require to make their decisions without fear or favour. At the heart of their independence is the guarantee that, short of mental decline, they are absolutely irremovable from their jobs.

But in the quest for independence there is a double mirage. First, in Britain these axiomatic conditions are not threatened. Respect for them is universal in politics and the law. The judiciary may suffer from all manner of social deformities through long association with a complacent and tenaciously conservative profession. But its members inherit a strong tradition. In the US, where 80 per cent of the entire federal bench now consists of Reagan or Bush appointees, the top judiciary has a shameless political bias. That is not true here. A measure of it is the expansion of judicial review of administrative and ministerial decisions. Applications for this rose from 491 in 1980 to 2,129 in 1990, with a steady 50 per cent being granted. For Thatcherite Whitehall, the judges were a curse.

The second mirage, however, is a more distracting illusion. Incantations about independence imply that there is no connection with the political world already. The judiciary, it is claimed, can only be true to their calling if their world is insulated from any other.

But it never is. Interpenetration is routine. Consider the highly political matter of resources. The judiciary, as is well known, consider they are overworked. They would like more judges and better support. They argue, although rarely in public, that the iron hand of the Lord Chancellor's Department in this sense operates against the quality of justice. Their perfect independence is violated by administrators telling them what they may and may not do, and by all kinds of pressure to increase their output. This is real life.

Nor do their cases take place in a vacuum. Most of them may be obscure and unnoticed, but the entire saga of the Birmingham Six, to take the case that brought Lord Lane to his knees, showed the intensity with which political realities sometimes efface the requirements of justice. The convictions were brought in on a wave of public feeling, supported by corrupt evidence which the judicial system felt no obligation to detect and challenge.

They were defended for years by judicial statements essentially political in character, from Denning's repudiation of the 'appalling vista' that would follow from their being mistaken, to Lane's own assertion, after a month looking at evidence now demonstrated to have been faked, that 'the longer the hearing has gone on, the more convinced the court had become that the verdict of the jury was correct'. When Lane said he had 'no doubt' the convictions were right, he was really saying he had no doubt the system could not have erred.

Where the interface is closest, however, is at the point of sentence. Sentencing is a judicial act with the closest political implications. Not only does it make a statement about the kind of society we are. Leave that aside, as the kind of philosophy which judges are perhaps as entitled as politicians to fashion. But a sentence is an imposition of costs on society. Upon many sentences are many prisons built. There could hardly be a more obvious arena in which judges and politicians should get together. And yet many judges resist it. Their sainted right to determine an individual sentence, often based on the flimsiest inquiry into either the convict's circumstances or the system's capacity to receive him, must never be infringed. Their independence would be sullied. Their priestly faculties would be compromised by association with the infidels.

When Lord Lane retired, his eulogy was spoken by Lord Donaldson, the Master of the Rolls. Lane, said Donaldson, had been the victim of a campaign of calumny, for which his colleagues on the bench could feel only 'anger and disgust'. But Lane had only been attacked for presiding over a massive blunder that cost six men even more years' freedom than they had already lost. Both Lane's own resentment and Donaldson's enraged defence spoke for a system whose leaders were blind to the collapse of public confidence in it.

This collapse was in no way invented. Quite the contrary. Unlike politicians, judges have enjoyed fawning public esteem. The public doesn't want to mistrust the courts, and readily gives them the benefit of the doubt. But now the confidence needs to be rebuilt, and that is Taylor's formidable task. He is right, in addressing it, to invite his brethren down from their pedestals. They are public men, operating in the public world, and should not be distant from the clamour that rightly surrounds public decisions. In the widest sense their decisions are sometimes as political as any other public official's, and they should acknowledge the fact by listening to criticism. With security of tenure, the pain ought not to be unbearable.

My life as a juror

BARRINGTON LEE SMALLIN is a dangerous young man. Not long ago he appeared at Wood Green Crown Court charged with assault, aggravated burglary, theft and unlawful wounding with intent to cause grievous bodily harm. I was a juror in his case and helped decide that he was guilty.

But being on a jury is not just an experience in judgement. On that level my week in court confirmed most of the good things ever written about the jury system. But sitting there offers a much wider canvas to explore. I've listened to parts of cases often enough as a journalist, but never had to stay from start to finish. Whatever else jury service does or doesn't do, it keeps you pinned to your seat for the duration. You're a captive audience for the whole panoply of the law.

This proves to be a more ambivalent experience. It's at the heart of the work of a new Royal Commission, chaired by Lord Runciman. Is the process working? Through questionnaires on thousands of cases Runciman is hoping to build a picture of how the judicial system is assessed by those (excluding defendants, it seems, but including everyone else) embroiled in it. After R v. Smallin, a typical mundane, unglamorous, unreported though bloody case, my ratings of the players may seem, given the verdict, a perverse indictment: Judge seven out of ten, Defence counsel five, Police two, Prosecutor one. The jury, I am quite certain, deserves ten out of ten.

The Wood Green Crown Court is in north London, seven stops up the Piccadilly line from King's Cross. With a single, flagrant exception, being a juror there was an acceptable experience. The massive Victorian building has been refurbished at a cost of £8.7 million, and both the courts and the juries' quarters are well-designed for the long haul. The chairs are comfortable and the light is good. Naturally it's a great bore to be called, disrupting all other plans. And it involves being plunged into a life of regimentation, herded in and out of different rooms at the lawyers' convenience. But as a herd, you're treated with decent respect. You, after all, have the decision to make. There was no hanging about. And after a case was over, the telephone hotline saved you a futile journey to court next day, telling you when you were not needed.

But there was this grave deficiency. In the morning, the train to Wood Green is always emptying, and by the time it gets there most of the occupants are black. It's the Brixton of the north. Yet in the jury assembly hall, with a hundred or so people waiting to do their citizen's duty, not one black juror was present.

This fact struck several members of the Smallin jury, since Barrington Smallin is a seventeen-year-old black. How can it have been? It plainly wasn't a calculated piece of racial discrimination. Among court officials the explanations ranged between poll tax-inspired non-registration to vote – the electoral register is the source of jury lists – and offhand insults about 'literacy tests'. When I later rang the Jury Summoning Office, the spokesman said: 'I'm surprised. Our system is totally random. I would certainly expect some coloured people to have been there.'

In court, however, the point occasioned no remark. The defendant looked blankly indifferent, his counsel made no challenge. Since the case turned in one way on an aspect of blackness, this came to me to seem doubly unfortunate. It could surely never have happened in New York City. Is it a reflection of British maturity, or of an innocence that can hardly last much longer, that almost every person in that court-room seemed to think nothing of it? At any rate, eleven white men and one white woman, chosen at random from this random herd (other Wood Green juries that week had a female majority) took their place to try Barrington Smallin.

The charges, though numerous, related mostly to a single incident. Smallin was alleged to have burst into a flat in Hornsey last April, beaten the two young whites who were there, tied them up, slashed one of them with a knife, stolen the usual gear (bikes, video, camera, etc.) and removed £500 from a bank cash dispenser, having extracted the relevant PIN number from its terrified owner. Smallin, if it was he, was accompanied by two other blacks, neither of them named at any stage, and both presumably still at large.

There was never much doubt about the law. On this kind of joint enterprise, as far as guilt goes it is all for one and one for all. The prosecution did not need to prove that it was Smallin rather than one of his accomplices who actually did the GBH. All they had to show, as was admitted by both sides, was that he was there. The case turned entirely on identification. Was this black youth, looking like so many other black youths, correctly identified by one of the two young whites?

In support of this, an earlier episode came into play. Smallin was also charged with attacking the same man five months earlier at another flat. It was someone, it turned out, who had been fleetingly at school with him. The recognition witness was unshiftably firm. The same Smallin he knew from school five years before had done both the attacks.

No other witness, however, could put a name to the face. This was the police and prosecution's problem. How, by the most elementary incompetence, they very nearly failed to resolve it was the issue that dominated my own instructive baptism as a functionary of the English legal process.

The prosecutor was a barrister named Williams, although this detail was not easily discovered. A feature of jury trial is that while the jurors' names are read out loud and clear twice, those of counsel are confined to episodic mumbling between them, and that of the judge is never mentioned at all. It can be discovered from the lists posted on a noticeboard, but otherwise judicial majesty evidently guarantees exemption from the Citizen's Charter: no name-tags for these officers of the state.

Mr Williams, it emerged from further inquiry, was a Mr O. Williams, or Owen W. A podgy man with a fruity voice, who looked around forty beneath his wig, he was of that school of oratory in which the double-breasted suit plays an important histrionic part, the elaborate procedure of buttoning it up being called into service as some kind of visual aid to authority. Unfortunately, in Williams's case, his smooth way with a double-breasted was not enough to conceal a half-arsed forensic performance.

He kept getting the names wrong. At one stage he was persistently referring to the defendant when he meant the victim.

Quite often the judge had to ask him to reframe his question, and each time Mr Williams conceded his error without a blink of embarrassment. He seemed quite used to it. 'Haven't you read your papers?' the judge tetchily inquired after one especially egregious omission. Maybe he'd only just got them. It was hard to know whether the sluggard pace at which Mr Williams examined his witnesses owed more to some special cunning he sought to invest in them or to the possibility, as he perused the texts of the statements they'd given the police, that he had forgotten what they were going to say next.

In fact, where Mr Williams met his Waterloo was not entirely his fault. Besides the single witness's evidence against Barrington Smallin, the prosecution's prize exhibit consisted of his finger- and palm-prints on pieces of newspaper strewn around the flat and photographed by the police at the scene of the crime. Plainly, if these were proved, Smallin's defence – that he was never there, that this was a case of mistaken identity based partly on the fact that white witnesses tend to think many blacks look alike – collapsed. It was the defence's contention that although Smallin's prints were incontestably on the newspaper, the relevant pieces were not the ones in the pictures but had been planted later among the exhibits, having been seized from one of Smallin's places of abode after the pictures were taken.

This argued for an elaborate conspiracy. It put the police in a disgraceful light, having taken a risk for which they needed, among other things, a strong motive. The defence decided to supply this in the form of Smallin's past record, which would normally, of course, have been withheld from the jury. But the defence produced a litany of brushes with the law, some of them serious, showing Smallin to have been a hardened juvenile criminal – but one who had sometimes escaped the penalties the police thought he deserved. This, the defence implied, was the big one: the moment the police thought they could nail Barrington Smallin and put him away for a long time.

Repudiating this subterfuge, however, was not assisted by what happened next. A crucial piece of evidence was mysteriously found to be missing. One of the newspapers most plainly visible in the police photographs suddenly turned out to have gone astray from the bag of evidence supposedly being kept in a secure place before the trial. Although this was not the incriminating item with prints on it, it was the salient piece that would most cogently attest to the claim that the papers in the picture and the papers presented as exhibits in court were the same papers: i.e., that the police were honest and the defence case was a pack of lies.

For the police, therefore, to have mislaid so vital an exhibit was a serious misfortune. The young detective constable in charge of the case, a Scotsman, DC Neil Murray, had no explanation for it. The solicitor from the Crown Prosecution Service – 'if service is the word,' the judge fumed – was absent from court at the moment when Mr Williams needed to produce the crucial newspaper. But it never appeared, even after a night to search for it. The defence counsel did not miss his moment.

Mr Philip Levy was a reassuring specimen of the kind of legal service available among the advocates hacking round the unchronicled crown courts of London. One must assume that, in keeping with the cab-rank principle of the Bar, Mr Levy does prosecution as well as defence work, but his demeanour on this occasion was that of a hardened defender. It is doubtless possible that DC Murray will some time find himself in court among the officers Mr Levy is leading rather than opposing, but one would have to assume that their professional relations might be a little strained in view of the disdainful manner in which counsel put it to the detective that he had cooked up the whole case of R v. Smallin, culminating with this mysterious loss of a vital supportive piece of evidence.

Mr Levy, a small man, with an interrogating style even slower than that of prosecutor Williams, none the less had an air of menace about him. Although his cross-examinations sometimes seemed forlorn, they carried a sense of heavy, if impenetrable, moment. When it became clear what he was seeking to show, his delivery accelerated and his lucidity became unmistakable. By the end of the evidence and the closing speeches, the weight of probabilities seemed to hang puzzlingly in the balance.

It was the judge's turn to hold the floor. Judge Jarlath John Finney. A circuit judge, *Who's Who* reveals, since 1986. Born in 1930, an habitué of the South-east Circuit, as barrister, recorder and judge for more than thirty-five years, and according to one of the middle-aged lady ushers whose job is to keep this show on the road, their steady favourite among the judges at Wood Green.

Judge Finney had thus far been a swift and vigilant presider: helpful to the witnesses, exigent towards the barristers, unpatronizingly courteous in his remarks to the jury as they were shuffled in and out of court while points of law were decided in their absence. He had his ways of lightening the wearisome days, revealing, for example, a Mastermind's ability to convert any imperial measure into metric equivalents in his head. This head, moreover, proclaimed a desire to escape from the imposed anonymity of his profession. Beneath the depersonalizing wig and above the uniform robes, Judge Finney cultivates a rich growth of facial hair suspended from his cheeks and tonsured at the jaw-line.

His address to the jury was a model performance. Since the law involved in the case was neither complex nor disputed, he had less to do than usual. By far the judge's most useful function is to remind the jury of the early evidence. He has taken a copious note, and can therefore recreate on the last day what is easily forgotten from the first. Judge Finney was good at this, in a calm and unloaded way. The only deviation that might have been held against him occurred when he was dealing with the plausibility of the defence's dramatic accusation, and in the course of this described one of the police witnesses, a civilian scenes-of-crime officer, as 'an independent expert'. This was not the most credible depiction of a man who, while not in uniform, works day after day alongside police officers. But this was a blemish. For the rest, Judge Finney dispatched us to decision with a clear and balanced remit.

At this point my story must become more obscure. So far everything I've written derives from being a mere observer, albeit one who was concentrating more than usual, in a public court. It would be open to anyone who turned up to make the same report. Once in the jury room, however, the law intervenes. Not only must jurors refrain from discussing the case with anyone while it's going on, but what is said in the jury room is protected by the Contempt of Court Act. I do not intend to break it by describing the course of our deliberations.

Some impressions can be conveyed, however. The first and overarching one is of our almost agonizing honesty. We were together for more than five hours, isolated from the world until we finished. At the start, there was a wide variety of opinion about the charges, the resolution of which was not assisted in any way by the inadequacy with which the police and prosecutor had presented their case. A finding of not guilty would have been crippling for the police. Although it could just about have been brushed aside as merely a technical failure to meet the normal test of guilt 'beyond reasonable doubt', the message shining more luridly out would have been that this was another frame-up. To a remarkable extent it was the jury, making its own examination of the evidence, including the exhibits and the photos sent in with it, who saved the police from this humiliating outcome and decided, unanimously, that there could be no trace of a doubt about Smallin's guilt.

This jury conformed to few of the familiar caricatures. Everyone could read and write, all without exception paid close attention to everything that was said, each one of us was palpably anxious to do our duty. Newspapers on display ranged from the *Sun* to the *Guardian*. In five hours of intensive discussion, it becomes pretty clear what people's arguments are made of, and in all that time not the faintest trace of racially-based opinion entered anyone's discourse. What people wanted was certainty and more. Even after certainty became clear, no hypothetical possibility was left unexamined, however outlandish, to test the possibility that Barrington Smallin might indeed, despite everything, have been framed.

Two thoughts especially impressed me as the court process neared its end. The first was that we were fortunate to be conducting it in the perfect laboratory circumstance: when the case started, we knew nothing whatever about Mr Smallin or any details of his life and work. This was the situation jury trial aspires to, where no pre-existing prejudice pollutes the course of justice.

The rules of court designed to this end often seem irksome. Not only does the jury come with empty minds; the way the case develops often contrives, especially at the start, to leave them confused. This is not a straightforward unfolding of the story, but one which is marked by obscure silences and mysteriously unput questions. Slowly you sense you are getting a case from which the procedural formalities exclude the search for total truth. At moments one wants to scream at the barrister to ask the obvious question, and one could never be sure in this case why he hadn't asked it. All the same, this sense of watching a case from a position of fresh innocence, through a glass that filters out some of the surrounding 'reality', is an aid to judgement. It made me look with new respect on the problems that must confront everyone concerned in any case where, through prior publicity, it is impossible to assemble a jury guaranteed to know nothing more than it hears in court. That seems to me, by definition, a seriously different trial experience even though the law does not say so.

Secondly, an invaluable accessory before the fact of jury service is television. It was slowly borne in on me that we English probably make good jurors partly because of the diet of whodunnits that contributes to so much of our television intake.

The law, in this respect, is quite different from politics. Take twelve good persons and true, and you couldn't rely on getting a decent political discussion going between them. Many would not even want to begin. But offer them witnesses to believe, facts to sort out, policemen to suspect, a judge to be wary of, barristers to scorn, evidence to examine, and you find that inside the skin of the average Englishman and woman there runs the blood of a meticulous, undeceivable descendant of Sherlock Holmes.

This was a case of Sherlock multiplied by twelve: each recalling different parts of the evidence, each assisting the others to piece the bits together, each displaying a mind ready to be persuaded of the truth. It was the most serious Platonic dialogue in which I have ever engaged. What it did not do, however, was to determine the final fate of Barrington Smallin. Finding him guilty was not quite the end of the story. He then had to be sentenced, which was where Judge Finney contributed his own lapse from perfection in my book, and called to mind another set of the problems to which Lord Runciman's Royal Commission should be addressing itself.

How and why judges pass sentence the way they do is already the subject of an abundant literature. In David Hare's play, *Murmuring Judges*, which no one interested in these matters should miss while it's in repertory at the National, the debate about sentencing policy comes out of the mouths of a High Court judge and the Home Secretary, perambulating in their black ties before a grand dinner at one of the Inns of Court.

Judicial independence, ventures the judge, is part of an infinitely precious tradition. The Home Secretary agrees but tentatively suggests there is always time to change. Picking his way delicately round the subject, he finally lets rip. 'To be frank,' he gasps, 'we're reaching the point where we'll run out of ways of requesting the judiciary to be less *trigger-happy*. We've nowhere to put these bloody prisoners you keep sending us,' he finally explodes. To which the judge retorts with a smooth, well-honed speech about how judges must decline to become 'an instrument of government convenience'. It is a telling scene, full of the velvety dialogue of the British establishment classes.

Barrington Smallin's crimes were serious, with grievous violence done. Moreover, he had been violent before and had not responded to non-custodial sentences with which he was favoured as a juvenile. All the same, a certain shock attended Judge Finney's abrupt exercise of his independence, compared with any number of other sentences handed down for offences involving as much or greater violence. With a five-minute lecture, he sent Smallin to prison for nine years.

The compromising of Lord Hoffman

THIS WEEK'S epic court case in the Lords would not be happening but for two men. One is General Pinochet. To him, a kind of life or death hangs on the outcome. But the other accessory before the fact cannot be forgotten. Lord Hoffmann's failure to disclose his links with Amnesty aborted the ground-breaking decision another batch of law lords made in November. The circumstances of that abortion leave a stain on the British judiciary which the system is doing its best to explain away as an unfortunate little accident. It wasn't little and it wasn't an accident.

Last Friday, Hoffmann's brethren released their reasons for ruling, before Christmas, that the decision he assisted could not stand. Perhaps because it was a Friday, the reasons attracted little comment. By historic standards, the lords were quite severe. They said clearly that the Amnesty link was an 'automatic disqualification' to Hoffmann sitting. But they didn't explicitly criticize him, and did not find him guilty of apparent, still less actual, bias. They let him off as lightly as they could.

More particularly, they decided not to examine what had happened inside the appellate committee when the first lot of judges were preparing to hear the case. This was, said Lord Browne-Wilkinson, 'irrelevant': as indeed it was, to the narrow issue they chose to frame. Did Hoffmann disclose his Amnesty link to his colleagues? Was it discussed? Did they disagree as to what should follow? Or did the entire case proceed in the ignorance with which, even after it was over, the Amnesty lawyers sought to enshroud the link, leaving it, as Browne-Wilkinson recounts the matter, to be revealed only by an anonymous phone call to Pinochet's solicitors?

Though these questions weren't addressed, they're in some ways the heart of the matter. As far as the credence owed to the law lords goes, they are crucial. Having talked around in their lordships' purlieus, I can't believe Lord Hoffmann failed to mention his link. Yet equally it is clear that, if he mentioned it, he wasn't compelled by his colleagues either to declare it or withdraw from the case. If they proposed such action, he refused. And having been permitted to stay in the case even after Amnesty had entered it as an interested party, he now has the opportunity to say that he was not guilty: that by failing to exclude him, his fellow law lords condoned what he did.

This seems a feeble talk-out for what we now know, even from the careful, sometimes convoluted, language of the Browne-Wilkinson court, to have been the judge's indefensible conflict of interest. In fact it has shocking implications. And unfortunately, this is not the first time Lord Hoffmann has skated to the edge of judicial propriety. In the summer of 1996, he allowed himself to be used by some desperate politicians to further their ends by exploiting his status as a judge.

The Major government was embroiled in trying to help the Tory MP, Neil Hamilton, in his desire to sue the *Guardian* for libel. Hamilton found himself obstructed by a clause in the 1688 Bill of Rights, which appears to define parliamentary privilege as not only giving absolute protection to anything an MP says in the House, but as preventing the courts from examining any aspect of an MP's parliamentary conduct. Since the issue was cash for questions, and the defence needed to go into precisely that, the court found Hamilton to be in balk and the case was stopped.

To give Hamilton another chance – and in so doing, the government hoped, shore up its own reputation in the sleaze wars – ministers decided on the extraordinary course of rewriting the great constitutional document of 1688 via an amendment to the Defamation Bill then passing through Parliament. They were aware this might look bad. They needed it to appear non-political, which, indeed, Lord Chancellor Mackay claimed it was. There was no official 'view upon the matter' he said. The government were 'neutral'.

The agent of this subterfuge, wittingly or not, was Lord Hoffmann. He met with the Lord Chancellor and the Tory chief whip, and agreed to bless the government's case for the Hamilton amendment by giving his name and speech to a new clause drafted by official draftsmen. His authority as a law lord was cited by

Mackay as proof of the apolitical nature of the amendment: itself a depiction falling disgracefully below the standards of exactitude to be expected of a Lord Chancellor, since the bill was unofficially whipped through by the government, supported in the lobbies by many ministers, and later bragged about as such by Prime Minister Major, who once asked an interrogator: 'Why did I help steer a bill through the House of Commons so that Neil Hamilton could take his case to court?'

Hamilton's part in this grotesquerie came to an abrupt end when he copped out of the libel action that then resumed. The constitutional alteration was all for nothing. Moreover, in time, the piece of work done that day has been heavily attacked. After the 1997 election, in the wake of the travesty, a joint parliamentary committee was set up to study the state of privilege. This hasn't yet reported, but virtually every witness addressing the point has testified against the hasty formulation which Mackay, Major and Hoffmann fathered between them.

For Lord Hoffmann to have been involved with such a crew was quite mistaken. He displayed his own tentative awareness of that by the half-baked expedient of withholding his vote from the amendment which he himself proposed and moved. A bizarre piece of double-think. Perhaps a parallel can be found between this concession to conflicted interest in the Defamation Bill and the tortuous mental process by which, though voting to extradite Pinochet, Hoffmann, unusually, declined to deliver a reasoned judgement.

One lesson of this saga is that serving law lords have no proper future as legislators. Dabbling in statutory amendment may occasionally be a proper use of their expertise, but it is vulnerable to politics and breaches the separation of powers, as Lord Hoffmann is not the only judge to have shown. The coming reform of the second chamber should address this. But secondly, Hoffmann has done damage that can't be undone. His recklessness is solely responsible for what is now unfolding *in re* Pinochet. His own credibility as a judge – impeccable repository of detachment, sagacity and an unseducible engagement with justice – is shot to pieces. He should break another precedent, and go back to advocacy.

The judges become politicians

IT ALL BEGINS WITH Lord Slynn of Hadley, a man you may not have heard of. By rights, having been there the longest, Lord Slynn should soon become the senior law lord, the top man in Britain's top court. But he will not. The prospect of Lord Slynn gliding into place when the present senior, Lord Browne-Wilkinson, retires, though precedent dictated it should happen, was unacceptable. He is highly qualified, and the only professional public lawyer on the bench of twelve, but he was, they said, too erratic, somehow too thin, maybe a little wanting in his output.

Something better, they thought, was needed. The legal system may soon be facing a crisis. When the Human Rights Act comes into operation in October, there will be a deluge of cases, and the need, therefore, for powerful leadership from the top to make sense of it. So a unique judicial reshuffle is set in motion, more significant than many Cabinet manoeuvres of the same name. It is not entirely the work of one man. The aforementioned opinion of Lord Slynn, though obliterated from all public talk, is commonplace in the most ferociously gossipy profession in England. But among the 'they' in question who have decided it, Lord Chancellor Irvine is first, and the rest are nowhere.

The politics of the personal is not unimportant here. It needed a big name to upset the Slynn succession, and nobody comes bigger than the Lord Chief Justice, Lord Bingham, who now moves in. Into Bingham's place comes Lord Woolf, the man who many lawyers said should have had that job in the first place but didn't get it, as many also thought, because Lord Mackay, the then occupant of Irvine's Woolsack, sensed Woolf's political unacceptability. Woolf was and is a penal liberal. Bingham was a clever man with no criminal form. Having done four years in a job that did not suit him, Bingham is translated to suit the game plan of another Lord Chancellor. Never, please, imagine judicial appointments are as devoid of the human, intensely political, touch as they are made to seem.

But that's not the end of it. A bigger fish thrashes round this pond. The fate of Lord Irvine himself, the masterful reshuffler, comes into view. Bingham moves from controlling the lower court system to leading the law lords at a time of acute controversy, looming but not yet quite upon us. The new entwinement of law and politics will put him fiercely to the test on two fronts.

First, he arrives in a court that is becoming heavily overloaded with work. The law lords handle not only the final appeals from British courts but, wearing other hats, have been in heavy demand as the judicial committee of the Privy Council, a hangover from the old Commonwealth. A recent spate of death-row appeals from the Caribbean has preoccupied them: cases in which, one told me yesterday, 'we can't field the second eleven'. The regular House of Lords work is getting behind, the ungiven judgements are piling up.

To this will soon be added Human Rights Act cases, where Bingham is expected to give a lead in law-making. Suddenly judges will become more exposed to a quasi-political atmosphere, requiring them to go beyond the letter of arid statute and investigate its connection with larger principles. As an early advocate of this reform, Bingham is well qualified for the job. He is a commercial, not a public lawyer, more the chilly intellectual than a man like Woolf, who connects easily with humanity and received an indelible penal education when conducting the Strangeways Prison inquiry. But Bingham has been good, for example, on free speech issues. He knows the ground.

This is a period when all courts are under pressure. The Human Rights Act is part of a wider public appetite to settle more by law than by politics. The law lords have the same kind of problem, writ a bit smaller, as the European Court of Justice, which groans under a weight of cases that its president said this week was insupportable. We live in an age of litigation for which society is chronically reluctant to provide adequate resources – unless, belatedly, the politics of asylum seekers makes a sudden demand for action. In these circumstances, it will be good to have the top court operating at the highest horsepower.

The very trend that is helping to produce a crisis of resources presents another kind of challenge to courts and judges, on which Lord Bingham may turn out to be a less dependable beacon. We must watch how he performs. Is he, at bottom, an establishment conservative, which means a judicial politician? Or is he a steely visionary, in favour of judges who are genuinely independent of politics?

The Human Rights Act will draw judges more into the political realm. Privacy, free speech, prisoners' rights and the right to life – all can involve both policy and politics. To begin with, the cases will come rushing forward, and some will have to go the distance. Conflicts between the Westminster and Edinburgh parliaments, which law lords have to judge under their Privy Council hats, will also have irreducibly political reverberations. The Irvine–Bingham regime – for that is what it will be, an alliance between two colleagues already very intimately acquainted – inaugurates a period of constitutional activism never before experienced by English law.

This requires a response that may seem paradoxical. The more political judges find themselves becoming in their legal work, the more resolutely apolitical they need to be at every other time. Their independence is on the line, and needs to be impeccable. They can afford no conflict of powers. This should mean the law lords withdrawing from all legislative work. Already a dubious luxury, a typically English mess, such double-hatting is now unacceptable, as several law lords seem to have accepted by quietly ceasing to speak or vote in second-chamber debates. Bingham has not done that. He intervened, for example, in strong support of Jack Straw's selective abolition of jury trial. To establish his scrupulous absence from the club of government, he should follow the lead of Lord Steyn and others, and renounce any role as a legislator.

At the apex of the double-hatted pyramid sits the Lord Chancellor: judge, minister, lawyer, politician, appointer-in-chief of judges who are supposed to have no rival avocation. He fights to keep all these hats, contriving to argue, with the speciousness that once made him millions, that only thus can his own and everyone else's independence be preserved. But the enemies of this self-serving rationale are closing in. Human rights law, with perfect symmetry, encroaches. In parallel cases probing judicial independence, the Strasbourg court is eating Irvine's case away. When the final test arrives, and Irvine is being preserved by politics alone, will Bingham have the guts to chuck the man who put him where he is?

Varieties of coercion

The murder of a journalist

NEWSPAPERS ARE NOT FAMOUS for sensitivity or restraint. Beating the competition into the ground provides a nervy and obsessive dynamic. One might have thought, none the less, that there were occasional exceptions to this rule: moments of sufficient enormity to penetrate the moral carapace of the *Daily Mail*, and for which the justification was sufficiently thin to persuade even those masters of perversity who control the inner regions of the *Sunday Telegraph* that here was one issue on which they were excused from bringing to bear their talent for patronizing derision.

Such an event, on the face of it, was the murder in Iraq last week of Farzad Bazoft. Although journalists these days die distressingly often in combat, innocent victims caught in the crossfire, the instances of their 'trial' and execution are rare. Here, however, was a man arrested in Iraq while on a journalistic assignment, held incommunicado, denied access to diplomatic help, brought to court for a secret trial without independent observers present, convicted on the basis of a confession extracted without the smallest safeguards, and hanged as a spy in defiant scorn for the opinion of the world. No Western government has proffered the smallest shred of justification for this chain of events; and none, one might have thought, existed. Such a judgement, however, proves grossly to have underestimated the ingenuity of the British press.

It soon emerged that Mr Bazoft's inhuman end could be softened in its impact by the disclosure that he had a record as a petty criminal. In fact, the more one chatted up former landladies and retired policemen, the shadier the fellow seemed to be. These discoveries were sometimes set against the reminder that his execution was, of course, very shocking. But the shock of it, to the unwary reader of the tabloid press, could be comfortably dispelled by these revelations of his fallibility, and of the *Observer*'s equal fallibility in employing such a character.

The next shock-absorber was the reminder that he was, after all, Iranian. Not a white man, not one of us, but a Middle Easterner himself and one who came from the wrong side of all matters Iraqi and should never have been near the place. This overlooked the fact that he was visiting Iraq for the sixth time as a guest of the Iraqi government, and that his credentials were as an anti-Khomeini Iranian who was *persona grata* in Baghdad. But the impression began to solidify: whatever happened to him was his own fault.

The clincher in this dossier was the suggestion that he was probably an Israeli – or was it perhaps a British? – spy. Offering themselves as authorities on this point were a variety of Conservative MPs: among them a former alderman from Birmingham, named Beaumont-Dark, who has been encouraged by the BBC and many newspapers to believe that there is no subject, however far from his experience, on which his opinion should not be taken seriously: and, more notably, a young man sometimes named Allason, whose immersion in subterfuge begins with his choice to go by a different name when he writes his books. The reckless suggestion that Bazoft was a spy, coming from someone whose literary work has brought him into close contact with the security services, conferred on itself a veneer of authority and was, all things considered, utterly irresponsible. But the tabloids loved it.

So did the *Sunday Telegraph*. Here, after the days of judicious rumination which are luxuriantly available to a Sunday newspaper, we reached the heart of the matter. The suspicion that Mr Bazoft might be slightly culpable was hardened into an all-encompassing explanation. For what he had been engaged on in Iraq was 'investigative journalism'. And between investigative journalism and spying, the *Telegraph* suggested, there might well be no definable distinction. So Mr Bazoft really brought the entire thing on himself. Bad luck, Farzad, for having had someone so idiotic as the *Observer* editor to send you to your death. Apart from a glancing reference to the 'horror' of the execution, the *Telegraph* wasted no tears on what happened.

This piece was not signed. It was an editorial 'opinion' from a coterie of journalists, it is fair to deduce, whose scorn for investigative journalism is matched by the extreme infrequency with which any of them has been known to insert a new fact into the public realm. Investigating nothing, save that which will confirm their unbreakable political prejudices, they yet have the effrontery to equate other people's efforts with spying, for which the ultimate penalty must, alas, in some circumstances be paid.

So remote was the *Telegraph* from fact-gathering disciplines that it could not even tell the story straight. It said the *Observer* sent Bazoft to Iraq five times, when the truth was that Iraq invited him six times, on two of which he offered stories, as a freelance writer, to the *Observer*. On this uncertain base, the pride of Tory Sunday journalism produced the most weaselling and morally insensate explanation that the Iraqi government can ever have expected to read: a propaganda gift from Peregrine Worsthorne to Saddam Hussein, with a subtext for Western eyes which says that investigative journalism is a punishable offence against the state.

Thus was an event of utmost horror rendered banal, even excusable. The deed was done not by politicians, criticizing journalists for some reason of *realpolitik*: all senior politicians, in fact, have been resolute in seeing the issue for what it is. The damage comes instead from journalists rounding on one of their own, on the paper he was working for, on the very function their profession is supposed to perform. The thirst to criticize and undermine, by publishing unverified allegations which all available evidence tends to refute, somehow exceeded and then completely obscured the scale of what happened in Baghdad last week. The first casualty of the circulation war is a sense of proportion.

Before Farzad Bazoft's name recedes over the horizon, let it be said clearly what happened. He was a journalist. He tried to get a legitimate story. He may have been naïve but by no code of justice did he deserve the gallows. Nor does Baghdad deserve one sentence of validating comfort. Bazoft was a victim, foully murdered. Period.

Terrorism against liberty

LAW, ONE OF THE FEW disciplines conventionally supposed to be above politics, is the most politicized of all the areas politicians grapple with. By 'politicized' I don't mean divided by party but united by sloganizing ignorance. Law and order is where politics enjoys its greatest ascendancy over discoverable fact. Many criminal problems are not amenable to categoric proof concerning the links between cause, effect and deterrent action. Even their scale is a matter of serious dispute. But instead of generating agnostic humility, this only intensifies the certainty with which remedies are proposed. Politicians vie to redouble popular fears, and allay them with populist responses.

The surge of panic about juvenile crime is a good example. A small number of cases, including a single quite horrific one, ignites a smoulder of introspection about the terrible state of youth today. It is inflamed by justifiable alarm concerning trends in a variety of fields, from drugs to joyriding. But the figures, awkwardly, do not entirely support the case. Home Office research shows that the number of known male criminals aged 10 to 17 has fallen by 32 per cent since 1985. Among those aged 10 to 13 the fall is 43 per cent. These are not marginal changes. Ostensibly they look like a rare case for public gratitude. Ministers might take some credit. Instead, because the figures get in the way of the alarmism they sense is at large, they say the figures must be wrong, and Mr Clarke pulls £75 million out of the hat to keep the public happy.

The Prevention of Terrorism Act (PTA), which comes to the Commons for renewal tomorrow, excites more invincible feelings of rectitude. It says it's against terrorism, doesn't it? Anything against terrorism must be good, mustn't it? Anyone against the Act must be in favour of terrorism, mustn't they? Let every suspect bomber be held as long as it takes. Let every suspect Irishman be sent back to Belfast without the option. Let the law do its worst against these bastards. I am prone to feel these surges myself, especially when travelling on the underground.

Labour, therefore, faces a hard political task when it opposes the renewal of the Act tomorrow, as it has done for many years. The party is an easy mark for the Tories on all these counts, to which will certainly be added the charge that Labour supports the IRA. With the government's back against so many walls, intimidation supplants rational argument. So Labour's consistent critique of the PTA is a reason to doubt the party's bona fides across the entire range of home affairs. Desperate men easily trot out the line. Even though it is untrue on all counts.

The PTA is a formidable measure. Passed after forty hours' debate in the wake of the 1974 bombings, it provides for arrest and detention without cause shown for seven days, and empowers the Home Secretary to impose exclusion orders sending residents of Britain back to the province. It greatly strengthens police powers to override civil rights whenever the police say they have reason to suspect terrorist-connected activity. Short of arrest, it provides for a massive amount of stopping and questioning that goes unrecorded. In the name of the anti-terrorist campaign, it legitimizes petty harassment, especially of Irish people in this country, on a grand scale.

It has not, in fact, been the source of any great swelling abuse. The numbers of people detained have remained fairly steady in the past few years. Although a species of police state in this respect exists, it is not expanding. But of those numbers, 160 last year, few are finally charged. Many are held in bad and demeaning circumstances for several days without charge or lawyer, in what is at best a fishing expedition for information they might or might not possess.

Of the 7,000 people detained under the Act since 1974, only 3 per cent have been charged under its provisions, and 4 per cent with other offences. Now these other offences are often heinous. They include murder, conspiracy or possession of explosives. But it is the case against the Act that most, if not all, the terrorists charged with such offences, or arrested on suspicion of them, could have been handled under the normal law of the land.

The Police and Criminal Evidence Act permits four-day, not seven-day, detention without charge. The police raid in Stoke Newington last week didn't need the extraordinary powers of the PTA. But they were, of course, deployed. Such is the habit of authority. If the law supplies a little bit extra, make sure it is used.

The Labour Party, which, long ago, was responsible for introducing the measure – Home Secretary Jenkins said at the time that it would last six months – has, alongside its overall opposition since 1983, proposed some reforms. When Douglas Hurd was Home Secretary, it privately pressed the case for subjecting the second half of any seven-day detention to the approval of the court.

Hurd was apparently sympathetic, but the judges, to their shame, let it be known that they preferred not to be involved. This year, Kevin McNamara, a Labour spokesman with impeccable anti-terrorist credentials, suggested a bipartisan approach, in which the party would support four-day detention with an improvement in the rules of interrogation and an end to the exclusion orders – a form of internal exile within the United Kingdom – which the government's own official, Lord Colville, has more than once attacked.

This was a sensible idea, which Kenneth Clarke instantly rejected. The official culture could never conceive of shedding powers it now has, even though their unique value is a matter only of assertion. But Mr Clarke would also be loath to lose an issue on which Labour can be made, in the degraded rhetoric that dominates the law and order debate, to look soft.

This is inconvenient for Tony Blair, Labour's Shadow Home Secretary, who has made a balanced pitch on current alarms, roughly halfway between panic and reassurance. He may be tempted to begin narrowing the principled aspect of Labour's stance on the PTA. He should not do so. The party has absolutely nothing for which to apologize. It is as opposed to terrorism as every other sane resident of these islands. All it challenges is the claim that the PTA is the only way of proving it. The Act is a distinct infringement of civil liberties. It lowers Britain's reputation. It forces Britain to evade the European Convention. It is an instrument of arbitrary power.

For all this, the justification needs to be unanswerable. What ministers say, by defaming all their critics, is that this burden does not lie with them.

The secret services declare themselves

ACROSS THE THAMES from the Tate Gallery, a new building declares itself with some flamboyance. Yellow and green, with receding terraced ledges, it looks like a ziggurat, standing out a mile from the concrete boxes around it. It could be a luxury hotel. In fact it's the new headquarters of MI6, the secret service, and its presence there is matched, on the Westminster side of the river, by an old building, expensively refurbished, the new headquarters of MI5. Together they constitute one of the unrecognized wonders of 1994.

For most of their existence, these agencies were based in dingy structures in south and north London respectively. When there was an incontestable need for their services, in a world filled with enemies of the state at home and abroad, MI5 and MI6 lived in a physical secrecy which matched the common pretence that they didn't exist. Hardly anyone knew where they were. Their offices hid in the shadows associated with their trade.

Exactly coinciding with the change in the world they're supposed to police, they have now gone public. In the US, this change has led to a debate about whether the CIA should not be abolished. In London, the CIA's counterparts have taken up grander establishments, defying anyone to spit them in the eye. It is an extraordinary coda to the Cold War, which some may suppose is part of a benign move towards greater public accountability, but which in fact says something else.

What we learn from the agencies' shift out of Euston and Lambeth into the heart of Westminster is not that they are regularizing their presence, but that their bureaucratic clout has by no means diminished in step with their relevance to the problems that face the country now. It was a formidable achievement for MI6 to capture its Thames ziggurat. It was even more impressive for the head of MI5, the famous Stella Rimington, to take her agency so close to Scotland Yard, whose functions she has already been successful in usurping.

All this happened with virtually no questions asked. The secret world is striding more brazenly into mainstream life. The Russians may be puppy-dogs, and the IRA may be trying to become our friends, but the machinery of doubt, and the weaponry of deceit and disinformation, are being kept in lavish working order. And this is sensible enough. The world is an uncertain place. But the legitimizing of MI6, like the Dimbleby-lecturing normality of Mrs Rimington, underlines what is for me the enduring moral of the Richard Gott affair: which is that for journalists to have dealings of any kind with the secret service of any country makes them a likely tool of the paranoia which is the professional condition of all secret services.

About twenty years ago, I had a memorable experience of this paranoia. I was calling on a minister from the lately fallen Cabinet of Edward Heath. Taking my coat, he told me that the man I had passed on the pathway to his door was the security chap who used to look after him when he was in power. He 'keeps me up to date', said the former minister who, it turned out, had discovered while in office evidence to support an attitude of unrebuttable clarity towards his political opponents. He had 'seen the files', he said. These had shown him that at least four of the top Labour politicians now in power were 'Muscovites'. He knew it for a fact. And he averred that one of them, Denis Healey, would, as far as he was concerned, preferably end up as 'a pool of blood on the pavement'.

In bearing and repute, this minister seemed a sane fellow, who later gave his party and the world distinguished service under Mrs Thatcher. But he was seized of a conviction, irrespective of observable evidence, which became an icy obsession concerning the other side. It was the same stuff of which was made the alleged plot by MI5 to destabilize the Wilson government and, just as important, Wilson's own obsession with the unverified existence of such a plot.

This condition is chronic among intelligence and security people. Arguably, their job is to harbour it. No doubt if more people at the *Guardian* had done so, the case of Richard Gott would have ended sooner and differently. But it makes secret services of every stripe a poisoned well for journalists, a devil with whom there is no merit, and much danger, in supping. This much is true, whichever side the secret world is coming from. Although clandestine consorting with the KGB is less defensible than secret contacts with the CIA, behind the old barriers journalists erect to protect their sources, the damage to the press can be just as great.

Common prudence suggests as much. I see no reason why MI6 or the CIA should be any more relied on than the KGB not to blackmail or expose a journalistic contact if it suited them to do so. They could be sure that, even on the *Sunday Telegraph*, such a revelation − perhaps even a revelation only half-proved − that the Foreign Editor, for example, took regular hospitality from MI6 would be something he would prefer his readers, and maybe his editor, not to know. It would be, or should be, professional death.

For me, therefore, the arrival of the secret world on the banks of the Thames is not a cause for rejoicing, but the most severe of cautions. It has very little to do with greater openness. It pretends to demystify their world, and make us more comfortable about them. I met a man at a party not long ago who told me the top rank he occupied in the service and, when I expressed mild surprise, proudly displayed his candour as living proof of the new, more open ethos that now gripped MI6. Even a *Guardian* journalist, he implied, was now on the same, trusted side.

But we are not. No journalist could be. These agencies' emergence into the high-rent district signifies not their waning sense of self-protection but their growing power. They are not afraid to announce their central role in government. Like every other department of government, their interests coincide only marginally with those of a free press that sets its own agenda and discovers its own truth. They're not a national enemy, like the KGB, but they are a professional enemy. They want to twist our words and steer our pens, and their interest in a conversation is not to pass the time of day, still less to assist us in reliably deepening our version of the facts.

During the Gott affair, Peregrine Worsthorne proudly announced what agreeable dinners he had eaten at the expense of the CIA. Because the Americans were on our side, he chortled, this was perfectly OK. Maybe that explains why, every week, the *Sunday Telegraph* shows how little it knows or cares about journalism, on just about every subject, that is not loaded in one direction.

Playing the race card

THE RACE CARD usually lands face down on the table. Its potency is surreptitious, and its playing, by otherwise respectable politicians, is always deniable. It is the joker that nobody at the despatch box would dream of admitting he or she possessed. But a party in desperate political trouble has persuaded itself that this card, though more like the deuce than the ace of spades, offers one of the few trumps with which it can be sure of taking a trick.

The Asylum and Immigration Bill, which began passage through the Commons yesterday, is not, of course, an overtly racist measure. The back of the card is clean enough. The bill's severities, which are without precedent in Britain, will apply to Bosnian and Nigerian alike in flight from oppression. It will abolish legal rights, destroy the relevance of appeal and, in an accompanying trick, withdraw social benefits so as to make it impossible for thousands of people to keep body and soul together long enough to exercise their rights anyway. But it is true that the victim of this could as easily be a Latvian as a Sudanese.

The race card, however, isn't confined by such subtle distinctions. It is blind to suits. What it addresses is the fear of influx, which in British history and psychology is coterminous with the immigration and/or asylum of non-whites. What it plays to is the evidence of private polling, done by both main parties, which shows that this issue, almost alone on the political agenda, is one where the Tories score better than Labour. We are, remember, at the beginning of an eighteen-month election campaign. Put crudely but not inaccurately, Labour is seen as being favourable to the advance and prospering of non-whites, and more people than not are ready to tell pollsters they don't like it. Here, as some Conservatives believe, lies a chance to limit the electoral disaster.

Many Tories, not least their leader, will be appalled to be labelled with such a strategy. Play the race card? What a nauseating insult to a Brixton boy. The party's innocence, however, depends on a belief in its good faith. Is its policy, in general and in particular, rooted in impulses that are manifestly decent – or indecent? The evidence is not encouraging.

The Asylum Bill does not fill a long-neglected need. Everyone knows there is immigration fraud, and not all asylum applications are justified. For a long time, the processing machinery has been getting clogged. But, barely three years ago, the Asylum and Immigration Appeals Act 1993 already both streamlined and restricted asylum appeals, especially for anybody arriving from homeland persecution through another country on the way. Designed to deter applicants, speed judgement, and curtail the grounds for appeal, the Act was draconian – but not enough.

The new bill moves with indecent haste to slam the door still tighter. These 'fast-track' appeals, to be exercised within ten days of a refused entry or not at all, will now be applied to almost all categories of asylum. Anyone coming from a so-called 'white list' of countries will face an insurmountable presumption that they do not qualify as persecuted individuals worthy of asylum: and white-list membership is at the supple discretion of the Home Office, which was once ready to designate both Nigeria and Algeria as quite safe. In virtually every case the power of the Home Office, to control supposedly independent adjudications by placing applicants within a category that preloads the case against them, will be increased.

The nooks and crannies of this pernicious bill, which will produce a great deal of misery with only minimal elimination of fraud, will be examined in the House. An idea of the attitudes that inform it, however, is already available from the performance of the new immigration minister, Ann Widdecombe, over two Nigerian asylum-seekers currently on the brink of deportation. The religious pieties that Ms Widdecombe took indelicately to flaunting earlier in the year seem to have left her political brutality, not to mention her Orwellian approach to moral philosophy, untouched.

Abiodun Igbindu and Ade Onibiyo are young Nigerians, both connected with the pro-democracy movement in their home country, who were about to be deported but who have now been granted, under intense political pressure, a few days' grace so as to exercise a final right of appeal. Ms Widdecombe's language in defending her insistence that they return may come from nothing more obnoxious than the school of political double-talk. She says that any applicant, even a democrat from Nigeria, must be able to prove he 'would be in individual danger'. But her mind-set, along with that of the minister, Mr Howard, who encourages and defends her, comes from the gutter, where any concept of moral decency is swilled down the drain of political opportunism.

Nigeria is a country affording no reliable promise of life, let alone freedom, to opponents of its ruling junta. Having recently hanged nine such, without benefit of fair trial, it has done more than most to demonstrate this beyond the most casuistical pretence. Mr Onibiyo's father, recently deported from Britain, hasn't been seen since. Yet Ms Widdecombe, insisting that each case must prove individual danger, refuses to admit even the most blatant general evidence in support of it. Only, it seems, when a Nigerian asylum-seeker turns up as a corpse at the gate of the British Embassy in Lagos might she and Mr Howard be satisfied that he was, after all, entitled to stay here.

This posture is so repellent, such a betrayal of the British tradition for supplying refuge against persecution, that it's hard to believe it will play well with very many voters. But, a reminder of the dark instincts some Tories, covertly venomous, are willing to satisfy, it constitutes the race card. And it presents Labour and Liberal Democrats with a problem. For the more they denounce the Tories, the more inexorably they help the card do its infamous work. Yet that is what they must do. They failed to get the bill sent to a standing committee, which was a sensible way of applying the test of evidence to its prejudices, and minimizing the injustice it will cause. These virtues made it, for the Home Office, unacceptable. But opposition must continue, on principle and in practice. For the only way to destroy the race card is to show, without the smallest ambiguity, that it cannot win.

Towards a police state

OVER THE POLICE and bugging, the road from complete public ignorance to a vestige of accountability is longer than we knew. We need to understand it. The Police Bill is by no means passed, and its iniquities are not extinguished. Jubilation over the passage of Opposition amendments on Monday is badly misplaced. Labour's amendment was, in fact, a fraud. It leaves Mr Howard in a mess, but that's not what matters. What matters is the bugging, the culture that permitted it for decades, the tolerance of it still by every governing politician and senior policeman, and the continuing inadequacy of the democratic response.

The House of Lords debate mattered far more than the result. It told, first of all, a story that hardly anybody knew. What it revealed was a laxness of practice and a casualness of attitude, about both law and truth, which show how unreliable is any authoritarian procedure that depends for its acceptance, as police bugging does, on the contention that the political system will ensure such powers are never abused.

The first discovery to come from the guardians of liberty was that police bugging – surveillance, device-planting, intrusion into private places of every kind – has been going on for literally more years than the Home Office can remember. Lord Callaghan (Home Secretary 1967–70) and Lord Carr (1972–4) said they had no knowledge of it in their time. To these pleas of ignorance, Lady Blatch, today's junior incumbent there, responded with a mixture of pity and incredulity. 'There were submissions to the department in those days about those activities,' she reproached Lord Callaghan. 'It is not possible for the noble Lord to say that none of these activities were taking place at that time.'

That she may be right is suggested by her next disclosure, that in

1977, the first year when some kind of record seems to have been kept, the number of times the police authorized their own buggings was '500 to 600'. The figure, she credibly claimed, can't have jumped from zero to 500 in a single year. Yet one must also believe Callaghan and Carr. They are unlikely simply to have forgotten. Callaghan was able to recall that the separate category of MI5 bugging, which he did have to authorize, added up to around 150 cases. Plainly, a massive quantity of police bugging was going on without a single politician even being informed.

We move to 1977. This was when the bugging came under 'guidelines' written in the Home Office. Callaghan by now was Prime Minister, but he said on Monday he had no idea about these guidelines either, and pronounced himself 'flabbergasted' that this system, of which he was entirely ignorant, had produced 500 to 600 buggings a year, which have now risen to more than 2,000 across the United Kingdom. The figures themselves, incidentally, are rounded up or down with an indifference to precision that surely signals a parallel insouciance about the bugging itself. Significantly, also, figures for the intervening years are just not available.

So that's one form of scandal: the readiness to tolerate unnumbered, uninvigilated police buggings. Another concerns the attitude to law. Here a further discovery emerged. Lord Browne-Wilkinson, a law lord, stated categorically that entry by the police on to private property without a warrant 'is today unlawful' and always has been. Lord Lloyd, another law lord, said: 'There can be no doubt that each one of those operations involved an unlawful trespass on private property', and was 'no less unlawful because they were carried out … in accordance with Home Office guide-lines'. Invited to respond to this, Lady Blatch said vaguely that the buggings were done 'under common law'. Every lawyer knows that to be unmitigated rubbish.

The official position is therefore as follows. There has been police bugging for many decades. It has always been unlawful. Some officials, and maybe some policemen if they hadn't lost all their moral faculties, knew it was unlawful. Successive Home Secretaries were kept in the dark and, whether out of idleness or lack of imagination, did not trouble to enlighten themselves. The bugging has continued, 'with a good deal of restraint' Lady Blatch proudly says, abated, she also pleaded, by the lack of resources for doing more. Every time she said that people's apprehensions of abuse could be set at rest merely by the tightness of police budgets, she revealed that her grasp of the principle is as slender as the thread which now protects all our freedoms.

This is the culture of apathy and negligence into which the Police Bill has been pitched. Only now have we learned the size of it. So appalling is this culture, so slap-happy and derisive of fundamental liberties, so steeped in secrecy and blind acquiescence, that one surely has to look pretty carefully at the statute designed to legitimize it. Prior approval by judges for police bugging does not stand a great chance of dramatically modifying the culture. But it would be something. However, it could be of value only if, in every case, it became the threshold a police chief had to cross before acquiring the lawful authority to trespass on these once-sacrosanct individual rights.

The Government, naturally, doesn't want that. Mr Howard is happy for the police to have every power they ask for. He finds it treasonable that anyone should think otherwise. But now, if he's to get the Police Bill through, he has to talk turkey with Jack Straw, who adjusted his party line and backed a role for Surveillance Commissioners, a cadre of present or former judges, to pre-scrutinize police requests.

The Howard–Straw conversations should be hard. In fact they may be all too smooth. For Labour's stance is essentially bogus. Yes to the commissioners – but yes, also, to exceptions. If it's 'not reasonably practicable' to seek prior approval, then this, Labour says, can be waived. Has there been a wider loophole through which a police chief will drive his surveillance machine? Since bugging is more likely than not to occur in an emergency, on what basis will any distinction be enforced between cases requiring prior consent and the rest? This is not a system of protection but the shoring-up, once again, of arbitrary power. Mr Howard shouldn't find it impossible to agree.

The Liberal Democrats, whose amendment the Lords also passed, are alone in taking a stance that begins to measure up to the ignominious history. They want a judge to handle every case. Home Secretary Straw, pretending to change his line, would differ from Home Secretary Callaghan only in that he knew what was going on.

One day to abolish a few freedoms

A CYNIC MIGHT SAY that the wisdom of Parliament was always going to be irrelevant to the Terrorism and Conspiracy Bill. With its majority, the government can force any measure through, whether the process lasts one day or a hundred. Any further debate than the single day in the Commons, and the next single day in the Lords, would therefore be academic.

Raison d'etat requires an answer now, the government insists. Yesterday Mr Blair and his ministers showed that they were, of all the cynics, the most cynical. They do not care what any elected politician has to say about the substantial change in law these clauses will effect.

A realist, equally, might argue that this is only right. Wasn't Omagh a terrible atrocity? Isn't the Real IRA a fragment of a fragment, and thus to be deposited in a special category suitable for extra-legal treatment? If Dublin, where draconian laws have been on the books for decades, is now prepared to turn the screw, how would we look if we failed to do the same? Doesn't *raison d'etat* mean that British–Irish lock-step congruity, above every other consideration, must rule this moment in British parliamentary process? Such was the argument pressed by Mr Blair, who has never before shown so completely how much he is a man of power and not a man of Parliament.

Neither the cynics nor the realists had a free run in the Commons yesterday. Led by Richard Shepherd, back-benchers declined to be unanimous in dumb acquiescence to the Blair–Straw interpretation of *raison d'etat*. They complained with bitter eloquence that the single day was neither adequate nor necessary.

For an hour, the first hour in the history of this government, the voices of disinterested principle wiped the floor with the stumbling ministerial vaporizers who barely attempted to answer their points. For this hour, the gravity of the Commons could be contrasted with the utter levity of the legislative process these ministers were determined to deploy.

The gravity was appropriate. The matters at stake are far larger than it suits ministers to recognize. Ministers ask us to put faith in the bill's minimal reach, its targeted approach, and the endlessly sensitive discretion with which it will be operated. Yet both parts of it are certain to compromise individual liberties and the rule of law.

The Irish part of the bill, which introduces the principle that a policeman's opinion is admissible in evidence to convict a suspect terrorist, was amended to say that this evidence would have to be corroborated. But how? The refusal of a suspect to speak will be enough. Corroboration need not consist of objective proof or other testimony, but simply the suspect's exercise of silence. Neither the opinion nor the silence will be solely sufficient, ministers piously insist. But the one, as they omit to say, will be enough to verify the other.

Silence, in effect, will be decisive. The existing rule of law is not being sustained, and nor are the rules of evidence. Yesterday, the successful spinning from Whitehall said suspects were being protected and there was nothing now to worry about. This is a travesty of the truth. For a narrow segment of suspect terrorists, who may not be terrorists at all, the rules are being drastically altered, and the courts invited to do their duty accordingly.

This is a matter on which Parliament should have something to say but in respect of which the sacks of potatoes lumpenly arrayed on the Labour benches voted for their own duty of silence. Accosted with complaints at their hysterical demand for speed, ministers retreated to a new legislative principle. The bill may turn out to be a bad law, they said, but we are providing for an annual review, so what does it matter? I can't recall, even in the lowest days of the Major government, such a combination of insensitivity to British norms, and ruthless indifference to the arguments against it, as we saw at the despatch box yesterday.

The second part of the bill shows this attitude at work with even more startling clarity. For some years, Whitehall has been searching for ways to respond to complaints from Middle East and Asian governments, with the US as their ally, that London is a haven for the enemies of local regimes. For just as long, officials have found a new law impossible to write.

Defining the foreign enemy, proving that he is a conspirator, distinguishing between freedom-fighters and terrorists: anyone who has studied the matter knows these are complex tasks. For the Commons to authorize the government's first-draft law in one day is a procedure that has a purely theoretical connection with deliberative democracy. Yet Mr Blair used this history not as a caution but, incredibly, as a defence. The global anti-terrorist law, he said, had been a 'long-held plan' and 'long on the stocks' – seemingly this disposed of the perverse anxiety that Parliament, dear old Parliament, might not have long enough to vet it. The fact that the Attorney-General, with the Foreign Secretary as a safety net, would be in charge of prosecutions was meant to allay fears. What it more aptly does is define the true nature of this entire measure: putting law at the service of politics, and individual liberties in the hands of a variety of Secretaries of State.

The Tory front bench – the official Opposition, invigilator of ministers – went blithely along with all this, seeking only to toughen it with outright internment. They were shown up by a handful of their back-benchers. The Liberal Democrats, while belatedly - whinging about the second part, were essentially compliant. They waved the Irish part through like redundant coalitionists, the party of liberty now reduced to flapping their acquiescent wrists: a contemptible spectacle.

There are principles at stake here, about the substance of the measures and about the role Parliament should play in considering whether they can be justifiably violated. This is solemn work. It is what we fight the terrorists to defend. But yesterday in the Commons, and today in the Lords, bear witness to the betrayal of due political process.

Stephen Lawrence and British racism

IN JASPER, ARKANSAS, right now, one sort of racist epiphany is being acted out. John 'Billy' King and two other white men are charged with murdering a black man, James Byrd, by chaining him to the back of a truck and dragging him three miles until his head was severed from his torso. This story does not summarize modern America, a society where the races quite often peacefully cohabit. But the event in Jasper is not universally detested there. The Ku Klux Klan has picketed the court-house. Racial violence is not only perpetrated but, sometimes, 'explained'. Think of Jasper in 1999, and you capture one defining picture of the current state of race relations in the USA.

Think of race in Britain today, and you think of Stephen Lawrence. The Lawrence inquiry has become our own defining image, and it seems an altogether better one. This has been Stephen's fate in death, though it took five years to materialize. Over his body developed, eventually, an argument that reaches deep into British society. The black man was the victim, but he also became a kind of hero, one of the very few black people to whom Britain has accorded iconic status. His name will never be forgotten, in connection with British virtue as much as British vice.

His murder was a racist atrocity, and the police investigation a failure in which the scandalous particulars – delay, prejudice, disbelief – also plainly rose in part from racism. But these have been investigated. The Macpherson inquiry has been, we may fairly say, magnificent. It ducked no questions and has apparently pulled no punches. By this means, society makes expiation for a shocking crime that was prejudicially mishandled, behind an unusual consensus. A tabloid newspaper, untainted by any history of liberalism, broke the law to force an inquiry to be set up, and a retired white judge of conservative demeanour, with no record of interest in the disorders of society, has put his name to a radical report.

The report will be a catharsis. Nobody, either, seems likely to dispute it. Its language may be questioned, but its premise, that racism of every kind is an incontestable evil, is not challenged. This is not Arkansas. The National Front is further underground, and smaller, than the KKK. In the aura of Stephen Lawrence's murder, every mainline voice in Britain is on the same side. By forcing policemen to disclose their racism in all its unconscious nakedness, the Macpherson inquiry did society a critical service, to which society will now set about responding. Won't it?

Only part of the response has to be about the police, and the least sensible part would be the resignation of Sir Paul Condon. Resignations by top people for misbehaviour by their subordinates are usually just symbolic: not proof of guilt but fulfilment of a ritual of accountability. In the case of the Metropolitan Police, the Macpherson process itself provided accountability in massive waves. Sir Paul may not have said what Macpherson wanted him to say – that his force was 'institutionally' racist – but he has been a more than adequate commissioner, who has fought racism, as well as corruption, throughout his life at the top.

His own battery of reforms, following the Lawrence and other cases, are testimony to such determination as society will allow him and his colleagues, like John Grieve, to muster. Racial consciousness has been raised. Training, recruitment, inspection, intelligence, the need for community partnership, the simple daily awareness of the racially charged environment in which urban police forces work: these priorities in all police management transcend the semantic question of whether or not the Met is rife with something that can be exactly called institutional racism.

The condition of the police, however, is only symptomatic. In the end, policemen mimic society. Working at the most jagged social frontier, their vices provoke most conflict, but the vices are not theirs alone. They have the greatest obligation to bury their racism, and need the most stringent rule-book to help them in this task. It is extraordinary, and now indefensible, that they should have been exempted from the ambit of the Race Relations Act 1968. Some of the blind and ignorant racists the Lawrence inquiry brought to light and put in the box should be sacked, notwithstanding the fact that many more like them will remain behind.

But the challenge the Lawrence saga makes is broader. It is to British complacency. Because we are not Arkansas, we may be tempted to believe we are close to a multiracial Elysium. Because we have a Race Relations Act superior in its reach to any similar Continental law, we might suppose that racial discrimination is being steadily eliminated from British life. Because we seldom have race riots, and would universally abominate any resort to the redneck tumbrils, it is easy for a white man to overlook the racial prejudice – the soft, silent, secretive, unexpressed but none the less decisive prejudice – that permeates the daily life of our society.

I do not know a black person, whatever their class, who does not feel this. Many survive and flourish in spite of it. But the job, the house, the kids, the schooling, the university, the promotion, not to mention the benefits, the passport check-in, the customs desk: for blacks each can be contingent on prejudice, whether in a public or a private person, in a way that doesn't happen to whites. This is the reality of British life: societal if not institutional racism, with corrosive if not necessarily violent effects. The peaceable but lethal infliction of a racism which is the more insidious for the pride it takes in never, but never, declaring itself.

The murderers of Stephen Lawrence declared their racial hatred. Some of the police who handled the case had their racism dragged out of them by Macpherson. The fact that they did not recognize it in themselves was the most eloquent subtext of the inquiry. It is the British condition. Somewhere deep down, unless I watch it, unhealthy racial awareness is my condition too. There are many specifics the Macpherson Report should help to change, greeted, as it will be, by a government falling over itself to do the necessary: the wasted years since Stephen's death at least saved us from the sight of Michael Howard responding on behalf of the people. But the larger effect is more to be hoped for: that whites get deeper into their heads the belief that racial justice is something rather more seminal than a branch of political correctness.

How Blair sabotaged freedom of information

THERE ARE CERTAIN MEASURES that tell the world how a government sees itself, what ruling species it belongs to. Is it open or is it closed? Does it trust the people, or suspect them? Is its priority invariably power or, just occasionally, accountability? Is it, at bottom, about control or, ever, about losing control? The Freedom of Information Bill, which starts its inspection by the Commons today, is such a bill. It reveals this government, at war with every previous principle, giving the wrong answer to every question. The artilleryman is Jack Straw. But the strategist and general is Tony Blair.

A month ago, when the bill was published, I made the mistake in this space of exonerating Mr Blair. The bill was terrible, but he was in the middle of the Kosovo crisis and, I thought, understandably distracted. This verdict overrated his heart and underrated his mind. On the contrary, the bill with which Mr Straw fashioned the burial of freedom of information as previously understood had the last nail in its coffin inserted, just in case the corpse made a final bid for life, by the minions at Number 10.

One exemplary clause is s.28(1)(a). Among a long list of classes of information exempted from the pseudo-right to know, it deals with an interesting category: information that relates to 'the formulation or development of government policy'. That clause, thus expressed, was not in the next-to-final draft of the bill that the relevant team of civil servants put together after weeks of ministerial argument. It was inserted at the insistence of the chief formulator and developer of policy himself.

It is worth a little deconstruction. It isn't limited to present policy-making, the crown jewel of contemporaneous Cabinet government. It covers all policy formation up until the thirty years have expired, which then requires the details to be released as public records. Nor is it confined to ministerial minutes and officials' advice, but can seclude every factual detail pertaining to every government policy decision. What facts did you rely on, minister, when permitting GM crop planting? Or squashing regional government? Or admitting Wal-Mart to out-of-town green fields? If the minister won't say, nothing in the bill will make him say.

Such a draconian law is apparently now essential. But it wasn't when the White Paper, published in 1997, said this kind of material could be withheld only after publication was shown to be specifically harmful. Nor does it appear in freedom of information jurisdictions elsewhere. Nor is it to be found in the open government code the Tories published and operated from 1994.

Under New Labour, however, we will have no right to know how, at the top, we are being governed. An NHS trust? Absolutely. A university? Sure enough. A parish meeting? Guaranteed by s.13 of schedule 1. The Broads authority, the council of the Scilly Isles, every pupil referral unit in the land? The words are there in black and white. All these bodies will have to be on their mettle, which is the main effect openness has. But on government itself, the light will not shine. No special mettle required. The irreplaceable test – were the procedures and reasoning that lay behind a government decision defensible in public? – will not have to be met.

This is one catch-all annihilation of freedom of information, in the Blair–Straw version. Another stands out. The many exempt categories can supposedly be challenged, in individual instances, through the agency of the Information Commissioner. In theory, she (Elizabeth France, already the Data Protection Commissioner) will guard the wider public interest The discretion of the state looks as though it might not be absolute. But the exact reality the bill sets out is different.

The Information Commissioner will have no power to order disclosure – another departure from the White Paper. Under the bill, ministers can't be overruled. All the commissioner can do is remind them to balance the interests: tell them, in other words, to make sure they go through the correct procedures to avoid being taken to court under judicial review for acting beyond their powers. The minister, not the commissioner, will be the arbiter of the public interest in disclosure. If, moreover, the minister decides, in his or her munificence, to let bits of exempt information out, the power will exist, under s.14, to control how the applicant intends to use it: in particular, to withhold it if this intended use includes – oh shock, oh horror – publication.

Such will be freedom of information, Blair–Straw style, unless the bill is radically altered. The fiasco has several causes. Accessory before the fact are the Liberal Democrats, sitting on the Cabinet committee that deals with the constitutional agenda. What, any longer, is the point of their presence if they let one of their own signature issues be travestied under their very noses, making them complicit?

As much to blame is the corruption of attitude that two years of power have visited on Labour politicians. They assume a position of total cynicism, reckoning that as long as they can claim openness has arrived in hospitals and schools, nobody except a crazed obsessive will be bothered by the barricading of the nerve-centre where the big decisions are made. They imagine, perhaps rightly, that most people are not concerned by the quality of Whitehall and its workings. They conclude, quite wrongly, that people can best be left in this sublime state of ignorance, and therefore palmed off with a bill that studiously breaks every promise Labour made in opposition.

Jack Straw comes to the Commons today to be questioned about it. Perhaps he will announce, with the pride he applied to ending trial by jury, another conversion experience: another liberal position, adopted in his youthful ignorance, now corrected by the discovery of the higher wisdom available only to the ministeriat. There's no knowing where the conversion habit might lead. But it seems unlikely to produce a sudden recanting on the bill, after the bloody bureaucratic victories that produced it.

This bill was not an accident. It tells us more about Mr Straw's special qualities, which Blair does not resist. We have the clinching proof that he's as right-wing as Michael Howard. The only difference is that whereas the Home Office detested Howard, it adores Straw. This says much about Whitehall, and just as much about Tony Blair. All are co-conspirators in a unique piece of legislative wreckage. A party that once said government would be different is exposed as another bunch of hubrists, incapable of imagining that information should enhance anyone's power but their own.

A policy of ethnic ostracism

JUST BEFORE THE second term launches, consider one thing the first has done. Catch it before it departs into the maw of another mandate where all is forgiven and much forgotten. See what power did in one particular zone, which I'm still prepared to call the moral sensibility of ministers. Not only have their arteries hardened and their consciences grown dull. That's to be expected under the weight of office. More startling is how easily the gates of perception, their sense of what they are doing, have been closed and locked.

When they came to power, one principle they seemed unbreakably attached to was a detestation of racial prejudice. Equality of racial justice and hostility to ethnic discrimination were ideals that united old and new Labour. To men like Tony Blair and Jack Straw they were articles of faith, which lay behind both the swift abolition of the Tories' primary-purpose rule challenging migrant spouses to prove they had any right to join their partners, and the later setting up of the Stephen Lawrence inquiry. To Blair and Straw it is unimaginable that they could be party to anything but the most impeccable correctness in all matters that touch on race.

Yet they have been. Two weeks ago, I wrote about the Race Relations (Amendment) Act 2000, which outlawed ethnic discrimination by public authorities but made an exception for the immigration service. I unearthed a ministerial order which authorized immigration officers to treat people of certain nationalities – unspecified, but to be identified at the future decision of ministers and officials – worse than other people. Replying to the critique, Straw pleaded a mere drafting technicality and termed my attack 'bizarre'.

But this order was only a beginning. There has now been a second one, dated 23 April, which extends the reach from nationalities to what it describes, in its own headline, as 'discrimination on ground of ethnic or national origin'. This time the ethnics in question are listed: '(a) Kurd, (b) Roma, (c) Albanian, (d) Tamil, (e) Pontic Greek, (f) Somali, (g) Afghan'. All persons of these origins are now to be subject 'to a more rigorous examination than other persons in the same circumstances'. They can be detained, questioned and rejected, as a class, more freely than other people because they are now deemed prima facie more likely to be illegal immigrants or bogus asylum-seekers.

They have something else in common, however. There is no Kurdish passport, there is no Roma passport. Identifying these people can be attempted through little more than their personal appearance, plus some inference from the flight or possibly boat they arrive on. So, not only is the bar on collective discrimination being ditched, but a peculiarly vicious form of sorting is written into statute, whereby immigration officers herd together anyone who looks like a Kurd or a Tamil or a Pontic Greek – regardless of whether these come, as Tamils do, from Sri Lanka, Canada, India or even the UK – and impose special oppression on them.

Ministers' handling of this law went through two phases. The first, during passage, was to pretend it was benign. The only purpose they cited was to make it easier to discriminate in favour of, say, Kosovan refugees. When pressed by Liberal Democrats such as Lord Lester, that was the scenario they repeatedly mentioned. They were lying. It is quite apparent from the 23 April order that what they wanted all along was the power to authorize state-sponsored mass exclusion of certain ethnic groups, without regard for individual justice, on a scale never before seen in this country.

Phase two came last week. The new law, said Barbara Roche, Straw's minion in charge of immigration, was merely giving formal shape to a practice that had been going on a long time. She was almost flippant in her incredulity that anyone should complain about a long-established pattern of ethnic selection. She talked about the need for 'objective evidence' against each migrant. But no one has explained how a Roma is meant to overcome the ethnic evidence against him, especially in view of the further sub-clause in the order which states, almost incredibly: 'If the information [needed to pursue an application to enter] is not available in a language which the person understands, it is not necessary to provide the information in a language which he does understand.'

Three conclusions can be drawn from this. First, whether or not ethnic selection went on before, it has now been systematized. If an apparent Kurd, or potential Roma, or notional Pontic Greek has by some oversight not been discriminated against, ministers may want to know the reason why. Immigration controllers are now on formal notice as to which ethnic and national origins are especially unwelcome in Britain. Their conduct will be policed by someone called a 'race monitor', but only retrospectively and without attention to individual cases. The monitor is plainly a PR stooge in the making.

Second, as the government's contribution to present discontents over asylum, this is political cowardice on a grand scale. No one disputes the need for immigration control. But faced by the mighty force of Ann Widdecombe, Blair and Straw are evidently terrified of electoral punishment if they can't match her rhetoric of national alarm with measures of ethnic hostility. Though all these politicians avow their respect for genuine cases, it's the tritest lip-service. Straw collaborates with Widdecombe in a discourse from which only the Lib Dems stand aside, that stigmatizes asylum itself as presumptively a bogus concept, eating away at the resources of the fifth-largest economy in the world.

Third, something unpleasant has happened to Labour in power. For all sorts of reasons, they need to win the election. I hope they do. They're the only plausible choice on offer and defend several important policies that will probably, given time, make this country a better place. But their immigration regime shows not only that they've become, in a vital area, as bad as the Tories, but that they have lost their intellectual as well as moral faculties. They appear not to know what they're doing. They sincerely believe they do not favour ethnic discrimination. Straw, the posturing anti-racist, thinks any challenge to his law can only be 'bizarre'. He is surrounded by a party that seems to believe the same – barely a squeak came out of it when the law went through.

Such, it seems, is today's corruption of power: not so much a conspiracy of self-interest as the building of a wall of righteous self-belief. A power-driven certainty that, because one is who one is, one can by definition do no wrong. This law of ethnic punishment is a disgrace. Perhaps only a party infused by belief in its own anti-racism would have the nerve to smuggle it past the frontier that separates a decent country from a shameful one.

Final proof that Labour is not liberal

PEOPLE WHO TAKE SERIOUSLY the civil liberties and human rights agenda have often, perhaps usually, voted Labour. They see themselves as progressive, on the left not the right, and have tended to assume that Labour, like them, believed in the importance of defending axioms that range across such issues as free speech, race and sex discrimination, the protection of the individual against abusive state power, and trial by jury. The assumption always was that, given the choice between the two main parties, anyone who cared about these things knew where they had to stand.

This was a triumph of optimism over experience never easy to understand. Beginning with Chuter Ede, post-war Labour governments have found no shortage of authoritarians to run the Home Office. Few showed natural sympathy for victims of state power, or resisted populist diatribes against fundamental rights and freedoms. Jim Callaghan was in the Ede line, and so was Merlyn Rees. It turns out that the entire weight of libertarian trust in Labour rests on the performance of one man, Roy Jenkins, whose record was epic in many of these fields, but who is now a Liberal Democrat – as is almost every politician now prepared to take risks for civil liberties.

The Blair government is, in this respect, old, old Labour. With one exception, it has run away from every libertarian challenge. It is profoundly illiberal. As Home Secretary, Jack Straw always wanted to make clear early in the conversation that he was not a liberal. Nor is Tony Blair. Liberal is a word that crosses Blair's lips as infrequently as socialist. The third way he seeks between these terms is the only one available: reliably and fiercely conservative.

A conservative stance was central to Blair's strategy before 1997. His most tenacious work as Shadow Home Secretary was to prepare the end of Labour's annual opposition to renewal of the Prevention of Terrorism Act. He also persuaded John Smith to abstain rather than oppose when Michael Howard's most extreme criminal justice bill came to a final vote. As Prime Minister, he maintained and extended his unreliable trajectory, insisting, for example, that the Freedom of Information Act, of which he spoke in opposition as a fervent supporter, should be operationally delayed for several years. With his support, Home Secretary Straw abolished the defendant's right to silence in criminal cases, again a reversal of the previous party line.

The exception to this pattern is the Human Rights Act, importing the European convention into domestic law. It was a big reform. But it was driven forward by the inescapable demands of history, together with Lord Chancellor Irvine's conversion to its merits. Straw seized on it, perhaps as cover for the anti-progressive things he wanted to do. Blair has never made more than passing reference to it. It doesn't grow out of the bowels of Labour, old or new, and certainly not out of the mind or sympathy of the present Home Secretary, David Blunkett, who refers to its libertarian impulse as 'airy-fairy', and furiously tried to wriggle round the constraints it placed on his anti-terrorism legislation.

This is the historic context in which to read Blunkett's White Paper on the criminal justice system. The progressive agenda places heavy reliance on the importance of law and judges; Blunkett has spent much time scorning what they say and do. Never has a Home Secretary done more to destroy confidence in the legal profession. Morrison and Callaghan were careful what they said about judges. Time and again Blunkett has whined and sniped at judgements that went against him. It shouldn't be surprising that a defining theme of the White Paper is the government's belief that the justice system has become a lawyers' ramp.

That hasn't produced a bad document. Blunkett's rarest virtue is that he's a listener, sometimes prepared to change his mind and challenge other people's conventional wisdom. The paper takes a radical and constructive swipe, long overdue, at some grotesque inefficiencies. At every stage from arraignment to trial, too many thousands of cases are bedevilled by multiple failures on the part of police, prosecutors, witnesses and lawyers. Seeking more reliable satisfaction for victims, and a better clear-up rate for crimes of every kind, is a worthy objective of government. The White Paper has many sensible ideas.

It is also good and grown-up about sentencing. Financial as well as social crisis has driven this Home Secretary to try to do something about the exponential growth that makes Britain the prison capital of Europe. Not a new aspiration – and the message is confused by doubling, as part of the strategy to speed up trials, the length of sentences magistrates can give. But most of the language and would-be policy on prisons is practical, not tabloid.

Blunkett has also listened on juries. Six months ago, in line with Lord Justice Auld's report, he proposed a system that might have halved the number of jury trials, drastically abolishing a fundamental right. Now he's gone back on that. That does not mitigate, however, the crucial shift this state paper expresses. The rule that determined the balance of the judicial system hitherto was this: it was worse for an innocent person to be convicted than for a guilty person to go free. Now that has been reversed. What drives the Blunkett White Paper is a demand for more convictions, no matter what collateral damage may be done to people who are not guilty.

That was the purpose of Labour's serial assaults on jury trial, two by Straw and one by Blunkett. Juries were thought to acquit more readily than magistrates. Though Blunkett was forced to pull back, he continues to eat away at his target. Juries will now be removed, if judges agree, not only from complicated fraud cases but complex cases of any kind that involve money: a burgeoning category. They will also be excused if in danger of 'intimidation', something easily manipulable by unscrupulous policemen. The truth is that these ministers dislike juries almost as much as they mistrust, and airily defame, the lawyers whose professional duty is to ensure defendants get a fair trial.

Even more offensive is Blunkett's willingness to open the way to more disclosure of previous convictions. This may already be done in narrowly restricted circumstances. Judges are now invited to extend them, to satisfy an explicit impatience with juries' present performance. The presumption of innocence is not being cleaved away with the axe that tabloid populism might like. But an insinuating needle can destroy the fabric of the system just as well, which Blunkett, detesting lawyers, seems only too happy to countenance.

These are a liberal's objections to his plan. To say the conviction of the innocent is more intolerable than the acquittal of the guilty sounds, these days, outlandish. But any system will be loaded to have one effect or the other, and Blunkett has made his choice. It's regrettable but not entirely surprising: the logical conclusion of Labour's unprincipled and treacherous history.

CHURCH AND STATE

Deliver them from theocracy

THE ONLY THING I envy about politicians is the ease of their convictions. They live in a world of intellectual absolutism, especially at elections. They are free from all doubt, except a lurking doubt about whether they will win. Contrary to much received wisdom, elections are a particularly undemanding time for any calls on judgement, choice or moral discrimination.

Take the economy. Even a semi-competent politician needs only a few selected figures in his head to prove his case beyond question. Press the button and out come the statistics. The condition spreads across the board. Hospitals, schools, taxes, pensions: the only difficult decision tends to be tactical. When and how to get the right words out to best advantage. On the substance, the good party man disengages his brain and consults only his affiliation. This untroubled context, wonderfully devoid of ambiguity, sometimes prompts the journalist who is not thus blessed to gaze covetously on the luxuriant polemical opportunities it opens up.

My own life of chronic detachment is marked by only one affiliation that imperils it. As a Roman Catholic born, bred and still roughly believing, I know something of the charm of absolute conviction. It is how I was educated to think about religion. It was supposed to make religious questions easy. Conviction, otherwise known as faith, dissolved all difficulties. This mental state, untouched by the agonizing of reason, has a facile attraction which disappeared some time ago, but its intrinsic nature – both its power and its horror – reappears in the most lurid imaginable light in the abortion case now before the Irish Court of Appeal.

I'm not in favour of abortion. No doubt that opinion is rooted in my past but it is not hard to defend. On the irresolvable question of when life begins, my bias is to say at the moment of conception. I believe abortion is a termination of life. If I was an MP, I'd vote to reduce the womb-age at which abortion was permissible. When I think about it, I'm repelled by the number of abortions, well over two million, performed in this country since the Abortion Act: but perhaps not decisively more so than by the squalor and destitution in which a million or two of the British are forced to live, when I think about those defilements as well. Each, it seems to me, is an outcome that represents some kind of democratic will, in which my private morality, like that of everyone else, has but a single vote.

This stance would no doubt be viewed with disapproval by the leaders of my Church. It is not a sufficiently absolutist position, but more particularly it rejects the claim that one opinion about abortion has the right to impose itself on an entire society. It allows for a different balancing of good and evil, which perhaps more people support. Tolerance, for me, must admit agnosticism. And besides: my brand of relativism now comes face to face with the perfect instance of absolutism against which it must be weighed.

The horrifying case of the fourteen-year-old raped in Ireland is one the Church and not just the State has to answer. The raped nun was the figure usually put forward as the notional example that most embarrassed upholders of the absolutist doctrine. Now the raped child is more than notional. She is required, unless the court finds a way out, to carry the product of this violation into the world; and is prevented even from travelling to secure the remedy, painful and unhinging as it might be, which her family, acting on their own private moral judgement in all the circumstances, wants her to have.

For this state of the law, the Church is essentially responsible. The 1983 constitutional amendment on abortion was backed ferociously from Irish pulpits, just as the 1986 amendment to legalize divorce was opposed. Yet the Church in the present crisis has been abjectly silent. Some hard-line anti-abortionists have been found who will say that the life inside the raped fourteen-year-old is the only life that matters. A lot more ordinary Irish people seem to be changing their minds about abortion: a weekend opinion poll found that 67 per cent now wanted to make abortion legal in some circumstances. But from the Catholic Church comes hardly a murmur of guidance, and not a whisper of apologetic accountability.

One may pity the priests their predicament. For once, absolutism offers no moral haven. Either way they will lose. If they insist, as absolutist doctrine requires, that the girl not be assisted to have an abortion, they will seem the incarnation of inhumanity. If they relax, they will have rewritten the law. If they collude in exporting the problem, as a spokesman has suggested, they will rightly stand accused of burying the moral issue.

In the circumstances, the silence of the hierarchy is perhaps not surprising. But it is also cowardly. It emphasizes not only the Church's failure to engage with an issue that discomforts it, but the Church's confidence that it will continue to exercise a power which it is not obliged to defend. Hard cases make bad law, but bad law makes atrocious cases. The emotional aura of even this case will one day be dissipated, however. When that day comes, Irish pulpits may be expected once again to resound to the narrow righteousness that is most comfortable when addressing abstractions.

Yet this case does have one redeeming feature. For it may be the moment at which such a self-evident truth, sanctified by the decades and centuries, no longer holds. The opinion poll is a straw in the wind. Perhaps its message will be more than transient. Perhaps this awful event, exposing the consequence of religious absolutism as graphically as any ayatollah, will mark a permanent reverse for the process by which one sectarian church, with such immoderate determination, is able to impose its practices on a society where significant numbers of people no longer agree with them.

Optimism could carry one into further realms of imagination. Overturning the Church veto on constitutional change would be a signal development in the evolution of peace in Northern Ireland. Dublin, when it chooses to think positively about peace, knows well enough that liquidation of the crucial remnants of a theocratic state are a vital precondition of Unionist trust. Legalizing if not approving abortion and divorce in Ireland will make or break the chance of mobilizing the Ulster people against their own demagogues. Perhaps the Catholic Church's contribution will lie in the defeat, at last, of its intolerable political pretensions.

For absolutism, it turns out, does not provide an answer. Reality is too strong for it, especially when reality encompasses the opinion of the people. Conviction must yield to judgement; general principle to particular exceptions. Priest and politician have reason thrust upon them. On reflection, I withdraw my confession of envy. Powerful men with easy answers are a menace to society.

The Pope in the world

WHEN KENNEDY WENT to Berlin, the world heard what he said. When Reagan spoke, the world was obliged to listen. When Clinton goes to Africa, the world thinks only about his private parts. But even if Clinton's life was simon-pure, there wouldn't be a great audience gathering to watch this rare excursion. For what he has to say will be utterly banal. It's drained of force by his fixation on the audience back home, and by America's paralysing lack of ambition to take a moral risk in the wider world.

President Clinton is not, except by formal measurements of economic size and military potential, a world leader. He does not lead the world. He does not seem to want to. He confers a fleeting blessing on Ghana, Uganda and other countries sufficiently reformed for the US to approve of. He'll be pleased to stand alongside Nelson Mandela, his sullied image absorbing what it can from an incontestable hero. But context as well as character debar Clinton from leadership. Americans are reluctant to see their leader take a difficult stand of any kind, and he would not dare disoblige them. Congress, in any case, wouldn't let it happen. Modern democracy consists of reading the polls, taking the pulse, struggling to be all things to all men and women, never confronting them with ideas they might not want to hear.

Leaving Africa as Clinton arrived was a real leader. Pope John Paul II is the only true world leader at large today. The frail old man who left Nigeria collects a massive audience, not just as the vicar of God but because he has a message. Can any other voice in the world draw such attention? No. The Pope poses a problem for liberals, especially liberal Catholics like me. But it's clear, in the end, where we have to come down. Regrettable though it is to say so, there are certain messages of transcendent wisdom that only an unaccountable autocrat now seems able to utter.

John Paul II, in his twentieth year, is, as far as politics goes, a failure. His conduct of his office has been, in the political sense, a disaster. This began with his view of the Faith, though that surely wasn't itself to be deplored. He may be rigid in his interpretation of revealed truth, unyielding in his rebukes for all kinds of sexual behaviour except one. He rejects all moral relativism. But if a Pope doesn't stand against moral relativism, who will?

Less easy to defend is his administration of the Church. It is possible for a Pope to reject moral relativism, while acknowledging the merits of the ecclesiastical reforms of the Second Vatican Council, which paved the way for a less authoritarian and Rome-centred regime, in keeping with the needs of the modern world. In several countries – Austria, Ireland, Brazil – many hard-line episcopal appointments have seen churches divided and congregations dwindling, with a consequent enfeebling of the very moral reformation for which John Paul has stood, from the start of his papacy.

So he is very poor at politics. And he has a complicated attitude to freedom. Terrible things have happened to the freedom of Catholic theologians, even as their leader has sent out the most resonant signals in favour of religious freedom elsewhere: he was the first Pope to enter a synagogue, and the first to visit a Moslem country. While internally he has been a policeman, externally he's a stubborn and innovative visionary.

This is the paradox historians will have to confront, but on which, I think, they should arrive at a favourable verdict. Wherever he has gone, especially in his later years, this Pope has been able to say the difficult things, and is often the only person whom his audience has ever heard saying them. So it was in Nigeria, an unusually squalid dictatorship, indulging in every kind of abuse of fundamental freedoms, against which our famous democracies have done no better than waft a limp-wristed hand, declaring for sanctions but not imposing them, muttering against the murder of Ken Saro-Wiwa but continuing to nurture the international oil company against whom he was mobilizing local protest.

John Paul II was magnificently clear. He told the dictator, General Abacha, to his face that Nigeria must 'strive for honest efforts to foster harmony and guarantee respect for human rights'. He railed against 'intimidation and domination of the poor ...

[and] arbitrary exclusion of individuals and groups from public life'. Every speech and sermon he gave, before enormous crowds, was of this stamp. One would call them fearless – except that the Pope had nothing to fear.

And that, surely, is the point of his journeys, and the justification for his life. Occupying a place of such eminence, he could easily descend into the same banalities as the political leaders, but never chooses to do so. He uses his invulnerability for righteous purposes. In Cuba he made the same defiant claim to a universal system of values as in Nigeria. In Latin America, while appointing bad bishops and viscerally rejecting the Marxist taint of liberation theology, he has usually spoken like a liberation theologian himself, and continued the transformation of the Roman Church from a supporter into an enemy of the dictators.

The uncomfortable part of this is that it springs from the same stem as his intolerance. John Paul's severity in defence of the married lifestyle, the all-male and unmarried priesthood, the unaborted foetus and the unimpeded conception is of a piece with his attacks on totalitarian politics and his ceaseless preaching against the evils of consumerist capitalism. He is saying: Here I stand, these are the rules of life that higher authority decrees, here are the standards to which we should aspire, such are the axioms by which humanity might do better for itself.

One doesn't have to accept all these rules to see the value of a public man who is prepared to speak for them. It has become an exceptional experience to be addressed by one who is a leader not a follower: who isn't sidling on and sucking up: who deals in challenges, not comforts: who gives us propositions to reject, not platitudes spun and doctored to be unrejectable. Liberal relativism has not turned out to make such a perfect world that we can't learn from its opposite. Which is why the Pope has more divisions, in a time when war no longer sets the moral compass, than Bill Clinton.

God and Basil Hume

WHILE BASIL HUME was dying, I did my best to enter his mind. This was certainly a bit presumptuous. But he had given us notice of his terminal condition. He wanted us to be clear, and we had time to think about it. I knew him for forty years, and in particular had known, in him, the only person of my acquaintance who did not appear to be at all afraid of death.

As a dying man, I can imagine, he was well prepared. This really was the moment to which his life was but the prelude. A headmaster at the monastic school where I first met him, when asked by an anxious parent to say what Ampleforth prepared its boys for – what traits would be bestowed, what niches opened up, what worldly successes guaranteed – he replied heavily: 'We prepare them for death.' Recounted to teenagers, these words sounded like a macabre and incomprehensible joke. But they summarize, of course, the Christian purpose: the living of a good enough life to conclude with a death that brings salvation.

Father Basil, as many people knew him, seemed to have the most perfect sense of this. He by no means believed he had all the answers. But he was, rather simply, a man of faith. He believed in God as the incontestable centre of anybody's life, could they but know it, and this was the sense he communicated without a trace of histrionics. Prayer was to him the oxygen, the natural resource, of sustainable existence. I liked to think of him, these last few days, in keen but tranquil anticipation of what, no doubt after a lengthy purgatorial interlude, was about to happen. And seeing him that way, one approaches the heart of what he gave the world.

As a schoolmaster, he got close to his pupils. Whether on the rugby field or in the history class, where he was a superb peda-gogue, he was demanding yet unintimidating. He could exude the greatest enthusiasm for winning the game or passing the exams, while somehow always reserving space enough to let you know that these were not everything. In a time when competitive triumph was in danger of being all that school was about, one dimly understood that here was a monk-teacher who genuinely – mysteriously, absurdly – reckoned every boy was of equal worth.

This innate belief in human equality was a key to the effect he had in a quarter-century of public life. He was not just admired and respected but, in a rare way, loved, and it was because he did not need the protection of a sense of grandeur. Nobody was less fitted to be called a prince of the Church.

It would be wrong, however, to call him meek. Though surprised to be summoned from Ampleforth to Westminster, he didn't flinch from the task. He was quietly critical of the state the Church was in in the mid-seventies, and, I think, welcomed the opportunity to address it from a place of power and influence. Humble before God, he was a willing, even assertive, leader of men, behind a demeanour that seldom failed to seem patient, tolerant and consensual.

This combination – effortless authority, human decency – ran through the three of Hume's qualities which in my opinion will leave the most memorable mark. The first, unexpectedly, was political. The cloistered monk had had to be a little adept in politics as abbot of Ampleforth, at a time when the Church was in turmoil after the Vatican Council in the early sixties. But that task was confined to a secluded monastery. Hume came to London as an unworldly innocent, yet was able to use this apparent guilelessness to many people's advantage.

He was trusted in Rome, and a particular friend of Pope John Paul II. This led to many years' service as president of the European bishops, and thus as a kind of offshore healer to a continent riven by extremely bitter ecclesiastical disputes. His steely mildness brought benefits closer to home, especially as regards Rome's baleful influence on church appointments.

The attempted incursions of the fundamentalist right were inexorably blocked. Almost alone in the world, the English branch of Catholicism went twenty years without a ruinous left–right divide in its college of bishops. For many complex reasons, church attendance here, as elsewhere in the advanced world, went drastically down in Hume's time. But the peacefulness attending this decline was largely his achievement.

Secondly, he was sparing in the use of his moral authority. He did not have a quote for every crisis, nor a passion for every cause. When he took up an injustice, as he did, for example, by leading the campaign for the Guildford Four, he therefore carried fearsome fire-power. When he preached against society's obsession with sex, as he did with more severity towards the end of his life, he managed somehow to save himself, even after a quarter-century at Westminster, from sounding predictable.

Not being the leader of the Established Church was helpful here. He could always stand a little on the edge, and mercifully resisted the contaminating notion that he should be received into the House of Lords. Though he did, by his own very Englishness, confirm RCs as no longer alien in late-twentieth-century Britain, he kept a nice distance, which enabled him to make his own agenda rather than being captive to the rituals and expectations of the state.

Finally, though, in the quest for Basil's uniqueness, one must return to his humanity, and the links he made between it and the Catholic faith. In all his time there never was a voice that better expressed the nature of religious conviction: expressed it, actually, by manifesting it in himself, and returning again and again to the exploration of what it meant.

He was a humorous man, and a natural self-deprecator. The affection he inspired in those who worked with him was matched by his own unpatronizing regard for the simplest people who worked or prayed with him. He followed Newcastle United and English rugby and cricket with a passion. He would jovially banter with any former pupil who crossed his path, whom he always seemed delighted to see.

But you knew, also, that this was a person engaged on a lifelong meditation about the meaning of life and death. Everything he did had that connection. He lived in the circle of final questions. To those of us who are all too easily, and almost all the time, distracted from those questions, his unflinching belief that God was at the centre of them worked as a rebuke, yes, but also a model to watch, and think about, and incoherently, occasionally, to follow.

The Christian millennium
that went wrong

THERE COULD NOT, as it turns out, be a more ominous moment to mark an epic Christian anniversary than 1 January 2000. In its European heartland, fount if not origin of the creed that captured more believers than any other in recorded time, Christianity has never looked in worse shape.

In the whole of the old millennium, no fifty-year span registered more committed godlessness than the past one. For priest and presbyter, 1950–2000 was the worst of half-centuries, and this, starting a new epoch, can hardly be a happy day.

Although it is supposed, as the calendar dictates, to be one of Christian celebration, it's more like one of Christian crisis. There is a crisis of belief, and a deeper one of institutions. Each was epitomized, in the run-up to the millennium moment here, by the churches' struggle to be heard, their relegation to the sidelines, the official reluctance to concede the Christian nature of the date in question, the apologetic embarrassment which Christian leaders have felt obliged to bring to their interventions. They seem to have few words more worthy of the era-shift than Tony Blair's speech-writers.

Every previous European century was, in one way or another, God-centred. In each, a personal God belonged to the natural order of things. From the Dark Ages to the Renaissance, God suffused the outpourings of the artists and thinkers anyone has remembered. It never occurred to Raphael to doubt, nor to Pope Julius II that patronage of artistic genius wasn't his natural duty towards immortal Christian belief.

The refinements of faith were, in all these times, often a source of appalling evil. Terrible persecutions – Henry's, Mary's, Elizabeth's – followed one upon the other, staining Tudor England. One cannot say – sweeping an eye across the martyrdoms, and wars, and burnings, and avenging crusades, and forced expulsions, and endless cascades of theological upheaval, often in the name of enumerating the true quantity of angels to be found on the head of a pin – that the millennium which Christianity dominated brought unbounded joy to the human condition. But at least there was belief. The Christian churches mattered, in this world and, all agreed, the next.

Now Christianity seems to matter only at the margins. The past 150 years have witnessed a slow but ceaseless decline. A. N. Wilson's erudite survey, *God's Funeral*, charts the loss of faith among nine-teenth-century European intellectuals. Carlyle, Eliot, Spencer, Marx, Darwin: these were the precursors of a great discarding that has gone on ever since, as science effaced belief and rationalism the irreplaceable notion of mystery.

What began in the nineteenth century spread wider in the twentieth. Non-belief, from being an act of meditated defiance that caused these Victorians the most painful agonies, is now a shallow norm which many Europeans, certainly many Brits, will defend with casual incredulity that there could be any other option. Lip-service is paid, at certain seasons of hypocrisy, to a tabloid God. But at the start of the new century, theism, rather than atheism, imposes confessional reticence in polite society.

Such collapse of confidence reaches high places. Pope John Paul II remains an iconic figure, proclaiming his own certainties in defiance of contemporary fashion. But not all his princes are so sure. *Le Monde* recently carried the millennial reflections of Cardinal Joseph Ratzinger. Even Ratzinger, who, as prefect of the congregation of the faith, is the Vatican's closest approximation to a modern inquisitionist, admits that Christianity is 'in profound crisis' – language seldom heard from under a red hat.

The crisis grows not so much from pervasive irreligion as from the Christian claim to be the sole agent of religious truth. Christianity, the cardinal noted, seemed to have become 'one form of religious experience, to be placed humbly alongside others'. The world saw it as little more than an 'expression of generalized religious sensibility', in a time that defined each religion as relatively true.

Ratzinger, of course, rejected this. The historic success of Christianity, he insisted, 'was based on a synthesis of reason, faith and life'. Why have people forgotten this? he imperiously asked.

Why, in particular, has reason been defined as incompatible with belief? To this timely question, however, the cardinal supplied no answer. He fell to waffling. Even the most skilful casuists, it appears, are drawn into an arena they no longer master by diktat alone, but grope in vain for other modes of persuasion.

No people seem more vulnerable than the British to such crumbling of conviction. There are few more godless countries in Europe than this one, measured by belief and church attendance. According to a survey conducted by Opinion Research Business and just published in the Catholic weekly, *The Tablet*, less than half the population (45 per cent) now believes Jesus was the son of God: in 1951 the figure was 71 per cent. Only a minority (48 per cent) claimed to belong to any particular religion: it was 58 per cent as recently as 1990.

All in all, it is now more fashionable than it has ever been to regard much that was once held as timelessly true as, after all, a 1,000-year hallucination: Michelangelo as a painter of fiction, Aquinas as a scholastic fantasist, Johann Sebastian Bach as pouring out his intricate creations to celebrate – poor fool! – a god who never was. This is a stimulating but frightful thought, perhaps congenial to the iconoclastic spirit of the age, after a millennium which, it turns out, the greatest minds of many centuries pathetically misunderstood.

You can say all that, and also say that the Vatican, epicentre of the Christian religion, made its own contribution to the century of waning commitment. Speaking as a cradle Catholic, I deplore, ever more fiercely, the choices Rome made, through the fatal years 1950–2000, when faced by the challenges of the modern world. If popes had taken less interest in sex and more interest in economic justice, they might have stood a better chance of allying moral conviction with popular assent.

As it is, Rome's core teaching on sex descended from propounding joyless inconvenience in the developed world, to insisting, literally, on a crime against humanity in Africa, where Aids must flourish, thanks be to God's vicar on earth. Meanwhile, passage through the eye of the needle for every insatiable capitalist, with his contempt for equity, remains mostly uncontested from the pulpit. With priorities like these, it might be argued, Christianity hardly deserves to survive as either moral code or system of belief.

And yet it has. Europe is not the whole of Christianity. Her nineteenth-century agonies of disbelief did not afflict much of America, nor did more recent withdrawal from church attendance. More than 80 per cent of Americans still say they believe in God. The churches continue to make a noise, and presidential candidates judge it prudent – compare 1960, when John F. Kennedy kept as quiet as possible about his Catholicism – to fulsomely declare their Christian belief.

Equally, in Brazil and the Philippines, and the Latin and Asian diaspora around them, not to mention stoical Africa, Christianity is often the only uplifting reality in the lives of the masses. The creed may be honoured in the breach, its leaders entwined in the corruptions of a military ruling class. But its vitality on the ground means we cannot take the unpriested deserts of Western Europe, with their divided hierarchies, ageing churchgoers and hand-wringing apologists, as conclusive evidence for global pessimism – always assuming some version of Christian practice and belief is felt to be worth preserving.

Even in Europe, the chances of this seem quite high. But whether it will adhere to the Ratzinger model is another matter. The survival of that model, with its assertion of unique and incontestable revelation, beside which every other religion, however godly, is a fiction, presages a reversion of pre-twentieth-century times. Christianity, some say, must revive itself by coming out fighting: precisely by resisting the relativism the cardinal abhors. They foretell, not least in Bible-punching Republican America, a new era of authoritarian intolerance as the pendulum swings back from the easy liberalism of 1950–2000.

But moods do not change merely because of a line in the calendar. Sceptical inquiry has become the deep habit of educated people, which they won't voluntarily eradicate. More plausible than an authoritarian Christianity is one that does seek coexistence, tapping into the spiritual sensibilities – the quest for values, the awareness that materialism has proved an unsatisfactory god, the longing for some undeciphered Other – which all opinion surveys these days uncover. Victorians, while beginning to experience Doubt, continued to go to church. Maybe the twenty-first century starts with empty churches – yet people trying to satisfy a new appetite for Belief, and to dispel the inarticulate melancholy of its opposite.

More plausible still, if we're talking millennia, is the likely appearance of a new religion altogether. Considered as a whole – Islam, Hinduism, Buddhism, even Judaism – the phenomenon of religion is not in numerical decline. The search for the Other will go on. Over time, human inventiveness will find new ways of conducting it.

One can still say that, in this search, Christianity, despite its enfeebled hold, has a head start. After all, its exclusivity is supposed to have been formally ended. The United Nations, spokesman for millennial correctness said so. According to the UN, we are now living not in 2000 AD but 2000 CE. The Common Era supplanted the Year of Our Lord some time ago. Yet hardly anyone noticed. The calendar itself, they decided, will never change. In that way, Christ still lives. Can His churchly interpreters seize their second chance?

CULTURE AND THE NATION

The philistine political class

MOST ARTISTS IN this country scorn politicians. Few politicians have any serious time for art, or even the arts. It is a relationship shot through with derision, and sometimes hatred. Now this attitude finds its policy, and its emblem.

In the East End of London, Rachel Whiteread's architectural sculpture, *House*, has been voted into destruction. *House* is a modern masterpiece. In it an ingenious idea is realized with great evocative power. Taking a derelict dwelling, Whiteread has turned it inside out by casting the interior in liquid concrete then removing the bricks. What is left is a monument to past domesticity, a coarse yet intricate edifice, alone in the space it once occupied with a hundred similar residences. It satisfies contemplative as well as aesthetic taste. Once seen, it makes you look at all houses in a new way.

On Tuesday night the Bow standing neighbourhood committee voted to pull *House* down. Six politicians, all Liberal Democrats, took the decision on the casting vote of the chairman, Councillor Eric Flounders. As an artefact of modern art, *House*, although puzzling, is among the most accessible. It arrests the eye and the mind. But Councillor Flounders, a man apparently not without the outward signs of education, called it 'excrescent', and 'a monstrosity', from the moment it was unveiled last month. He was determined to expunge it from Tower Hamlets at the earliest moment.

More telling than the vote, however, was the extremely modest request which it overrode. This was not that *House* should stand for ever. The limited life of the excrescence was contractually prescribed from the start. What disappeared this week was merely a stay of demolition until January. It seems to have been inconceivable to either the artist, or her sponsor, Artangel, that this structure, once created, might deserve indefinite preservation. They were just pathetically grateful for their chance. The notion that *House* might improve Mile End Park, or that, once emerging from experimental darkness into the light of widespread acclamation, its fate might be reviewed, was beyond the imagination of anyone in the art world, let alone the political. 'A park is a park,' the Lib Dems said, and the work just disappears.

Such routine philistinism, however, does not belong to Tower Hamlets alone, or the Liberal Democrats. Councillor Flounders speaks from the heart of the body politic in all its grim bipartisanship. The massive cut in next year's national arts budget comes straight out of the Whitehall school that believes in equality of misery for all, with the caveat that some are less equal than others. At the bottom of this is an attitude to culture of which the vandalism in Tower Hamlets, unremarked as far as I know by a single politician high or low, is but a congruent instance.

This attitude begins with the personal. Not everything in politics is determined by the personal. A great deal of the next public spending round is more mechanical than discretionary, though this time the proposed assault on welfare digs up ministers' personal prejudices more than usual. But as to arts spending, the questions are essentially personal. How central do you believe culture is to the health of the country? How much more willing are you to see massive overspending on rip-off motorway contractors than minimal public sustenance for the arts? How hard will your personal commitment induce you to fight for a vibrant cultural life?

We know rather little about the cultural predispositions of the present Cabinet, but I will attempt a synthesis. They begin, I think, with an infirm belief in the place of public culture at all. The right would like to eliminate public subsidy altogether, the rest would like to feel the heritage is being preserved at the lowest possible expense. Neither group likes a fuss, but if the fussing can be stigmatized as an emanation of the chattering classes then its serious purpose can be politically neutralized. If culture can be fitted into the matrix of the economic ideology – as a tourist-booster, a customer-maximizer, a bottom-line-in-the-black exemplar – it may make a more acceptable call on public funds, although in the current assault even the passing of those tests is no guarantee of survival. Culture is vaguely good for national prestige. The Tories wouldn't like to preside over a wasteland. But the more this can be kept at bay by private money the better.

The personal cultural habits of ministers start with the absence of time to take any culture seriously. Mr Portillo, like Mr Major's wife, is known to be keen on opera. Mr Hurd plainly has time to read, as well as write, some books. Mr Heseltine has his trees and Mr Gummer goes to church. Mr Brooke reveals the traces of a classical education. There have been ministers recognizably possessed of cultural passion. But the names of Stevas, Gowrie, Patten (C.) and Ridley have long since gone missing. Far better represented are overworked political obsessives who are unlikely to make space to go to a movie, let alone visit a challenging exhibition. As a serious follower of modern painting, Richard Ryder, the chief whip, is wholly eccentric.

So the median cultural stance of the people in charge of the cultural budget would appear, on all available evidence, to veer between negligent and hostile. They think they're doing us a favour by allocating any money at all. As for promoting an open-minded attitude to the nature of art, almost no politician in any party can be relied on. The idea that art must innovate, still less that it might dare to offend, is one that most politicians, if they ever address the question, are incapable of accepting. To the always urgent problem of distinguishing between pretentious trash and real creative excitement, they make no contribution. And yet they have great influence, which goes beyond the budgetary. They make room for the Queen Elizabeth Gate, a tinselly kitsch embarrassment nailed for ever into the heart of London, but see *House* destroyed without a blink, righteously declaring, if asked, that green spaces must be saved from artistic defilement.

'We must let the artist fail,' said Lord Palumbo, in an eloquent little speech before awarding Rachel Whiteread the Turner Prize. More, the artist must surely be let to live when she has succeeded. In Britain, philistine revelling underpins niggardly public provision. It wouldn't happen in France, where politics has fathered great cultural boldness. It doesn't happen in Germany, where the political class has a secure hold on the connection between money for the arts and contentment for the nation. Only in Britain do politicians, as a conscious act, while resentfully putting up with artists, actually disdain the purpose of art.

The martyrdom of Salman Rushdie

CHRISTMAS EVE IS a strange day to remember an Islamic story. But on Christmas Eve a year ago the latest chapter in this story began. What has happened since, and what may happen next, offer among other things a challenge to the Christian idea of the sanctity of individual life, and to those who in their public role purport to be guided by it.

Salman Rushdie is a modern martyr. He is plainly not a Christian martyr, but he stands at least for the kind of tolerance, a secular liberty of conscience, which contemporary Christianity, shaking off the worst tyranny of decades and centuries past, comes closer to upholding than any version of Islam. Nor is he by any means alone. Until the gulag is purged of its last forgotten inhabitant, there will be martyrs whose punishments exceed those of Mr Rushdie. From Burma to Kenya, from Indonesia to Peru, this world abounds in martyrs to conscience and belief, with whom the rest of humanity chooses undemandingly to live.

For Britain, however, Rushdie is unique. Not only does he appear to be the only foreign non-Muslim ever to be subject to the fatwa or death penalty, he is probably the only British citizen, and certainly the only British writer, now alive who endures the daily threat of execution. There are no more British hostages in Lebanon. Iran and Iraq have released the hostage British businessmen. Salman Rushdie exists in solitary, horrific dignity, while our capacity for astonishment at his condition insidiously slips away.

Last Christmas Eve, he made an attempt to help himself. Two years after publication of *The Satanic Verses*, he issued an emollient statement agreeing to suspend any paperback edition. This had been the prime demand of all but the most extreme Muslims and he met it. At the same time he did something odder. He engaged in a kind of religious education, sitting at the feet of sundry Islamic divines to inform himself about the creed whose core he had so deeply offended. The process issued in a crude report that he had 'converted'. His road to security, if not salvation, appeared rather smoother.

This turn of events had two consequences, of a kind any martyrologist would recognize. First he was denounced by his friends. Never mind the 'conversion', many said, the concession on the paperback showed that poor Salman must be out of his mind. Seldom has a rebuke from the salons seemed more complacently insensitive. Suspending the paperback was a reasonable gesture, as argued here among other places. It showed an earnest intention to avoid further bloodshed without fundamentally violating free speech. A million copies of the book were already in circulation.

Secondly, however, the gesture only further enraged Rushdie's harshest enemies. There was no similarly peaceable response. The price put on his head by Iranian authorities was upped to three million dollars, and it was established through diplomatic sources in Continental Europe that a mercenary hit-squad had set forth to claim the bounty.

Rushdie, in other words, had within reason tried his best. He had laboured to persuade Islamic authorities that his book had no intention of insulting the deity. He ceased to be the stiff-necked martinet of a liberalism blind to all consequences, but this got him nowhere. When he made a daring speech at Columbia this month, remarking on these events and reclaiming his right to paperback publication, his reward was not only the reaffirmation of death-threats – albeit vicariously, as a deceiving submission to English law – by sundry British mullahs, but denunciation by Hesham el-Essawy, a one-time ally, who claimed to have been conned by Rushdie's 'conversion' and now handed him back to the fanatics. Last week, Essawy contributed the most nauseating article the *Guardian* – for good reason – published in 1991.

Britain, however, is not personified by Muslims soft or hard, and the British way of handling the challenge Rushdie presents is determined elsewhere, namely by the government. The government does have a choice which can affect the matter. It may not be long before it has to make it.

No one can say ministers have been unsupportive. They have not stinted the personal protection. When they resumed diplomatic relations with Iran in September 1990, it was on the basis that neither country would interfere in the other's domestic affairs, a stipulation understood to mean that Tehran had withdrawn secular backing from the mullahs' decree.

It wasn't long, however, before the bounty was raised and the hit-squads set off. And over the last year there have been various reasons for London not to alarm Tehran by asking too many questions. Iran was an ally in the Gulf War. Iran was the ultimate jailer of the hostages in Lebanon. Iran required to be exonerated from all blame for the Lockerbie bombing, if Libya was to be put in the dock of world opinion. All in all, Iran's deep desire for acceptance in the Western world has received significant satisfaction in 1991. In this intermeshing of many strands of high politics, the fate of a single writer, especially one who makes no great appeal to the Conservative Party or the admass media, may easily vanish from view. Perhaps it would be a different matter if all this was happening to Jeffrey Archer.

The completion of Iran's return to the undemanding world now awaits. Britain is poised to exchange ambassadors, the final stage of diplomatic normality. This was foreshadowed last month, with a little-remarked easing of trade. For the simple reason that there were many unfulfilled contracts to be completed, and much heavy commercial business to be done, the Foreign Office opened up medium-term export credit guarantees for Iran.

There would have been no question of exchanging ambassadors if any British hostages were still in captivity. Is Rushdie in the same category? One reason why diplomats doubt he should be rests on their contention that the Iranian government cannot affect the fatwa. But one result of this case having lasted so long is that more people understand reality. They know that these diplomats are talking self-serving nonsense. No one close to the case doubts that Tehran could lay off the contract killers, which would dispose of 90 per cent of the problem. The question now to be tested is whether Tehran wants world recognition badly enough to see that this is done. Which in turn means: will Britain, for the sake of this narrow cause, make Tehran sweat until it complies?

It is a question of values. The values of a nation, not just of its leaders. The case of Rushdie can easily be buried under a few reassuring, brutal words of the kind the Foreign Office is trained to write in its sleep. They would quietly inter his last best chance of relief: also, however, the last claim Britain could make as safe asylum for the rights of a man.

The eccentric art of being British now

A PRIME CASUALTY of the European war is the greatness of Britain. I don't refer, for these purposes, to British power but to the meaning of Britishness. It is being appropriated and perverted by those who make the Union Jack their political stock-in-trade. Daily it grows more narrow and self-referential.

Its most feverish expression is not in politics, where Britain has its back to the wall and can scarcely pretend to any real power, but in culture. More and more, we're invited to exalt British values and icons that depict a country revelling in its inwardness, wallowing in heritage, and proudly flaunting a grim-faced self-regard against the defiling hordes of Continentals.

We're in a period when only history seems to matter, a condition Britain is periodically prone to, but which now burns with particular intensity. This coincides with the discovery that British children's knowledge of detailed history is sketchier than it has ever been, but that's another story. In general, the past is not another country, and we don't do things differently here. The rejection of Europe requires, it seems, the narrowing of nation, and with it a spreading stigma on modernity in all its forms.

Yet all is not quite lost. Mike Leigh's new film, *Secrets and Lies*, is at one level the quintessence of Britishness. It could only have been made here, only explored the tensions of a British family. The bourgeois anxiety of Monica is pure Scots priggery, uprooted to London. Cynthia, the confused, pathetic mother-figure, could exist, in her specifics, nowhere else. This is a film, created with precision and acted to perfection, especially by Timothy Spall and Brenda Blethyn, that's hewn out of the soul of the island race.

Yet it is a rebuke to the all-devouring vogue for reactionary Britishness. It has no trace of nostalgia about it, falls into none of the categories most commonly associated with our defining cultural brilliance. There's no deflecting irony, none of that deflating jokiness through which, in the British way, arch parochialism undermines all messages about the human condition. *Secrets and Lies* is a film of universal power. In that sense, its Britishness is accidental. Like *Trainspotting*, it may not be a 'better' film than *Sense and Sensibility*, *Chariots of Fire* or *The Lavender Hill Mob*. But it asserts that the most famous outputs of British culture need not be confined to escapes from sometimes ugly modernity. It is artfully contrived but unflinchingly real. It looks forward and out, not back and back.

This is the only way great art is made. Nostalgia never made a masterpiece. Narcissism and nostalgia, encroaching again as the British paralysis, are the enemies of a culture anyone can care about. There were many ways to watch Andrew Graham-Dixon's brilliant series on the history of British art, which has just finished on BBC2. One of them, you could say, was as a history in pictures of British Euroscepticism, beginning with the destruction of Catholic art perpetrated by the Reformation and continuing with repeated proofs of what Graham-Dixon, in his helpful book-of-the-series, calls the 'irrepressible, vigorous eccentricity at the heart of the national imagination'.

I prefer to see another rebuke to the conventional wisdom about Britishness. British art has never been purely British at all. Its most formative figures, the series showed, were two Europeans, Holbein and Van Dyck, whose influence stretched through two centuries. There are even more ethnic strains in the history of British art than there are in the English cricket team, a fact which complicates the diagnosis of modern patriotism and should teach a lesson to those who want to see it corralled into the past they can't stop trying to protect.

Equally, British art became void of power whenever, as in the Victorian era, it was lusting after history, real or imagined. Graham-Dixon calls the Pre-Raphaelites 'pathological' in this respect. The British disease they exemplified grew out of two afflictions: a lack of 'consuming moral and emotional conviction' and 'a chronic inclination to subside … into a tame and soft compliance with genteel taste'. The great men of British art have been innovators and boat-rockers: solitary geniuses, Stubbs and Turner chief among them, whose passion was for incautious creation that made its own rules.

British art today, although at the forefront of international esteem, sometimes seems as empty and self-referential as the definition of Britishness which the reactionaries themselves insist on. But Graham-Dixon makes a persuasive case for Damien Hirst, in the vanguard of modernism while trying to reconnect with the tradition of Stubbs.

To watch the transmuting of Britishness into the worship of nostalgia is a frightening experience. It's a political happening. Political reaction is married to cultural reaction in a way that has become almost predictable. Britishness, in this sense, is a dismal commodity. The words it brings to mind are retreat, cul-de-sac, escape, exclusion, complacency, closed doors: along with more directly political manifestations such as aggression, jingoism and, let's face it, xenophobia.

The latest cultural target the political machine is closing in on is the design (a foreigner's, of course) for the extension to the Victoria and Albert Museum. To judge from the photographs, this promises to deliver an arresting, beautiful, modern shock to a structure that deserves revitalizing. The regiment of philistines, the Prince of Wales's Own, did not wait one day to start condemning it out of hand. The best of British never was like that. The old art and the newest film show it. Britishness reaches out and gathers in. The redemptive moment in *Secrets and Lies*, when both the secrets and the lies are blown apart, is achieved with the reception into the family of the black stranger, the newest and most optimistic personification of Britishness.

True Britishness is not all of the above, retreat and vengeance and the rest, which is what the sceptic Right increasingly makes it look like. It is open and unafraid. In its palmy days, it always embraced the modern world, didn't run away from it. What it's in danger of becoming is the lowest common denominator of a society gazing with sentimental defiance at its own wrinkly navel.

Mad dogs and Englishmen

THE CURSE OF this small island is the onward march of sameness. One country, one system, and the devil take anyone who tries to do it different. My most exhilarating half-hour yesterday was on a London Tube train in the company of a boisterous crowd jabbering away in what I eventually realized was Welsh. Same island, different language. Wonderful! Perhaps they were in town for today's mass eruption in Hyde Park on behalf of the country against the city. I think this rally of rural outsiders has to do with more than the rights and wrongs of hunting.

It's about the hideous blight of centralized uniformity, which has already almost throttled a country apparently not big enough, in any sense, to resist it. The Thatcherite force for sameness, commerce, is succeeded by the New Labour equivalent, which is correctness. Together, unless the rally finds a voice the Blairite legions in the Commons cannot miss, these mutually reinforcing opposites will soon have presided over the death of all particularity.

Go down any main street in a British town, and you find almost nothing that is not the same in Hell, Hull or Halifax. The takeover of city centres by identical superstores, and shopping logos that promise the uttermost predictability, was complete long ago. Apart from newsagents and corner-stores, the appearance of any one-off local shop without chain connections has become a matter of remark and an offence against nature. As a result, Britain, with odd exceptions dotted round London, is the most tedious rich country on earth in which to shop.

Why has this happened? A lot of it has to do with the centralizing power of an economic arrangement whereby commercial rents have never been controlled. Big money drives out small, just as relentlessly as bad money drives out good. The mighty weight of

Boots, facelessly deployed from central control, crushes the life out of the local pharmacy. But the locality has also brought this on itself, because local people are no less susceptible than anyone else to the uniformity that the big name, deployed on every high street in the land, apparently guarantees.

The instincts taught in the Age of Thatcher ferociously underwrote these trends. The likelihood of any social norm prevailing over the economic law of the jungle was excluded, as a matter of conscious and virtuous policy, for two uninterrupted decades, though other aspects of the same law met different local responses. When another branch of central control ordained the building of new motorways by the hundred-mile, on behalf of the Gross Domestic Product, pockets of locality perceived the destruction of their way of life and tried to stop it. But they never succeeded. Localities were more swiftly linked, but in the process lost ever more of their localism. Between roads and housing together, more of the particularity of the parts of Britain has been concreted over in the last twenty years than in any other twenty years in history.

The most conspicuous victims of this homogenizing juggernaut are people who live in the country. Everyone is the loser, but those noticing it most are those whose sense of locality was the last to be violated: whose ways of life preserved uniqueness, and who stood furthest from the domination of the one city, the Great Wen, Londinium itself, whence all this, both politically and economically, proceeds. In the lives of rural people far from London or any other semi-metropolis, the diabolical combination of hard commerce, political Thatcherism and the prairie agronomics of the European Union has done much to wreck what once made them special.

And now comes New Labour. I'm not interested in hunting, and am deeply squeamish when faced by animals alive, dying or dead. I don't understand why drag-hunting, without an animal to kill, doesn't offer just as satisfactory a day out on horseback as chasing after the blood of deer or fox. As a bit of a lawyer, I'd have to be among the first to argue the case for minimum standards and fundamental rights that apply nationwide and would not be left, even in a federal country, to the precious cultural quiddities of Hicksville, Alabama, or even, shall we say, Drumcree, Co. Armagh.

But a ban on hunting is the demolition of a particular way of life, to satisfy a prejudice which may be that of the majority, but destroys the freedom of a minority to do what it has done for centuries. Hunting may be cruel, though the antis never show very convincingly why snares and traps and traffic collisions bring a less painful end: nor does their concern extend to throat-torn fish. Hunting may be superfluous, though nobody has answered Ted Hughes's eloquent account, on this page last Saturday, of a history which shows the contrary. Hunting may offend the sensibilities of the centre, but does the centre have no duty of respect for the jobs, the economies, the pleasures and the preferences of the periphery?

Hunting, in other words, is in danger of taking its place on the altar where offerings are burned before the god of British uniformity. It's not one of those hard issues, where the rights of one citizen must be balanced against another's and there's never a perfect answer: criminal against victim, rentier against tenant, Conran against Conran. Hunting in the countryside could carry on with perfect impunity for the people in the city and their representatives in the Commons, were it not for the absolutist determination of this putative majority to impose, from Land's End to John o'Groats, their dislike of hunts and all who ride in them.

The dislike isn't hard to share. Personally, I'd as soon down a stirrup-cup with the Beaufort Hunt as venture a Highland jaunt in the company of Michael Howard. But the British sensibility cannot be truthfully defined by people whose soul is urban and heart is centrist, in possession of a transient majority sufficient to convert their gratifying piety into law. In the New Labour dawn, these pieties are as relentless as the pressure that keeps them on-message. Committed to setting up a Scottish parliament, for example, the Cabinet has just decided that Scotland can't ever be left to make its own abortion law. Far too risky. Letting the locals decide for themselves. Where will it all lead? To a country with some differences. Can't have that.

First came the concrete wasteland, where the same bricks of Mammon ring every cathedral close. Now looms the moral wasteland, where one orthodoxy insists on ruling. Hyde Park is about much more than the right to wear the pink.

Diana saves the monarchy

THE PRINCESS IS dead and buried: long live her successors. Going to her grave, that's where she has left the monarchy. Last week was unique for many things, and unforgettable in the experience of many people. Among its defining properties, however, none will last longer than the life it breathed into royalism. Republicans, eat your hearts out. What happened, in the end, was a triumph for royalty, not the disaster many diagnosed at first; proof of royalist ardour, not the beginning of the end of the magic.

The week was spent in fantasy-land, a theatre of pleasure as well as pain. Royalty takes the place of religion in sating, in the British case, all people's need of myths. But let's not continue the fantasy into the realm of post-funereal judgement. If I were a serious republican, I'd have to concede that all the excitable talk about monarchy being on the verge of destruction by the popular will was rendered ridiculous by the spectacle of two million people crying their eyes out on Saturday. Has there been a more breathless case of wishful thinking than the notion of this life and death being a platform for the ultimate constitutional reform?

There were bits of Saturday's beautiful ceremonial that showed royalism, and all who who march with her, on the back foot. When the Queen and her little clan went down to the palace gates to watch the coffin pass, they seemed a depleted bunch. Dragged down to the people's level, they didn't know how to look. Compelled to be ordinary, they lost so much of what their separateness bestows.

Earl Spencer, also, socked them. Never has a figure of total obscurity more brilliantly seized his moment to deliver a message to the world. It won't quickly be forgotten, even though he chooses exile from the country in which he couldn't cut it. What the earl had to say about the hunter-killers in the media spoke for what many people think they think. What he implied about the record of the royal family as rearers of happy children, and their need for help from another dynastic line, was laid out vividly before us in the marital wreckage scattered round the front pews.

But monarchy? The tumbrils rolling, by popular demand? Royalty, royalism, royal-ness, all the forms and declensions of the regal, in jeopardy? And proven to be so by the quality of Britain's emotional apocalypse? Not only is that an improbable political conclusion to draw about the most conservative country on earth, it seems to me utterly to misread what's going on out there in the hearts of men and women. It's the fanciful conceit of those who think there can be no proper reform of ancient Britain without the ending of the monarchy, joined by those who have such contempt for what happened to Diana at the hands of the royal family that they believe the only redemption is to be found in abolition.

The princess wasn't a movie star. She wasn't Madonna. If she had been, her death would have been a one-day wonder. If she hadn't been a royal, she would have been close to nothing in the calendar of celebrity. Only accoutred with royal status did she gain access first to the people's fascination, then to their adoration, finally to their imagined love. She was beautiful, caring, a consummate populist. She acquired a large part of her identity, and much of her popularity, by being perceived to fight the royal family, after being atrociously victimized by them. She was the best of the royals but what mattered, miles ahead of everything, was the royal. Only royalty reaches the millions and ties bouquets to railings up and down the land.

So what happened last week turns out to be not the end of monarchy but, more likely, its rebirth. That depends on the learning of lessons, which the incumbents will find very difficult to absorb. You can't invent public warmth in a seventy-one-year-old woman who has made an ideology out of enshrining what is past. You can't discover overnight a capacity for popular connection in a stiff, neurotic, autocratic middle-aged man who, in the verdict his late wife gave to the editor of the *New Yorker*, was not born to lead the country but to hold house-parties for artists in Tuscany. None the less, such loosening-up, such levelling-down, the *improvement* not the *death* of royalty, is what will surely now be attempted.

For this task, the royals have the right Prime Minister on hand.

Tony Blair, it should always be recalled, is a social and political conservative. No particle of him has even the smallest leaning towards anything so radical as the end of the monarchy. His constitutional reform programme, though in the British context portrayable as almost revolutionary, is in fact pretty modest. Only when the Blair government provides for an elected second chamber, and a fully proportional electoral system, will we know they have judged the rules of our politics, the constitution, to be radically defective: a judgement which the years of incumbency will soon, I confidently predict, debar them from endorsing.

Blair is an ameliorist. He wants to make things better but without changing anything in a way that alarms too many people or, indeed, makes a single identifiable enemy. You can find many positive things to say about him, but his desire to challenge fundamental precon-ceptions is pretty limited. This is as true of his approach to the pillars of the constitution as it is of anything. What interests him is advancing what is practical, feasible, not unpopular. It does not necessarily have to be congruent with some grand doctrinal scheme. Clauses and canons are anathema to his way of politics. He's not interested in the textbooks and the theories and the wonderful constructs that hope to render the monarchy terminally illogical. He is monarchy's most potent friend.

But that's also because he, too, is a populist. His entire political record has been based on an understanding of what the people want and, even allowing for the preposterous excesses the voting system can produce, his majority in April proved a point. What the people showed every sign of wanting last week wasn't no monarchy, nor the erstaz aridities of republicanism, nor some man-made artefact that would preserve them from all that emotion: but a better monarchy, a monarchy that came down to their level without depriving them of residual awe, a monarch whose passing might reliably command a display of national grief half matching that accorded to Diana.

Adaptation, the Blairite watchword for almost everything, is the name of the royalist game as well. It's the quality that has kept this country, for better or for worse, conservative. In the eighteenth and the nineteenth centuries, our kings did not have their heads chopped off, when all around were losing theirs. If this fate is spared them in the twenty-first century, Diana will have played her part, in death as in life, by jolting them, at the final hour, into doing what the people want them to do. Ask not for whom the bell tolls, it tolls for the Republic.

Two years before the Dome

IN THE BEGINNING, there was time. And time had its natural home. The home of time is Greenwich. That is an official statement from the British government spokesman. He spoke the words on 19 June 1997. Time began at Greenwich. Two years ahead of the anniversary of time's beginning, there's still a little time to challenge the blackmail being directed at any dissent from this analysis, and at any criticism of the way the British are proposing to mark the moment. This day two years from now, the national appropriation of time will have been declared a triumph. Before our feelings are compulsorily herded under the shelter of £758 million-worth of Greenwich Dome, consider what it will really mean.

No other country is spending so much, with such gigantic presumption, on a national focus to celebrate 2000. Some nations, like the most powerful one in the world, appear to be doing almost nothing. But the British are deemed to need this Millennium Experience, crowned by the Dome, 'to take stock of ourselves' or alternatively, according to the Prime Minister, to 'make a statement for the whole nation'. Maybe this is what the Dome will do. If so, we relinquish any reputation, as a nation, for political straight-dealing or, which is more millennially revealing, much intellectual coherence as to what we are about. The saga is a scandal that rises from the swamp of politics to the heights of aspirational vacuity.

As a process, the Dome shows the old country still steeped in political deformities. Beginning, under the hand of Peter Brooke and Michael Heseltine, as a private project, it was obliged to lurch, after a couple of wasted years, into the public sector. Private business continues to handle the public money, unembarrassed by the judgement of the Disney Corporation, whose activities have become a sought-after model for Dome crisis-managers, that none of those in charge had 'ever run, managed, designed or promoted in any way whatsoever a major international leisure attraction'. In millennial Britain, the gentleman-amateur lives on, personified by the ungentlemanly buccaneers of other trades to whom the government has turned to run the project.

Another emblem of modernity is these people's casual attitude to accountability. When civil servants insisted on a normal account-ability procedure for the £147 million of direct taxpayer's money involved, it was attacked by Heseltine as 'quite unnecessary'. As for the £450 million which the Millennium Commission is funnelling from the National Lottery, public money in all but name, the filing of accounts for this was described by the relevant officer as an 'excessive' task, likely to stop the Dome builders 'getting on with their work'. Questions about who, in the assembly of overlapping, semi-public, semi-secret bodies, was responsible for particulars were met by the sublime anaesthetizer that the work was 'a partnership' and 'we are all in this together'.

The Dome, in short, is above the rules. It has started, so it must finish. If costs overrun, the purse is as good as bottomless. The government has said: 'Should these commitments unavoidably increase in the future, we will take steps to ensure – through the lottery – that the Commission is able to meet them.' Nothing could more helpfully underline that this has become a wholly political project, to which high reputations are staked so tightly that the men in question will do anything to ensure it does not too obviously fail. Heseltine, the architect of the grandiosity, may be yesterday's man, but Tony Blair and Peter Mandelson, his inheritors, are not.

What, however, is the test of success? Here we clamber out of the swamp towards the thin, hot air at the mountain-top. For all this investment, compounded by such ruthless corner-cutting, is there an intelligible goal? The efforts to define one bring to mind the baritone voice of an American TV commercial by which they are surely meant to be intoned. 'The diversity of culture and experience and aspirations around the country,' said the chief executive. 'A living, evolving millennium destination, a place which the people of Britain had helped create,' said the first creative consultants, who have since retired. 'It's going to be quite wonderful, but don't ask me how,' said Heseltine, rather less baritone. Neither a museum nor 'a tacky theme park', but something with a spiritual element, and 'one of the country's very, very great achievements,' whistled Mandelson, sole shareholder in the Experience and the official appropriator, cited above, of time as a British possession.

These are the philosopher-kings now spending our millions to make sense of the millennium, and this is the best that they can do. Here's the most outrageous aspect of the Dome. It may be unfair to demand exactly what's going into the place, but we shouldn't be discovering so late that the unloaders of all this money began without any concept of what they were doing, beyond a vast, inchoate grunt expressed through the emptiest, as well as biggest, project in the world: jejune hysteria pumped up by Heseltine and timidly adopted by Blair–Mandelson, against collective Cabinet opinion, for fear of looking insufficiently aligned with British greatness.

What is already being revealed is not the greatness but the void, a country barren of philosophy other than the image-man's feel-good and the adman's soundbite. Anybody with enough money can reclaim a piece of derelict land and erect upon it an impressive structure. It takes inner seriousness to proclaim a more convincing reason for doing this than the fact of a millennium arriving. We learn that, as a crafter of public projects, Tony Blair is not François Mitterrand. He relies on the intimidation of selective history: those who defiantly argue that all great projects have been preceded by public scorn, or, with Heseltine, whinge that 'it's virtually impossible to do anything in this country of any imagination without the media trying to vilify and ruin it'.

There's no chance of ruining this one. A normal public project, national or local, advanced so loosely would be laughed out of the Treasury. No one even has to say whether the Dome will last five, twenty, a hundred years, or merely one. Existentially, it is needed. Not by the nation, but by a small group of frustrated public egotists, with the lottery as their cash cow, who want to build something big. We have two years to watch it rise, and its linguistic apologias grow fit to burst – while high culture, the product of 1,000 years of history, is allowed to wither on the vine.

ACKNOWLEDGEMENTS

I would like to thank Peter Preston and Alan Rusbridger, editors of the *Guardian*, for the unfettered space they have given me for two decades. Never a line suggested, nor a word changed. There could be no more congenial place for a columnist to work.

I also thank Toby Mundy and Alice Hunt at Atlantic Books, for urging me to make this collection and shepherding it to publication.

INDEX